SHE KNEW SOMETHING TERRIBLE
WOULD HAPPEN....

The path cut through a brushy, wooded area and it was hard to see from the road. As Suzi walked onto the path, she was seized with an ominous sensation.

Someone's watching me, she thought. She looked all around but didn't see anyone. A creepy feeling had come over her and she felt like something was telling her to get out of the woods.

It was about then that she heard a noise and looked around to see a stocky man, who was about five-eight, with a dark complexion and dark combed-back hair. He had a thick, full mustache, and he was carrying what looked like a clothesline in his hand. She figured it was a leash for his dog that he'd let run loose on the path.

Suzi turned back around and stopped walking. As she waited for the man to pass her, she took a few drags of her dwindling cigarette and threw it down into a puddle at the end of a drainpipe.

Suddenly she felt something on her neck.

Then she was up in the air and she couldn't breathe. She looked down and saw the man's face. He looked mad. Really mad. His face was hard. Out of the corners of her eyes, she saw the rope and his hands holding it so tight. So tight. It hurt.

Oh, my God, she thought. *He's going to kill me.*

THE
BIKE PATH
KILLER

MAKI BECKER and
MICHAEL BEEBE

PINNACLE BOOKS
Kensington Publishing Corp.
http://www.kensingtonbooks.com

PINNACLE BOOKS are published by

Kensington Publishing Corp.
119 West 40th Street
New York, NY 10018

All Kensington Titles, Imprints, and Distributed Lines are available at special quantity discounts for bulk purchases for sales promotions, premiums, fund-raising, and educational or institutional use. Special book excerpts or customized printings can also be created to fit specific needs. For details, write or phone the office of the Kensington special sales manager: Kensington Publishing Corp., 119 West 40th Street, New York, NY 10018, attn: Special Sales Department, Phone: 1-800-221-2647.

Pinnacle and the P logo Reg. U.S. Pat. & TM Off.

ISBN-13: 978-0-7860-1997-7
ISBN-10: 0-7860-1997-2

First Printing: June 2009

10 9 8 7 6 5 4 3 2 1

Printed in the United States of America

Dedicated to Lois, Lydia, Randy, and Duncan

Acknowledgments

We would like to acknowledge the following people for their contributions, guidance, and help in putting this book together: Margaret Sullivan, Stan Evans, William Flynn, Gene Warner, Donn Esmonde, Dan Herbeck, Lou Michel, Matt Gryta, Derek Gee, Harry Scull, Charles Lewis, David Duprey, Jake Elwell, Mike Shohl, Donald Beattie, and the members of the Bike Path Rapist Task Force.

1

Joan Diver

Joan Diver could never have guessed that on the morning of September 29, 2006, when she set out for a brisk run on the neighborhood bike path, she would come face-to-face with an unrelenting evil that had plagued Western New York and confounded the local police for almost three decades.

The day, a Friday, had begun unremarkably for the forty-five-year-old mother of four children.

This was a normal day that started routinely, Steven Diver would describe the morning's events in a written statement he was asked to submit later that same day to detectives with the Erie County Sheriff's Office (ECSO).

That fateful morning, Joan, a nurse turned full-time homemaker, and her husband, Steven, a chemistry professor at the University at Buffalo, drank their morning coffee together in their home on Salt Road in Clarence, a well-to-do suburb east of Buffalo. As the house filled with the noisy clatter of their rousing kids—Conrad, fourteen, Collin, twelve, Claudie, nine, and Carter, four—Joan and Steven discussed where to go for dinner that night. Steven also brought up the idea of buying electric toothbrushes for the kids.

Just as they always did, the three oldest children hurried off to school. Then Steven Diver said good-bye to his wife before heading to campus at about 7:50 A.M. An hour later, Joan hopped into her blue Ford Explorer, strapped little Carter into his booster seat, and took him to his preschool.

With her husband off at work and all four children at school, Joan Diver had three free hours to herself that Friday morning. And, as she often did with any of her rare, spare time, she prepared to go for a good, hard run.

Joan worked hard to stay fit and healthy. At five-five, she weighed a trim, but certainly not unhealthy, 140 pounds. She was a vegetarian. Her exercise of choice was running, particularly because it was a chance to be outdoors, which she loved. With four children and a household to look after, Joan had few precious moments to herself like this. That made the Clarence bike path a perfect place for Joan.

The path was just a two-minute drive from her house. She had two routes on the path: one that started at Saw Mill Road heading west and the other just down her street on Salt Road, which headed east. There was a small parking lot conveniently located next to the path where it intersected with Salt Road. Joan liked to leave her car there while she ran, allowing her to increase her exercise time.

Closed to motor vehicles, the bike path is 6.5 miles long and its entire length is paved with asphalt. It was built on the remnants of an old railroad track bed. Tall trees and thick brush lined the straight, well-kept pathway, creating an oasislike corridor that transected the town.

Clarence is home to middle- and upper-middle-class families seeking a quiet and safe escape from Buffalo's urban woes. Most everyone in this tight-knit community of twenty-six thousand votes Republican and drives big SUVs with four-wheel drive, perfect for plowing through Western New York's bountiful snow. It's a wealthy town, with household incomes averaging nearly $75,000, and most of the houses reflect that wealth: they're spacious and new, with big plots of land, and many boast swimming pools used during the Buffalo area's gorgeous, albeit short, summers.

Clarence is just one of many commuter suburbs that surround the city of Buffalo, a once-bustling metropolis nestled along the corner of Lake Erie and the edge of the Niagara River. Buffalo has suffered from a lack of jobs and the exodus of the young and ambitious. The city has shrunk by nearly half from its peak of 560,000 in the 1950s. Factories and warehouses, a sad majority of them vacant, make up Buffalo's semblance of a skyline, and a web of old railroad tracks from the city's days as a freight port still crisscross the cityscape. Stately, century-old mansions and a lush, people-friendly park system, designed by the renowned landscape architect Frederick Law Olmsted, are among the more eye-pleasing remnants of a more prosperous time for Buffalo.

Steven and Joan Diver were not natives to Western New York. They met and married in Utah, then moved to Madison, Wisconsin, where Steven got his Ph.D. in chemistry. They then moved to Boston, where Steven did his postdoctorate work at Harvard University before he landed a prized tenure-track position in 1997 at the University at Buffalo, the flagship school of the New York State school system, referred to locally as UB.

Joan had worked as a hospital nurse, specializing in the care of the critically ill. But with four young children, she had temporarily put her career on hold. She was planning to return to work the following fall when Carter started kindergarten. But in the meantime, she was happily devoted to raising her family. It was a sacrifice she relished.

Joan Diver loved to make her home a beautiful place for her husband and children, especially their garden, which she filled with colorful flowers. She was fond of sharing her love of nature with her children. She took her family camping and on hikes and volunteered with both the Boy Scouts and the Girl Scouts, helping out with everything from bake sales to teaching first aid and prepping them for outdoor excursions.

By the time the Diver family moved to Western New York in 1997, it had been three years since the last known attack of a much-feared serial predator who had been raping and murdering girls and women across the Buffalo area.

He was a most unusual, and sadistic, criminal. This was a rapist and killer who lurked in broad daylight. He most often struck during the warmer months, generally between April and October. He had a sick penchant for using a rope or cord to subdue his victims. He would quickly, deftly wrap the cord around his victim's throat twice, rendering the woman unconscious—sometimes dead—and always leaving a distinctive mark: two deep, dark red lines across the throat. The double ligature mark came to be regarded as this killer's calling card. He was infamous for targeting his victims in isolated areas—in vacant lots near railroad tracks, on running trails in parks, and often on the bike paths that wound through the region's suburbs. It earned him the moniker "the Bike Path Rapist."

But in 1994, after the Bike Path Rapist raped a fourteen-year-old girl on her way to school in an industrial part of Northwest Buffalo, the attacks had suddenly and mysteriously stopped. The authorities had begun to speculate that whoever this psycho rapist was, he had left town, been locked up in prison for some unrelated crime, or maybe even died. And as the years passed with no new cases, news reports on the rapist-killer dwindled, and girls and women had begun feeling safe being alone on bike paths again.

As a runner, Joan Diver may have heard about the rapist's most famous victim, Linda Yalem, a twenty-two-year-old student at her husband's university. Yalem was attacked while running on the Ellicott Creek bike path that skirts along the edge of the campus, located in Amherst, another suburban town located between Buffalo and Clarence.

Pulled from the path, Linda Yalem had been raped and strangled. The murder of the coed sent shock waves through the region, not only because of the vicious nature of the crime but because it had taken place in Amherst, a town that year after year had been ranked among the two or three safest cities in America. Every year since Yalem's murder, the university sponsored a memorial run in the young woman's honor. The race was always held on or near the day of the anniversary of her death: September 29, 1990.

When Joan Diver went running exactly sixteen years to the day later on her neighborhood bike path, the significance of the date would likely have never occurred to her.

It would never have crossed her mind that when she chose to park her car at the Salt Road lot and began running east, that she was running toward danger. She would have had no reason, on that perfectly pleasant September morning, to feel afraid as she ran alone on the near-empty bike path.

Not even when she turned around and saw the stocky, middle-aged man with the close-set eyes, dark eyebrows, and salt-and-pepper mustache closing in on her from behind with a cord in his hand.

2

Missing

A call came in at 12:42 P.M. on September 29, 2006, to the Erie County Sheriff's Office's 911 dispatch center.

It was Steven Diver. He wanted a deputy to come to his house. He explained that the UB campus police had just called him at his office at the university's chemistry department to let him know they had just heard from his youngest son's preschool teacher. The teacher told the campus police that Joan Diver hadn't come to pick up Carter, as scheduled. She was supposed to be there by noon. He told the dispatcher that he was leaving the Amherst campus and would be back at his home in twenty-five minutes.

It was the sort of call that every police department in America got several times a day. Almost always it ended up being nothing. The person was just late. Or had a flat tire. Lost track of the time. Was with a lover. Almost always the person turned up and was usually terribly embarrassed by all the fuss he or she had caused.

Regardless, the sheriff's department was duty-bound to respond. It was what law enforcement did.

The request was dispatched to Deputy Michael D'Alfonso, one of eighty deputies in the Erie County Sheriff's Office assigned to patrol the outskirts of the county. Unlike Buffalo and many of the other two dozen towns and villages that make up Erie County, Clarence does not have its own police department. That meant the sheriff's department was responsible for patrolling the town and investigating any crimes that had taken place there, as well as other parts of the county without their own police force.

Clarence's arrangement had recently become a point of contention within government circles. The county executive Joel Giambra, a brash, budget-slashing politician, had begun suggesting it was unfair for the rest of the county's taxpayers, who already pay local taxes for their own police departments, to pay for the sheriff's protection of areas without police departments. But the idea was shot down quickly, with many Clarence residents feeling they'd be wasting their money on their own police department in the normally sleepy little town.

In the meantime, the sheriff was struggling to keep up with the patrol demands while dealing with steep budget cuts. Sheriff Timothy Howard, a former state trooper elected the year before, was operating on a relative shoestring, with dozens of positions already cut or in danger. The crime scene investigation (CSI) unit had been virtually eliminated. And its detective squad, which once boasted forty members, had been whittled down to a dozen investigators. These detectives handled everything from drug busts to homicides, although homicides were few and far between.

Up until September, there hadn't been a murder on the sheriff's turf in over two years. But a couple of weeks prior to September 29, the sheriff's office was faced with a bizarre case of a young man who was found shot dead at point-blank range in his pickup truck in the parking lot of his workplace in Clarence.

Deputy D'Alfonso had not yet arrived in Clarence when Diver called 911 again at 1:15 P.M. Diver told the dispatcher that he had gone home to see if his wife had arrived, but she was still not there. He said he then drove to the Salt Road parking lot, next to the Clarence bike path, where he spotted his wife's blue SUV, a Ford Explorer. He told the 911 dispatcher that his wife would park her car there when she went for a run and that when she ran from that location, she would always head east before turning back. Steven Diver also said he saw a full one-liter Poland Spring water bottle inside the SUV, which meant to him she had not yet returned from the run. He said he had also seen a white pickup truck in the lot. The dispatcher told him that a deputy was on the way to meet him at his home.

Ten minutes later, Carter's preschool teacher, Wendy Kelkenberg, called 911 from the Diver house. She explained that she was at the home watching Carter and that Steven Diver had returned again to the bike path to go look for his wife.

D'Alfonso pulled up at the Salt Road parking lot at 1:34 P.M. It is a small, open lot with no hidden areas. He saw a car that turned out to be Steven Diver's. But there was no SUV there, nor was there a white pickup.

He called back to headquarters to report there was no sign of Joan Diver's Ford Explorer. He then drove up the bike path and found Steven Diver on his bike searching for his wife. He told him the Explorer was gone from the lot.

It sounded like Joan Diver had come back to her car and was probably on her way home. That's how it seemed the situation would end.

But when Diver and D'Alfonso returned to the Diver house on Salt Road, Joan was still nowhere to be found. D'Alfonso called headquarters and it was decided that a search was warranted.

Sheriff's lieutenant Ron Kenyon was working the mysterious Clarence murder from earlier in the month when the call about Joan Diver came in. He didn't know what to make of it. He knew missing person cases hardly ever turn out to be much. But it sounded like there might be more to it. Perhaps she had been injured while she was running.

Kenyon sent out more deputies to begin looking for Joan Diver on the bike path. He also headed out from downtown Buffalo to Clarence to get a better picture of what was going on.

Kenyon didn't know what to think of Steven Diver's assertion that he had seen his wife's SUV at the Salt Road parking lot. Just eleven minutes had lapsed between the time Diver had called 911 to tell them about the car and by the time Deputy Alfonso arrived he found Steven's car there, but not Joan's. All anyone knew for sure was that Joan Diver was still missing.

At 2:30 P.M., deputies, on all-terrain vehicles (ATVs) on the western end of the bike path, spotted a blue Ford Explorer. It was parked just off Shisler Road by the bike path, a little over a mile southwest of the Salt Road lot. There was no parking lot there. The SUV was simply parked along the side of the road. It was locked, but there was still no sign of Joan Diver.

Steven Diver was told about the discovery of his wife's car. He had never known his wife to park her car on Shisler, he told the deputies.

Kenyon alerted sheriff's Special Services chief Scott Patronik, who ordered a full-scale search. He set up a command post at the Clarence Fire Hall on Main Street, about the halfway point of the bike path. The sheriff's mobile command center—a giant RV outfitted with a communications system—was brought in and parked outside the fire hall.

The sheriff's SWAT team, which is trained to do woodland searches, was called to take part in the search. Nearly eighty firefighters from eleven surrounding volunteer fire departments arrived at the firehouse to help scour the bike path.

The prevailing theory at the time was that Joan Diver was hurt somewhere along the bike path, so Patronik ordered what's known in law enforcement parlance as a "quick, hasty search." The aim was to cover as much ground as quickly as possible. If Joan was hurt and unable to move, it was critical to find her fast so she could get the medical attention she needed. This was not to be a careful, detailed operation. They weren't looking for a body, a suspect, or even evidence. They were looking for a live person who needed to be found fast.

Patronik formed four search parties, each with two SWAT team members and one paramedic. Two teams headed west and two teams went east. On each side, one team took the north side of the path, and the other took the south side. Each team had a thermal imaging camera to help search the thick brush along the sides of the bike path. Searchers on ATVs were also ordered to ride up and down the path to continue looking for her.

The sheriff's department helicopter was down for repairs that day, but Patronik was adamant about having aerial support for the search. He was able to get help from the border patrol, whose helicopter—normally used for surveillance along the nearby Canadian border—was equipped with infrared cameras.

Don Burrows, a sheriff's deputy from neighboring Niagara County, and one of the region's police K-9 handlers, brought his scent-sniffing dog, Hope, to the spot where Joan Diver's SUV was found. Hope was shown a "scent pad," which had been rubbed on the car's front seat, and the dog instantly perked up. It began tracking the scent eastward on the path to a town parking lot just off Main Street. The dog picked up the scent again at the Salt Road parking lot, but then nothing. The scent pad was packed up as evidence.

The sheriff's officials didn't want to jump to any conclusions. They weren't even sure that Joan Diver was really missing. Perhaps there was nothing to this at all, they thought. Maybe she had simply left her husband and taken off with a boyfriend. After all, the investigators figured, there was no sign of any foul play. Not yet. All that was certain was that Joan Diver was missing.

As the search continued into the night of September 29, Kenyon had his detectives question Steven Diver about the day's events. They grilled him for six hours. They asked him to write out a statement detailing everything he could remember of that morning.

He also accompanied them as they drove up and down the bike path and all around Clarence. Steven pointed out places to the deputies where he thought they should look more closely for his wife. "This is a good spot," he would say.

The detectives found Diver's behavior a little odd. In fact, the deputies found a lot of what Steven Diver was saying and doing strange. They couldn't figure out this chemistry professor. They thought that to be that smart, you just have to be operating on a different plane.

As the sun set and the search continued, Kenyon made a phone call to one of his most trusted detectives, Alan Rozansky. At the time, Rozansky was working a second job: traffic detail at a Friday-night high-school football game.

"It doesn't look good," Kenyon told Rozansky.

"What doesn't look good?" Rozansky asked him.

"Come by here," Kenyon said.

"I'm going home," Rozansky said. It was the end of a long week, and he had been looking forward to a relaxing weekend with his wife and two daughters.

"No, no. Swing by here. I want to brief you on this case. It looks like she's missing. But we don't know."

Rozansky reluctantly made his way to Clarence. He spoke with the detectives. No one really had a good handle as to what had happened to Joan Diver.

At about 9:00 P.M., another veteran sheriff's detective, Sergeant Greg Savage, came to Clarence to help with the search. A cold, drizzling rain had begun to fall by then. A light wind had kicked up. The weather made it a miserable search.

"It was really cold. It was unusual, because it was in the twenties that night," said Savage, who ended up searching all through the night for Joan Diver.

The media picked up on the case that evening. It was the top story on late-night broadcasts and the local radio.

The search went on until about 5:00 A.M. on Saturday, September 30. Patronik's shift as commander would be over in two hours. With no trace of the missing woman anywhere along the bike path, he ruled out the likelihood that Joan Diver was lying injured somewhere. He knew that if she really was still out there, then she probably wasn't alive. It was time to switch gears. He called a neighboring county to ask them to bring in their cadaver dogs.

The search for Joan Diver proceeded into the afternoon. By then, searchers were stumbling over each other. They felt like they had been looking at the same spots over and over. They believed they had exhausted any possible leads. So at around 3:00 P.M., the search was officially called off.

The decision was made to concentrate more on the investigative side of the case.

Steven Diver was stunned. He knew in his heart that his wife was truly somewhere along that bike path. His neighbors and friends came to him and volunteered to help continue the search. Once the sun came up Sunday morning, they set out on the bike path in their own search parties.

Among them were the Boy Scouts that Joan had volunteered for.

At 2:10 P.M., a couple of the Boy Scouts and their leader were combing through a wooded area on the northern side of the bike path, just past the border of Clarence into the town of Newstead. A quaint bench marks the border. Just south of the bench is a chicken-processing plant. The Sunoco gas pipeline runs along the side of the path.

Deep into the brush, about forty feet north of the path, one of the boys saw something.

"Hey!" he yelled to the Scout leader.

The troop leader ran over, and there before him was what everyone in the search party had been dreading they'd find.

It was hard to see it through the dense foliage, but there it was. A hand. As they looked closer, they saw the rest of the body. It was Joan Diver. And she was dead.

The scout leader called 911.

Two deputies hightailed it over to the site and tried to keep the members of the search party away.

There lay Joan Diver. Her eyes were closed. Her face was dirty, bloodied, and bruised. Her blond hair was matted and wet. Her running shorts had been pulled down and hung from one leg. A navy sweatshirt had been placed over her torso. It was clear to anyone looking at the body: This was no accident. Someone did this to her.

Unraveling yards and yards of yellow crime scene tape, the deputies established a perimeter around the body.

Rozansky, like many of the other deputies, was getting ready to work security at the Buffalo Bills game that Sunday afternoon in nearby Orchard Park when he got the call that Joan Diver was no longer missing. The case was now a homicide. He would be the lead detective in the investigation.

With the crime scene secure, detectives carefully removed the sweatshirt that covered her body. They found that her gray T-shirt had been pulled up. She was naked from the waist down. They took note of two purple lines—one across her neck and one that went up across her chin.

They began to discuss the possibility that this was the work of the Bike Path Rapist.

Were the dark lines on her neck the infamous "double ligature mark"? they wondered.

All of the Bike Path Rapist's victims, those who survived his rape attacks, as well as the two that didn't, bore the same gruesome marks across their necks.

The survivors all said that when their assailant pounced on them, he wrapped a cord or rope of some sort around their necks, immobilizing them almost instantly. He pulled on the rope so hard it knocked many of the victims unconscious. In some cases, he would pull on the cord, then let it loose just enough so the victims would regain consciousness in the midst of the rape. It was an especially cruel act that criminal profilers said was evidence of the killer's total lack of humanity.

Rozansky was still at the crime scene when he got a call from an old friend, Lieutenant Kevin Hoffman, with the Amherst Police Department (APD).

"Hey, Al," Hoffman said. "Do you know what the twenty-ninth is?"

"I don't know," Rozansky replied.

"That's the Linda Yalem day," Hoffman explained.

Rozansky didn't know what to make of that piece of information. Could the Bike Path Rapist really have returned? Could he be celebrating a sick anniversary? Maybe it's a copycat? He didn't know.

The Amherst Police Department sent its top crime scene investigator, Captain Mike Melton, to help out at the scene—to offer his expertise but also to check out whether this killing could be the work of the Bike Path Rapist. Every cop in Amherst had been aching to catch this guy ever since the Yalem murder, and it had been a sore spot to this polished police force that the killer was still on the loose.

Sheriff's sergeant Greg Savage was shocked by the discovery of Diver's body. During the search, he had been right past the spot where Joan Diver's body was found. "I had a team on the other side of the path," he explained later. "We walked right by her."

3

Detective Lieutenant Ray Klimczak

Ray Klimczak, a retired Amherst police detective, was driving back to his new home in Clarence on the evening of September 29 when he heard on the radio that a woman had gone missing from a bike path in his neighborhood.

It felt like a stab to his heart.

He couldn't help but think about Linda Yalem. Sixteen years later, he could still see her body lying out in the brush off the Ellicott Creek bike path. Her lifeless eyes, the way they were wide open and staring up into the sky, flashed before him.

Then he realized what day it was. It was the anniversary of Yalem's murder. *There's no way this is a coincidence,* he thought.

Klimczak called Amherst police chief John Moslow.

"John, he's back," Klimczak told him. "And there's no doubt in my mind we're looking for the same guy."

His next call was to Detective Lieutenant Joseph La-Corte. The two had worked on the bike path case for over a decade before Klimczak retired in 2002.

"Nobody was shocked," LaCorte would say later. "The

one thing we knew," he said about the killer, "was that he would never stop unless he was dead or in jail."

Klimczak knew it was just a matter of time before Joan Diver's body would be found.

But when the news came two days later—that she was indeed dead and that there was a double ligature mark on her neck—it still left Klimczak an emotional wreck.

Klimczak had spent fourteen years trying to find the bike path rapist-turned-killer. He was darn near obsessed with the case.

For Klimczak, it began in 1990, in Amherst, with the second bike path rape.

Klimczak wasn't assigned to the first case. On August 24, 1989, a fourteen-year-old girl walking to cheerleading practice at her high school was attacked.

The case had come as a total shock to the entire police department. As far back as anyone could remember, there had never, ever been a rape in broad daylight by a stranger anywhere in Amherst.

The detectives working the teenager's rape had learned that there had been a series of sexual assaults in Buffalo that fit the same description. Two high-school girls had been raped in the northwest part of the city over the past two years. There had also been a woman jogger attacked in a park in 1986. All of the attacks had happened in the daytime. And all of the victims had been strangled with a garrote during the rapes. They believed that it could all be the work of one psychotic rapist.

Amherst was still working the case, when on May 31, 1990, the rapist struck again.

At 7:30 A.M., a thirty-two-year-old secretary had been out for her daily walk on the Ellicott Creek bike path. She walked every morning before going to work at a local office. She did it to help keep in shape for her other favorite pastime, ice-skating.

She was headed down an incline and had just passed a rest shelter when she was attacked from behind.

She never saw her assailant. She felt someone put a rope around her neck and pulled her from behind. Then she blacked out.

A couple of hours later, joggers heard strange noises coming from the brushes. They found the woman semi-conscious, moaning incoherently.

Klimczak was working the day shift at the detective's bureau when the call came in about a woman who was raped on the Ellicott Creek bike path.

"As detectives, we instantly knew," Klimczak would later recall.

Oh, my God, they had all thought, *we have a real, real problem here. . . . We have a serial rapist.*

Klimczak was assigned to interview the woman. She had been taken to Millard Fillmore Suburban Hospital in Amherst, where she remained unconscious for about ten hours.

Klimczak waited outside her hospital room for much of that time. He remembered walking into the room to talk to her when she started waking up. "Her eyes were completely reddened and swollen and black-and-blue," he said. "I thought she had been beaten."

It was not until later that he would learn that asphyxiation from a garrote punctured blood vessels in the eyes, leaving victims appearing as if they had been punched in the face.

He noticed deep purple marks on her neck. He was also struck by how tall she was. About six feet, he figured. It was also apparent that she was in excellent physical shape. Whoever did this to her had to be very, very strong, he thought.

The woman was groggy and confused as she slowly regained consciousness. At first, she had no idea where she was or what had happened. Klimczak tried to explain to her what had taken place and she slowly began to remember some things. She told him that she remembered going down a hill when she felt something going over her neck and then the sensation of being pulled back. And that was it.

She said she hadn't seen the attacker and had no idea what he had done to her, but a medical exam had proven she had been raped and choked.

This second rape sent the Amherst police into high gear. There was no way the department was going to let this rapist get away with it again. The officers were determined to get him.

The Amherst police were used to catching their suspects, Klimczak said. "We always solved our crimes." But here they had a repeat offender: someone who had struck innocent victims twice in their town and gotten away.

Every patrol officer was ordered to take down plate numbers of any out-of-place cars on side streets anywhere near the bike path. Among those officers was a young Joseph LaCorte, who was not yet a detective. A tip line was also set up for anyone with information about the cases.

Klimczak volunteered for a special detail. Knowing that the rapist liked to strike in the early morning, Klimczak began spending just about every morning, starting at five-thirty, hiding in the brush in a spot off the bike path, right in between where the two rapes had taken place. He would dress in full camouflage and endured many an insect bite as he would wait and watch for any suspicious characters walking or jogging by. When he'd see someone like that, he'd get on his walkie-talkie and tell a patrol officer to stop him and get his information.

He kept up the detail until September 29, 1990.

Klimczak wasn't working that day so he hadn't been out on his undercover morning detail. That night, he got a call from another detective letting him know that a UB student had gone missing on the Ellicott Creek bike path.

"My heart sank," Klimczak said, "because I knew. We have another victim."

Linda Yalem was a twenty-two-year-old Southern California woman who had just transferred to UB from a college in Long Island, New York. She was a communications major and was also training for the New York City Marathon.

Every day, she went for a long run along the Ellicott Creek bike path, which ran along the side of UB's north campus. At about 11:00 A.M. that day, she clicked a Tears for Fears cassette tape into her portable tape player and began running.

At 9:30 P.M., her roommates reported her missing. She was supposed to meet them to catch a movie, but hadn't shown up or called.

Campus cops and Amherst police began a search, which went through the night. It continued into the next day. Klimczak was among those out looking for Yalem, when at about 5:15 P.M., a couple of officers found her body.

She lay in a dark clearing surrounded by brush, several yards off the bike path. A footbridge that went over Ellicott Creek was nearby. There was a clear view of the path from Interstate 990.

One leg of Yalem's running tights and her underwear had been pulled off. Her bra was pulled down. Her shirt was pulled over her head. Two pieces of duct tape covered her nose and her mouth. Her eyes were wide open.

Those eyes would continue to haunt Klimczak.

He was especially sickened when he saw where Linda Yalem had been murdered.

Months earlier, he had taken an FBI profiler on the bike path to show him where the rapes had taken place. He vividly remembered pointing out that spot.

"Look at this area right here," he had said. "No homes here. Completely isolated. This would be a great spot if our guy ever comes back."

He couldn't stop regretting those words.

The Linda Yalem murder put Amherst on red alert. The case had become national news. Every detective was under strict orders that they were to make any tip that came in on the case a top priority. They were to drop whatever it was they were working on and follow up on every piece of information that could be gleaned from it.

Years went by and tips trickled in. Hot leads came in and went nowhere. Dozens and dozens of suspects were interviewed and eliminated. Klimczak went to the FBI Academy in Quantico, Virginia, where he met with profiler Gregg McCrary and other crime analysts. He presented the case to them and the profilers told him three things.

First, the killer was escalating in violence. He was no longer satisfied with just rape. He now had a taste for taking a life. Second, they said, he would probably stay away from Amherst and would strike again in the place he felt most comfortable. And third, he probably led a very normal, unremarkable life.

It was all intriguing information, but it didn't get the Amherst police any closer to their killer.

By the time Klimczak decided to retire in 2002, Yalem's murderer still had not been caught. That bothered Klimczak, but there was nothing more he could do.

Even in his retirement, Klimczak hadn't stopped looking for the killer. He would find an excuse to take I-990 so that he could look over the edge and see if anyone was lurking around on the Ellicott Creek bike path.

Every morning, he also would take a walk on the section of the Clarence bike path that ran through his part of the neighborhood. He couldn't help himself, as he would take mental notes of everyone he saw walking, jogging, and riding past him. He'd remember the cars he'd seen parked around. He always, always kept his eye out for any man who was on the short side, with dark hair and a mustache.

And now, the killer had struck again. It haunted him to know that the murderer he had chased for over a decade had struck in his own neighborhood. Klimczak especially hated knowing that it had happened in a section of the bike path to which he had never gone.

4

The Diver
Investigation

Clarence and all of Western New York were aghast by the grisly murder of Joan Diver—a mother of four, one of their own, had been strangled, possibly even raped, in a quiet suburban neighborhood.

And it could have been the work of a long-feared serial predator, the Bike Path Rapist.

The death sent a chill through the UB community. The wife of one of its faculty had been brutally murdered on the anniversary of the murder of one of their students.

The university president e-mailed a message of condolence to the entire campus. A second e-mail was sent to students warning them to be careful. Clearly, the university leadership was fearful that the same man who had killed Linda Yalem in 1990 may now have targeted the wife of a UB professor.

With the homicide that has occurred near the Clarence Bike Path, members of the university community are reminded that they should not travel alone on the Ellicott Creek bicycle path near the North Campus or on other Western New York pathways, the message read.

There is always safety in numbers. If you intend to walk, jog or bicycle on a bicycle path, please do so with a friend.

The sheriff's office was reeling. Normally, its detectives handled burglary rings and drug busts. It was now faced with a horrific murder mystery that had all of Western New York on edge.

The sheriff's investigators began making pleas to the public for any information that could help solve the crime.

The Erie County Sheriff's Office is requesting the public's assistance in the investigation of the Joan Diver homicide, an October 4 news release read. *Anyone who was in the parking lot near the bike path on Salt Road in Clarence on Friday, September 29, or who saw any vehicles in the parking lot on that date, is asked to call the sheriff's office.*

A local businessman posted a $100,000 reward for anyone who came forward with information leading to the arrest and conviction of whoever killed Joan Diver. The tips began to pour in. The sheriff's office received hundreds of calls and dozens of e-mails.

As they sifted through the leads that poured in, the investigators received some curious news from the medical examiner.

Joan Diver had indeed been strangled. She also had suffered some form of blow to the head.

Ligature strangulation and multiple blunt force injury, read the cause of death from Dr. James J. Woytash, the Erie County medical examiner (ME).

Diver's neck bore the angry, double red ligature marks from a garrote. The blood vessels in her eyes had burst— a condition called petechia—which characterizes a strangulation death.

Woytash's examination also showed a deeply lacerated lower lip, bruises on her face and scalp, a deep bruise on her right shoulder, abrasions on her right leg and knee. It was clear that she had gone down fighting.

But, and this was very strange, there was no physical evidence that Joan Diver had been raped.

When there is suspicion that a rape has been committed during a murder, the medical examiner will perform a special exam on the victim. It is almost identical to the kind given to surviving victims of sexual assault who are brought to a hospital after the attack. These exams are commonly referred to as "rape kits," a reference to the box of evidence collection devices used during the procedure. They are on hand at nearly every emergency room in the United States.

The exams not only provide a way to document all the injuries, but they also preserve any possible evidence that could be used in the criminal investigation.

In cases of rape, the body is the crime scene and forensic science can unlock the mystery of who the rapist is.

The rape kit can be a difficult experience for a victim, especially coming right after the trauma of having been sexually assaulted.

The victims' clothes are removed and preserved in bags. Their bodies are photographed to document any bruises, cuts, or other injuries. Nurses scrape any material from under the victims' fingernails. Sometimes they clip the nails. The material often contains skin cells from the attacker if the victim was able to scratch her assailant. The nurses perform a thorough pelvic exam, noting every bruise and tear. Any semen, saliva, or blood is swabbed and preserved on slides. They also take samples of any other material found on the body: dirt, grass, leaves, anything that could be used as evidence. The nurses comb through the victims' pubic hair looking for hairs or fibers from their assailants.

Such rape kit exams were performed on all the Bike Path Rapist's victims. Many of the exams uncovered the mystery man's semen and other fluids. The DNA proved it was all the same man, but there was no way to know who that man was.

The rape kit performed on Joan Diver indicated there had been no sexual assault whatsoever. In fact, there was not a single drop of foreign DNA anywhere on her body.

In almost every other case linked to the Bike Path Rapist, he had earned his moniker. He had violently sexually assaulted all his victims, almost always leaving behind his DNA-rich semen and other fluids on their bodies.

With no DNA whatsoever, and no other physical signs that Joan Diver had been sexually assaulted, the investigators began leaning away from the idea that the Bike Path Rapist was the culprit.

Also, the Bike Path Rapist was almost always able to get control of his victims instantly. All the survivors had said the garrote around their neck had left them unable to move. They all said he was very strong and very calculated. The injuries to Joan Diver indicated that there had been a serious struggle.

The lack of a sexual attack made it look like maybe this wasn't the Bike Path Rapist, so the investigators began to turn their attention elsewhere.

Being seasoned detectives, they knew they also couldn't even begin to consider such an incredible scenario as the Bike Path Rapist returning before ruling out the man closest to the victim.

In this case, that was her husband, Steven.

"Most times," Detective Greg Savage explained, "when a woman disappears, there's a ninety-five percent probability it's their husband, boyfriend, or some guy that they know that's involved."

There were things Steven Diver had said and done that had raised their antennae. First, it didn't make sense to the cops that Steven Diver reported seeing his wife's car at the Salt Road lot, when it was actually found a mile away on

Shisler Road. The investigators knew that the Bike Path Rapist had never touched his victims' cars before.

Second, there was the fact that when they pressed Steven Diver on whether he had seen his wife's car at the lot when he went there the second time with his bike, he said he couldn't remember. How could he not notice? the detectives asked themselves.

Could Steven Diver have been trying to hide something? They began to wonder.

Steven Diver had indeed been extremely cooperative on the day his wife disappeared and had allowed the police to search her car and even handed over a set of spare keys to them.

But once Joan's body was found, things changed. The detectives came to him and asked him to take a lie detector test. He refused. They asked him to formally sign papers giving the authorities the right to do a comprehensive search of the interior and exterior of the SUV. He refused, and told them to get a warrant.

When they asked permission to bring dogs to his house to sniff for clues, he refused again, saying he didn't want the animals near his property.

He hired a lawyer, which raised some eyebrows among law enforcement.

The attorney told investigators that Steven needed some time before he could make any decisions about signing any paperwork.

The detectives let the lawyer know they wanted Steven Diver to consent to a DNA sample—a swab from his cheek. Once again, his attorney said he wasn't ready and asked for a little time.

There was also some other strange behavior that the deputies didn't know what to make of.

The very next day after Joan Diver's body was found, Steven Diver put his three older children on the school bus and sent them to school. A school administrator called the sheriff's office, worried about the welfare of the children.

Friends of Diver's seemed to be protecting him as well. A colleague began acting as a spokesman for him.

There was also the mystery surrounding why it took so long for Joan Diver's body to be found. The autopsy showed that she appeared to have been killed on the morning of September 29. Yet, a massive search-and-rescue operation failed to find her until some of the volunteers stumbled across her remains. Even cadaver dogs had failed to pick up her scent. Had her body been moved?

The press began to seize on Steven Diver's apparent lack of cooperation.

But as suspicions grew, Steven Diver barely took any notice. He was too busy taking care of his four children, trying to help them cope with the awful tragedy that had befallen their family. He also had a funeral to plan.

On the day of the funeral, Zion Lutheran Church in Clarence Center was packed with mourners, both friends and strangers who had heard about her untimely death through the media. Joan Diver was remembered as a loving mother and wife who enjoyed reading, photography, music, volunteering with both the Girl Scouts and Boy Scouts, the outdoors, and, of course, running.

Her daughter, Claudie, read a poem about her mom that she wrote on what turned out to be Joan's last Mother's Day:

I like other people's moms, but mine is ahead of the rest!

I remember and will never forget the time my mom and I went to the mall. First, we went walking, just laughing and talking. My baby brother did too, even though he didn't know what we were doing.

Whenever I am with her, I feel safe. I feel like I'm holding on to the edge of a cliff and the bottom is all rocky. But then out my mom comes and pulls me out!

My mom is always the best and always will be the best in my book!

About the same time, sheriff's detective Alan Rozansky was given the chore of checking out Diver's alibi for the morning of September 29. He went to the UB campus and began interviewing Diver's colleagues and graduate students. Several put Diver at the campus the entire morning.

Rozansky also reached out to one of Joan's sisters. She was in tears as he interviewed her by phone. She swore that her sister never told her of any tensions or problems in their marriage.

In the meantime, another more promising lead popped up. Several area residents reported having seen a strange man who wore thonglike shorts and some sort of mask over his mouth while jogging on the path in recent weeks. One woman said that a couple of weeks before Joan Diver's disappearance, she saw "Thong Man" running in and out of the woods on the bike path near the Salt Road lot. Several days later, she spotted the man in the same area again. She told her husband, who followed him, and wrote down his license plate.

Using the license plate information provided by the witness, Detective Dennis Fitzgibbon tracked down the car to a twenty-nine-year-old man who lived in an apartment in Amherst. They brought him to the sheriff's headquarters in downtown Buffalo for questioning. He appeared nervous, wouldn't make eye contact, and clutched his stomach as they talked. But he insisted that he was not near the Salt Road lot on the morning of September 29.

During the interview, another Niagara County Sheriff's Department (NCSD) K-9 handler was called in. His dog,

Billie T, was given the same scent pad that Hope, the earlier dog, had tracked on the bike path. The dog was taken to the man's Toyota Corolla, parked in a nearby lot. The dog tracked that scent from the lot to the sheriff's office.

Fitzgibbon was alerted to the dog's reaction. On the morning of October 11, he obtained a search warrant for Thong Man's apartment and car. At the apartment, detectives found a pro-wrestling video, which included some especially violent footage of men stepping on and grabbing female wrestlers. Investigators also found video surveillance footage from an apartment complex security camera near his home on the morning of September 29. It showed that he had left his apartment at 9:41 A.M. and returned at about noon—a perfect window of time to have committed the crime.

On October 12, as investigators continued to sift through tips and evidence, snow unexpectedly began to fall in the region. It would turn out to be a freak storm that dumped nearly two feet of heavy, wet snow on Buffalo and its surrounding suburbs. Trees and power lines came crashing down. The electricity went out. Snow clogged the streets. Every sheriff's deputy was suddenly busy answering emergency calls. The press threw its attention to the storm.

The Joan Diver case seemed to be growing cold.

5

Steven Diver

Corey Hogan was standing in line at the Urban Funeral Home on October 6, which was packed with friends and admirers of Joan Diver who had come to pay their respects for her wake.

Hogan, a lawyer and partner at Hogan & Willig, a twenty-five-member law firm in Amherst, had only met Steven Diver once, but his wife knew Joan through advanced math classes the Hogan and Diver children were taking at the University at Buffalo.

"I'm looking at Steven, just looking terrible, standing there with his four children," Hogan said. "And all I can think is that he might have killed her."

Hogan had read a story in that day's *Buffalo News*: DIVER'S HUSBAND NOW LESS COOPERATIVE, the headline read.

In a new development, the story said in the fifth paragraph, *law enforcement sources say that Diver's husband, Steven T. Diver, has become "less cooperative" as the investigation into his wife's murder has progressed.*

The *News* story said that Diver had refused investigators permission to search his wife's blue Ford Explorer without a warrant. The story also said that Diver had hired a lawyer, Kevin Peinkofer, who could not be reached for comment despite repeated phone calls.

"I may not be the brightest guy in the world," said Hogan, who later came to be friends with Diver because of their children, "but the idea I took away from that story is that the police were looking at Steven Diver."

The story also said that Diver had not been named a suspect, or even a person of interest in his wife's murder. However, Hogan said, the message of being less than cooperative came through clearly to him.

Diver had a good explanation for looking so physically terrible. He had spent five hours that day weeping over the death of his wife. After the stress of the bungled search the previous weekend by the sheriff's department, and having to remain strong for his children, he had broken down and wept over the loss of Joan Barney and the end of a marriage that seemed to get stronger every year.

"The month of August 2006 was the best time of my life," Diver later said. "Joan and I were like teenagers in love. Our family was whole and we were living our life the way we wanted to live it. Before school started, we went for family walks on the bike path right after dinner. Earlier in the summer, we did several trips like this to break in our new hiking boots. I carried my youngest son on my shoulders. Joan and I held hands while the kids rode their bikes or scooters."

Diver, who at thirty-nine was six years younger than Joan, looked even younger in his photograph on the Web site for the University at Buffalo's chemistry department. Dressed in coat and tie, unsmiling and wearing glasses, with his longish hair, Diver looked more like one of the chemistry graduate assistants in his research group.

Steven had met and started dating Joan while they were both students at the University of Utah, and while she graduated with two degrees, a Bachelor of Arts in 1986 and a

Bachelor of Science in nursing three years later, Diver's career was eventually the one that took precedence.

After they both graduated in 1989, Joan went to work in a hospital in Utah, while Diver went to the University of Wisconsin to get his Ph.D. in chemistry. They kept their relationship going long-distance.

Diver proposed twice. She turned him down the first time because she didn't think he knew what he was doing, because he was so much younger than she was. Diver admitted that.

After she accepted the second proposal and they married, she moved to Madison, Wisconsin, to be with him and started working in the intensive care unit at the Veterans Hospital. They had two sons while Diver got his doctorate, and the family then moved on to Boston, where Diver did his postdoctoral research at Harvard University.

With a third child now, their first girl, he took an offer for a tenure-track job at the University at Buffalo in 1997. Four years after coming to UB, Diver won a $510,000 grant as a National Science Foundation young investigator, and then a grant for twice that amount from the National Institutes of Health (NIH).

The money allowed his research team—led by Diver, it comprised ten graduate and two undergraduate students—to develop new reactions for the synthesis of complex organic molecules. The group also was looking at the synthesis of potential anticancer compounds from natural products.

A rising star in chemical research, he had written sixteen scientific papers since 2004 alone.

Nothing in his life had prepared him to face what he now was looking at: a life without his wife, his best friend, and the mother of his children. The fact that she was brutally murdered in their community, and her body left by the side of the bike path they had both come to love, made it even worse.

And now, people coming to the funeral home, and to Joan's packed funeral the following day, had read in the newspaper that he was not cooperating in the investigation of her murder.

Diver understood—as anyone who watches crime shows on television does—that police first look at the spouses of murder victims as possible suspects.

A third of all female homicide victims in 2005, the last year studied in a U.S. Justice Department analysis, were killed by someone intimate with them. The percentages have dipped slightly over the years, but are consistently about a third. But if the category was further refined to husbands who killed their loved ones, the percentage drops to 10.8 percent.

Diver said he began sensing on Friday night, while the search for Joan was under way, that sheriff's detectives somehow felt he was involved.

Two detectives were assigned to him, and Diver took them to the Salt Road parking area, where he had seen Joan's car, and described to them what he saw. They asked him to write out a statement, which he did.

"I wrote a long statement. It was very detailed and it was truthful," he said. "I am not sure if they understood that I am a scientist and I am very observant and detail-oriented. I think it was the detail in my statement that led to their concern that I was somehow misleading them."

Diver let the detectives look around his house, gave them Joan's slippers to use as a scent for the tracking dogs, and let the detectives take the family's home computer to see if Joan had received any threatening or unusual e-mail, even though he thought it absurd. If she had gotten any e-mail like that, she would have told him.

At the sheriff's mobile command post, Diver and Huw Davies, his colleague from the chemistry department who later became the family spokesman, were purposely kept separated by the detectives. Diver said the detectives talking to him had no knowledge of Clarence or the bike path, and he was suggesting that they search east of the Salt Road parking lot, her normal running route, instead of searching the area where her car had been found.

"The turning point was the map I drew," Diver said. He drew the map of Joan's running route because the detectives did not seem to know the Clarence geography. He thought it logical that he if could draw a map, show them where Joan usually ran, they could search those areas.

"I knew right then I was getting into trouble, because they drew in closer and then asked me where did I think something could have happened," Diver said. "I told them I had no idea, but they wanted me to guess. I identified two spots where I felt the woods were close to the path and that she could be snatched.

"They basically seized the map as evidence and left the room," Diver said.

Diver insisted on helping search for Joan, but he said the detectives put him in the back of a cruiser as they drove up and down the bike path. Diver kept suggesting they search the area where he knew she ran, but he saw most of the search parties near Shisler Road, where her car had been moved. They stopped twice near areas Diver thought might be likely spots, but the detectives, with one flashlight between them, failed to find anything.

"It was mostly driving along the path, we didn't walk it," Diver said. "This struck me as odd, since we were trying to find Joan. Again, it was as if they were squandering the opportunity to search for Joan in a cumbersome effort to get information from me. They saw it as an opportunity to vet my story again by putting in another detective. 'What do you think happened, Steve?' I told him I thought she was injured, lying out there, killed, or abducted. His look suggested he didn't believe me. I think they figured she left me at this point and I was trying to cover it up."

Diver grew more and more uncomfortable with the questions and the insinuations. He knew his wife. He knew she wouldn't have abandoned Carter at preschool, that she wouldn't just leave him and the kids.

"If she was hurt," he said, "I felt they needed to find her fast. It was cold that night. I felt that they had formed an idea of what happened. First, she had run off. Maybe she met someone. Maybe I knew and was hiding this, insisting that she had ran. At some point, they considered that maybe I moved the truck, because it would be strange and risky for the murderer to do so. Second, they probably considered that if she was murdered, it was possible that somehow I was involved."

That evening ended when Lieutenant Ron Kenyon, of the sheriff's department, said that Diver would need to take a lie detector test the following morning.

Diver knew that polygraph tests were inadmissible in court. Why should a scientist take a test that didn't meet scientific standards? His wife was missing, perhaps dead. He was under incredible stress. What if he failed the test? What then? Would they arrest him and leave his four children without either parent?

Diver had told them no. He wouldn't take the test. He was hiring a lawyer.

The following day, Saturday, the bike path was still blocked to the public by a sheriff's cruiser for most of the day. By day's end, the sheriff's search teams again had not found Joan. And then, to Diver's amazement, the sheriff's department called off the search.

Diver had remained proud of the way his neighbors reacted. When news of the sheriff's department calling off the search reached them, they called Diver and offered to help.

Lieutenant Kenyon advised Diver not to do a civilian

search, but he and his neighbors disregarded the advice. They also planned to paper the area with posters showing Joan's picture.

A couple of Boy Scouts, whom Joan had helped, went looking for her body east of the Salt Road parking lot, right where Diver had earlier told the sheriff's department to search. That was where her body was found.

Diver and his neighbors were angry. His wife's body had lain in the woods for three days, under an off-and-on rain. Had the sheriff's search parties taken his advice and searched the area east of the Salt Road parking lot during daylight hours on Friday, Diver believed, they would have found her then. And the crime scene evidence would not have washed away. Instead, they searched that area mostly at night and came up empty.

After her body's discovery, as Diver was trying to explain to his children that their mother was dead, he said the sheriff's investigators returned to his house. They seemed angry, now that they knew she had been murdered.

"They basically demanded to speak to me, despite my right of counsel," Diver said. "I was in distress, in the living room, trying to explain to our kids that Joan was dead. I was dull to it then, but, in retrospect, this showed unbelievable insensitivity on their part."

Diver had already given sheriff's investigators the spare keys to Joan's truck and they had impounded it, but Diver said he and his lawyer decided to make them get a warrant to search the truck.

Diver knew the detectives had the legal right to search the SUV, but given their attitude toward him so far, he felt he needed the protection of a warrant.

"From a legal standpoint," he said, "I would not be able to challenge this if I had given consent."

Besides Diver's actions making them suspicious, the sheriff's department investigators also had something else that they never disclosed to him.

Diver's written statement was shipped to a New York Police Department (NYPD) detective who analyzed it using a forensic technique known as scientific content analysis (SCAN). It's a quasi-psychological approach that holds that people sometimes say different things than they mean by the language they use.

An example of the analysis, which an investigator later dismissed as "garbage":

8. *The subject said:*
    "(We had spoke about where to go to dinner tonight, and about my idea of getting the kids an electric toothbrush)."

Please notice the following:

a. *Anything written in parentheses includes information which is not part of the statement, but it is related to the statement. Therefore, the existence of parentheses indicates that the statement did not come out of a vacuum—it is quite likely that the information included inside the parentheses is truthful.*

b. *"We had spoke..." and not "We spoke..." —the subject used past perfect, indicating this conversation was earlier.*

c. *"We had spoke..." and not "We had talked..." —"spoke" usually refers to a formal conversation.*

d. *"...where to go to dinner tonight..." —"tonight" indicates that the subject gives the statement during the day in question.*

e. *"...the kids..."—missing possessive.*

f. *"...an electric toothbrush."—One should note that when this specific activity ("brushing the teeth") is mentioned in an open statement, it indicates that the subject will conceal other*

> *information later on in the statement, and it is
> likely about a relationship.*

Eighteen pages later after parsing each sentence of
Diver's statement, the analyst reached a conclusion.

Bottom line: the report stated, *based upon all the above,
the subject committed the crime.*

The sheriff's department on Friday, the day of Joan's
funeral, stressed that Diver was not suspected of involvement in the killing.

"He is not a suspect, nor is he a person of interest,"
Lieutenant Kenyon told a crowded press conference.

Kenyon confirmed investigators' suspicions that Diver's
attorney had been stalling sheriff's investigators who
wanted to search the car, but said he understood that Diver
had a lot on his mind.

"We're very sympathetic," Kenyon said. "I can only
imagine what he's going through."

On October 9, the Monday after the funeral, the Diver
family issued a statement to the press in the hopes of
quelling any suspicions about Steven.

*Although our family just said goodbye to Joan this
weekend, we are hurt by some of the misinformation that
appears to be circulating,* the statement read. *We would
like to provide some information and clear up some mis-
understandings.*

The statement argued that Steven had been more than
cooperative and thought he had already given the sheriff's
office permission to search his wife's SUV.

*We were unclear why any consent was necessary at this
point,* the statement continued. *We are glad to see that this
has been cleared up and that the police have taken the
necessary steps to continue the investigation.*

The statement also addressed the DNA sample issue:
The Buffalo News *reported on Saturday morning that
there was no DNA found [on Joan Diver's body], but other*

*reports in the media suggest that law enforcement want
a DNA sample from Steven. Because we want to keep the
investigation moving forward, Steven will willingly provide
his DNA. Hopefully this will help the police in focusing
their investigation.*

Steven Diver signed the consent forms for the search of
the SUV and had his cheek swabbed for DNA.

6

The Hunt for DNA

On October 9, as detectives were busy looking at Steven Diver and Thong Man and their possible involvement in the Diver homicide, Deputy Jim Mirusso came in to work.

For years, he had been the sheriff's only crime scene investigator, but he had recently switched back to patrol because of budget constraints.

With no foreign DNA found anywhere on Joan Diver's body, sheriff's investigators knew that their only hope for any traces of DNA was on her Ford Explorer.

It seemed like a very real possibility that whoever killed her also moved her car. Also, a cadaver dog that was brought in for the search "hit" on the back of the car.

With so much at stake, the sheriff's department asked Mirusso to wear his old hat again. So on October 9, Columbus Day, on what should have been Mirusso's day off, he came to the Central Police Services (CPS) building in downtown Buffalo. (The building had a special garage for forensic testing.)

Working with Mirusso were Detectives Kevin Mahoney and Steve Mirbooth.

They started on the outside. Mirusso noticed bits of orange material on the tires. Perhaps the car had driven over a traffic cone?

They also found scratch marks on the top of the car, possibly from a bike being thrown on top.

Mirusso then opened up the back door of the SUV and began the painstaking process of swabbing the area for DNA. There's no way to tell with the naked eye whether there's any DNA present. So, what crime scene investigators must do is take samples from any spot they believe might have a chance of having a trace of some sort of bodily fluid or oil from the suspect.

First he peeled open the packaging to a large cotton swab. He dipped it into a little sterilized water and then carefully dabbed the spot where he felt there might be some DNA. He then bagged the swab and labeled it to identify where it was taken from. He would repeat this for each place he believed could hold some evidence. It's a grueling, tedious process. Mirusso always got a good laugh out of shows like *CSI,* in which crime scene investigators instantly find evidence and can catch a criminal in a tidy sixty minutes.

As Mirbooth and Mahoney worked on the backseat, Mirusso moved on to the driver's seat.

"Look at this," he called to his colleagues.

He pointed toward the front passenger seat. It was a little messy, like what you'd expect in a family car. A little dirt, lint, and bits of paper were all around.

Then he pointed to the driver's seat.

"Pristine," Mirusso recalled. "The guy cleaned the car." It looked so clean he wondered whether it had been vacuumed.

He then took a look at the steering wheel. He shined a high-intensity light on it. It was smooth all around. "Your hands sweat. You leave grease," Mirusso later explained. "If I were to do this to your car, I'd be able to show you where you put your hands."

But the steering wheel appeared uniform in color.

"It looked like someone had wiped off the steering wheel," Mirusso said.

His next task was to try to preserve any fibers or hairs from the scene.

Some crime scene investigators use a specialized vacuum to suck up those hairs. Mirusso preferred a less scientific, but equally effective, approach. He took masking tape and laid pieces, one by one, on top of the driver's seat and pulled up whatever was stuck to it.

Each piece of masking tape was placed in a Baggie and packed up.

He then began swabbing the driver's-seat area.

Mirusso stopped to think about where the killer may have touched inadvertently. He took a swab from the rearview mirror. "Most people, when they get into a car, they'll wiggle the mirror," he said.

He swabbed the radio dial. Maybe Joan Diver had left it on and her killer wanted to turn it off.

Mirusso then went to the steering column and swabbed the ignition switch.

In the end, it took nine hours to complete the painstaking forensic search. The three men had no idea whether their meticulous work had accomplished anything.

The samples taken from Joan Diver's car were brought upstairs to Dr. John Simich, a member of the Erie County forensic lab, for testing. His job was to search for any trace of DNA belonging to someone other than Joan Diver.

Over the next five weeks, Simich's lab systematically went through the swabs and masking tape swatches that Mirusso and his crew had provided.

During that time, Simich came to the swab Mirusso had taken from the ignition switch. A quick test found that there was a tiny droplet of sweat there. He ran a DNA test on the speck of sweat. A few days later, on November 15, Dr. Simich came to an astonishing conclusion.

Simich's first call was to Ken Case, the assistant district attorney (ADA) handling the Diver homicide.

"Are you sitting down?" Simich asked. "I just finished the

testing on the DNA from Diver. It's the Bike Path Rapist."
The tiny sample of DNA matched, within a degree of certainty of close to one in a trillion, and proved that the man who moved the car was the Bike Path Rapist.

The hair stood up on the back of Case's neck.

Case's boss, District Attorney (DA) Frank J. Clark, was not in the office. So Case went to his immediate boss, Deputy District Attorney (DDA) Frank A. Sedita III, the homicide bureau chief, to tell him.

Case closed the door. "I just got off the phone with John Simich, and he told me all of our speculation about who it could have been—Thong Man, Steve Diver—was wrong."

Case called his boss, District Attorney Clark, and told him the Bike Path Rapist was back.

Scott Patronik's cell phone rang as he was headed to work. It was one of the secretaries at work, telling him that the sheriff was holding an emergency meeting to discuss the DNA results.

"Unbelievable," Patronik remembered thinking. A chill ran down his spine.

Rozansky was at the office when one of his colleagues came up to him and whispered the shocking news.

The local media hadn't gotten ahold of the stunning information yet, but Rozansky didn't want his buddy to get in trouble for leaking the news to him. He switched on the TV. There was mostly static, but he pretended he could hear it. "Look at what's on TV!" he yelled so that he could tell everyone the news.

Mirusso, the evidence technician, got a call from a captain at the sheriff's office.

"The DNA in the car matches the Bike Path Rapist," the captain told Mirusso.

"Get out," Mirusso exclaimed. "You're yanking my chain." He thought for sure someone was playing a joke on him.

"No. Really."

7

Sheriff Howard
Forms the Task Force

When Timothy Howard, the Erie County sheriff, got the
call from the district attorney on November 15 that the Bike
Path Rapist had returned after twelve years, Howard drew
on his nearly twenty-five years in the state police, an agency
with a long history of working together with local police
forces to solve a major crime.

He wanted to form a task force of experienced investigators who would go over each and every rape and murder the
Bike Path Rapist had committed. This guy had been allowed
to go free for too long, taunting the police with his ability to
strike at will, disappearing for as long as he wanted, and
scaring the hell out of any young girl or woman who walked
or ran alone. He wanted to throw everything at him.

At fifty-six, Howard was familiar with inter-police department politics in Western New York. He also knew how they
sometimes held on to information. He began his law enforcement career as a patrolman in the tiny Erie County village of
Gowanda, then became an officer in the nearby Town of
Eden before his name came up on the state trooper's list.

He spent the next twenty-four years in the state police,
starting out as a trooper and working his way up the ranks to

staff inspector. Along the way, he picked up a master's degree in criminal justice from Albany State University. He spent most of his career in Western New York before he retired from the state job in 1998 to work as Erie County undersheriff for another state police veteran, Patrick Gallivan. When Gallivan stepped down as sheriff in 2005, Howard ran for the job, and defeated a former Buffalo homicide commander in a bitter race. He became Erie County's fifty-third sheriff, a job once held by Grover Cleveland in 1871 before he served the only two split terms as U.S. president.

Howard's three brothers are local cops and his two sons and a nephew are state troopers. There wasn't much that went on in law enforcement in the county's town and village departments that Howard didn't know about.

He had known about the Bike Path Rape cases before Diver had been killed three months ago, and since then, he had come to realize how little Amherst and Buffalo talked to each other about their separate murders. That had to change.

Like any unsolved case, the Bike Path Rapist gnawed at him. And now with the DNA from Diver's car, it was his case as well. It didn't help his mood that the county lab gave the DNA test results first to District Attorney Frank J. Clark, even though it was Howard's evidence technician who took the DNA swab from Diver's car. Lab protocol meant Howard should have been the one called—it wasn't a good start.

Howard called John Moslow, the police chief in Amherst who had just returned from medical leave for prostate cancer, and H. McCarthy Gipson, the police commissioner in Buffalo, told them what he wanted and asked whether they wanted in. There would be no holding back. Each department would share everything. He would share everything from the Diver homicide, and he expected Amherst to share its files in the 1990 Linda Yalem homicide and its Bike Path rapes, and Buffalo would do the same with its rapes and the 1992 murder of a Buffalo prostitute, Majane Mazur.

"We wanted to have a fresh set of eyes looking at everything from a little different perspective than what was done before," said Howard, a big man with a salt-and-pepper mustache who, at over six feet tall, still looked like a trooper. He expected each investigator from the different departments to read the crime reports of every rape and murder committed by the Bike Path Rapist—at this point, there were ten attacks tied to him—visit the crime scenes, talk to the victims, take a new look at old clues. It would be starting all over again.

He also told his fellow chiefs that he wanted to bring in the state police as an equal partner and would call on the FBI for its national crime lab and criminal profilers. State police investigators almost always worked with local departments, so it was nothing new to Howard.

In the mid 1990s, as a state police lieutenant, he and Thomas Beilein, then a Niagara County sheriff's captain, and now the sheriff of the county to the immediate north, had headed a task force looking into unexplained questions in the shooting of a Lockport police officer, Steven L. Biles. The task force stunned the community by concluding that Biles had been shot by a drug dealer he had been protecting.

Howard also had the respect of his fellow cops, who, like him, had spent decades in police work. Howard was no bureaucrat. He was a certified hero. In 1982, his patrol partner, Trooper Gary E. Kubasiak, was shot and killed by a mental patient, James Swan, who was holed up in his home in Dayton in the Southern Tier's Cattaraugus County.

Kubasiak had gone to school with Swan and tried to use that relationship by going into the house to persuade Swan to give himself up. Instead, Swan shot Kubasiak with his .30-30 rifle at point-blank range. Howard climbed through a bedroom window, and when Swan swung around and pointed the rifle at him, Howard shot him in the chest.

Howard received the Brummer Award, the state police's highest award for heroism, for his actions.

Howard's department had the last crime—the Joan Diver murder—but his detectives had never investigated the Bike Path Rapist case before, so it was natural for him to propose a multiagency team of investigators.

Howard was also struggling with budget cuts in his one-thousand-plus-member department, which patrolled county roads, staffed the jails, ran marine and snowmobile patrols, and flew the county's police helicopter. The county's fiscal crisis had decimated his detective division, and the county executive was threatening to charge towns and villages who used the sheriff's services.

In addition, Howard's department was still reeling from the escape in April from the Erie County Correctional Facility of Ralph "Bucky" Phillips, who shot and killed a state trooper and wounded two other troopers during his statewide flight from the police. Howard might not have been dealing from the strongest position, but nothing had worked at bringing in the Bike Path Rapist yet. He wanted a task force.

Howard met with Chief Moslow, Commissioner Gipson, DA Clark, and Captain George Brown, of the State Police Bureau of Criminal Investigation, the next morning before the press conference where they would announce that the Bike Path Rapist was back.

"I have always believed in interagency cooperation, the best service to the public is best served by getting as many people as possible working on the case," said Howard. "Let me put it another way. If you said it would take a thousand hours to solve the case, I would rather put one hundred people on it for ten hours, than ten people for one hundred hours. This is the kind of case that needs to be solved quickly."

The police chiefs and district attorney agreed on the formation of the task force and went out to face the press.

"We're saying with certainty at this point that the DNA from the Joan Diver homicide has been clearly and irrefutably linked to what has been referred to as the Bike Path Rapist," Howard told the assembled reporters.

"For a twenty-year period of time, this person has been preying on women in the Western New York area," said Gipson, the career Buffalo cop who had that year become Buffalo's first black police commissioner.

"It has been very frustrating for us," said Moslow, who had risen through the ranks in Amherst to become chief in 1999, after he outscored everyone else in the department on the chief's exam. "It is frustrating, obviously, but we're not going to give up on it."

Clark, the two-term district attorney and a federal prosecutor before that, said the evidence pointed in one direction, and one direction only.

"Right now," the longtime prosecutor said of the Bike Path Rapist, "we have one viable suspect, and it's the same person who did the other nine. Anything else is pure conjecture."

8

Suzi Coggins

It was like the floor had dropped out from under Suzi Coggins when she heard that the Bike Path Rapist had returned.

She hadn't seen it coming at all. When the initial reports came out about Joan Diver's body being found, she had thought it was a copycat.

Coggins was all too familiar with the Bike Path Rapist. She was one of his victims.

All the other times he had struck since he raped her, she swore, she felt it coming. She maintained she could almost feel him growing itchy. She could feel the pressure building . . . but with this last one, she didn't feel anything.

Ever since she was a child, she'd had strange, unexplainable extrasensory experiences. She vividly recalled the time when one of her parents' friends had died. She was a little girl then. She believed he came to visit her that night. She told her mother about seeing the friend. "Honey, he's dead," her mother told her.

Then Coggins described what he had been wearing. A black suit with a bow tie. Coggins hadn't been to the funeral, but she somehow knew that the friend had been laid to rest in a tuxedo.

So it took her by surprise when twelve years after his

last known attack, her rapist had returned and she hadn't anticipated it.

A flood of memories came pouring back.

Suzi had awakened late on the morning of July 14, 1986. It was a Monday and she had summer school that day.

She had flunked math the previous semester at Frontier Central High School in Hamburg, a town just south of Buffalo. It wasn't that she wasn't smart. She was, in fact, and she often did get good grades. But she always had a hard time with math, especially when the answers weren't multiple choice. Years later, she'd learn that she was dyslexic.

But in 1986, in the summer between her junior and senior year, she was still undiagnosed. So, instead of spending a lazy summer sleeping in and hanging out with her boyfriend and her buddies, Suzi, then seventeen, had to get up every weekday morning to go to math class at summer school.

"Mom, can I get a ride?" she begged her mother.

It was a twenty-minute walk to school from Suzi's house—a good mile or mile and a half. Suzi had lost her sneakers over the weekend, and all she had to wear were some uncomfortable, worn-out clogs.

"No," her mother told her.

Okay. Fine, Suzi remembered thinking. *Screw it.*

She put on her clogs, grabbed her cigarettes, and headed out the door.

On the street, she ran into a couple of girls from school. Real goody-goody types. The kind of girls that Suzi just couldn't relate to.

Suzi was a bitter and angry girl back then, the inevitable result of growing up too fast. Her parents ran a biker bar and they liked to party with their customers. Suzi and her brother were often left home alone to fend for themselves. And as Suzi became an adolescent, she began to rebel.

Her rebellion had landed her in the hospital the past two Mondays. On June 30, she was riding on a dirt bike with her boyfriend, against the wishes of her mother, when she cut her leg on a sharp piece of metal that had been sticking out of the back of the bike. She needed seventeen stitches. Her mother was furious and told her she was absolutely forbidden from getting on a dirt bike again.

The following Monday, she disobeyed her mother again. She got onto a dirt bike with two friends. They were going so fast at one point that Suzi just couldn't hang on. She fell off and sprained her ankle badly. Again, she was in the emergency room.

On the morning of Monday, July 14, as Suzi ran into those girls she couldn't stand, she decided to take a different route to school. Normally, she would have stopped at the corner convenience store to buy a soda or maybe a cup of coffee and have a cigarette or two. But with those girls going in that direction, Suzi headed for the bike path next to her school's outdoor field.

The path cut through a brushy, wooded area and it was hard to see from the road. As Suzi walked onto the path, she was seized with an ominous sensation.

Someone's watching me, she thought. She looked all around but didn't see anyone. A creepy feeling had come over her and she felt like something was telling her to get out of the woods.

But she went against her instincts. As she continued on the path, walking fast and puffing on her cigarette, she had another strange thought, *I'm going to be in the hospital today.*

That's weird, she thought, then brushed it off. After all, she had spent the past two Mondays in emergency rooms for accidents she didn't predict.

Then she had a jarring vision: a body lying naked in the bushes. It freaked her out. *Why are you thinking all of these things?* Suzi silently asked herself. She shook it off and kept going.

It was about then that she heard a noise and looked around to see a stocky man, who was about five-eight, with a dark complexion and dark combed-back hair. He had a thick, full mustache, and he was carrying what looked like a clothesline in his hand. She figured it was a leash for his dog that he'd let run loose on the path.

Suzi turned back around and stopped walking. As she waited for the man to pass her, she took a few drags of her dwindling cigarette and threw it down into a puddle at the end of a drainpipe.

Suddenly she felt something on her neck.

Then she was up in the air and she couldn't breathe. She looked down and saw the man's face. He looked mad. Really mad. His face was hard. Out of the corners of her eyes, she saw the rope and his hands holding it so tight. So tight. It hurt.

Oh, my God, she thought. *He's going to kill me.*

He then started dragging her through the brush.

"Keep going," he ordered her as he made her run with him about three hundred yards to a cutoff.

He began pulling at the rope again and Suzi tried grabbing at him to try to loosen his grip. She started feeling herself fade. Her legs began to buckle and suddenly the man let go of the clothesline.

Suzi felt a rush. Her head was spinning. She felt high. *I can't think straight,* she thought.

"Lie down," the man told her.

He then told her to take off her shirt. Suzi unbuttoned her button-down black-and-white–checkered blouse, and took it off. The man grabbed it from her and put it over her head, tying the sleeves into a knot behind her head to form a blindfold.

Then, in an eerily calm voice, he asked her: "Have you ever been fucked before?"

She told him she had. She wasn't lying. She had been sleeping with her boyfriend for a while by then.

"How old are you?" he asked.

"Seventeen," she answered.

"Bend over," the man ordered. He pulled her pants down, bent her over, and began to rape her.

I'm going to die. I'm going to die. Suzi was terrified. She didn't know what to do.

She then felt herself go into another mode. Without realizing what she was doing, she began pretending that she wasn't being raped by a horrible stranger. In her mind, she was with her boyfriend. She kept pretending, and then everything seemed a little less scary.

The man stopped abruptly. It seemed like he didn't finish. Suzi later realized the man probably got turned off when she seemed unafraid of him.

"What now?" Suzi asked him.

"Nothing," he growled. He seemed angry with her. He grabbed her, and then, with what felt like either the back of his hand or maybe his foot, he pushed her into the mud.

"Lie down and stay here for twenty minutes or I will kill you," he said.

And *boom,* he was gone. He took off running.

Suzi began to panic. She took off the blindfold, pulled up her pants, and put her blouse back on. She grabbed for her cigarettes and sat down on a log. She smoked one cigarette, then a second, as she tried to figure out what to do next.

She had a terrible feeling that he was still out on the path waiting for her.

So, instead of going back on the path, Suzi began to run through the brush. She ran fast and kept running until she got to the field. She ran to the parking lot at the school, where she ran into a boy she knew.

"What happened?" the stunned boy asked her.

"Fuck you, you fucking asshole!" she screamed at him. "Stay the fuck away from me!"

The boy didn't know what to do. Suzi was covered in

mud and crazed with fear and anger. "Where's the nurse?" she bellowed.

Someone went to fetch the nurse. "What happened?" the nurse asked.

"I was just fucking raped!" Suzi screamed. The nurse brought her into her office and closed the door. She called the police and Suzi ended up in the hospital for the third Monday in a row.

The rape kit exam at the hospital was almost as traumatic as what had just happened. Suzi had never had a pelvic exam before. This would be her first time. She was mortified and scared as the doctors and nurses examined every violated inch of her. To this day, she will cry remembering that experience. She was in terrible pain too. All the way from her ears down to the bottom of her neck was raw and bright red from where the man had tried to choke the life out of her.

A couple of days later, she met with two detectives from the Hamburg Police Department (HPD): Daniel Shea and Bobby Williams.

They were there to take the report. The two men couldn't have been kinder to Suzi.

As a rebellious teenager, she had no respect for authority, especially cops. But the detectives took her seriously and believed what she told them. She was grateful for that. It was the first time she had an adult treat her with that much respect.

The detectives told her they'd do everything they could to find the man who had done this to her.

She believed them.

The next few years were hard ones for Suzi.

She broke up with her boyfriend. She couldn't stand the thought of having sex with him again, not after those thoughts she had during the rape. He didn't understand, but Suzi just couldn't be intimate with him ever again.

For half a year after the rape, she refused to leave her

house. Then when she did, she insisted on being with someone. And when she did venture outside, everywhere she looked, she would see a man with dark hair or a mustache and think: *That's him.*

She was feeling herself lose her grip. She began carrying a knife.

It took until the one-year anniversary of the rape. On that day, Suzi knew what she had to do.

She walked back to the bike path and began to follow the route she took exactly a year ago. The weather was just the same. Her heart raced.

If I go through this, it's not going to happen again, she kept repeating to herself. She walked, and kept walking, and finally came to the field, into the open summer air.

Suzi felt free for the first time in a year.

She came to the realization that she could either be bitter and angry and afraid of the world or accept the fact that her life—anyone's life—can end at any moment, and she'd be better off enjoying every moment she'd been blessed to have on this earth.

She went to counseling. She began writing down her thoughts. And she got her life together. She got married, had two kids, and went to college.

Suzi had a few relapses as she would hear about the Bike Path Rapist's subsequent victims. She said she always had a hunch that something was about to happen when the killer would resurface. She could almost feel him itching, she said.

As the years went by, Detectives Shea and Williams would keep her informed of any developments in the cases. They would call her up all the time. They'd bring her to their station house to help them with a new sketch or to look through a new photo array or a book of mug shots. She hated doing it, but she just couldn't say no to the two cops who had been so kind to her. A couple of times, she thought she recognized a man in a mug shot as the man who had raped her. Once, she had even called the police station after she spotted a man driving by who looked like him. She got his license plate number. However, they were all false alarms.

Suzi eventually came to a point where she decided to forgive her rapist. She didn't condone what he had done, but she felt she was wasting too much energy hating him. She figured he was some loser who had no friends or family and lived in a basement. As the years passed, and he wasn't caught, she figured he had died or ended up in jail for something else.

But even having made peace with what had happened, she could never forget it. She couldn't shake those memories. She would find herself at the gas station, at the mall, or at the corner store and see a man with a mustache or dark hair and become choked with fear. *That's him,* she'd think. *That's him.*

And now, suddenly, here he was again for real. The police had found incontrovertible evidence that the Bike Path Rapist was still here.

Oh, my God, Coggins thought as she watched the news. *He's alive.* It was like Frankenstein's monster coming back to life. The creature was back.

9

Christine Mazur

Christine Mazur saw the phone number with a 716 area code on her cell phone that day and she knew what that meant: there had been a development in the unsolved murder case of her mother, Majane Mazur.

She was only five when her mother's body had been found by a man and his daughter looking for thistles in an open field off Exchange Street, on the edge of downtown Buffalo. She was too young for her mother's funeral, but through her maternal grandmother, Elizabeth Phillips, she had kept track of the hunt for Majane's killer all these years.

Christine was now nineteen and was living in South Carolina. The call she got with the 716 number was from a TV news reporter from Buffalo. The reporter had called her several times before over the years, asking her for comment on this aspect or another of the case. But this time, he had some huge news—that the man who had killed her mother in 1992 had murdered another woman.

Mazur had mixed feelings that the killer was back. When investigators had contacted her and her grandmother, Elizabeth Phillips, they always mentioned that it would probably take another attack or killing for the cops to catch him. Now it had happened.

Christine Mazur felt terrible for this latest victim's family.

But she had to look at the silver lining. The more crimes he committed, the more likely he'd be caught.

Among the Bike Path Rapist's victims, Majane Mazur had stood out. The others were all either students or career women. The others were either taking a shortcut through an isolated area or were running on bike paths. Majane Mazur was a drug addict who had turned to prostitution to feed her self-destructive habit.

"*She smoked crack, and she was like the devil,*" her husband, David Mazur, told the *Buffalo News* after his wife's body was found a week before Thanksgiving, 1992, and long before police realized his wife had been another victim of the Bike Path Rapist. "*It wasn't my wife that was doing it; it was the drugs.*"

But Majane hadn't always been like that. She was born Majane Elizabeth McCauley to an upper-middle-class family with deep roots in Greenville, South Carolina. Her name was pronounced "May Jane," and she was named after her maternal grandmother. Her father was a successful businessman, and her grandfather had been the mayor of Greenville.

Majane led an idyllic childhood. She was the oldest of three siblings: she had a brother, Jack, and a sister, Jo Anne. She went to private schools and took every kind of dance lesson, from tap to ballet. She was something of a tomboy. She was never into dolls. She spent much of her time outdoors. When she was little, she loved to collect bugs, particularly butterflies. When she got a little older, she devoted all of her time to her horse, Blackjack. Every day she'd rush home from school and run out to the barn to go tend to and ride Blackjack. She would show the horse at contests and won numerous ribbons with him.

After graduating from high school, Majane attended Anderson University in South Carolina, where she earned a two-year degree in education. She graduated with honors. She then attended Lander University and got a second degree, once again with honors. Her plan was to become a physical education teacher.

While Majane was in college, she met and married David Mazur. He was from Dunkirk, New York, about fifty miles southwest of Buffalo, and had been visiting Greenville. It was also at college where she started using drugs.

"Back in college, she would do it as a social thing— snorting cocaine and stuff," her husband told a *News* reporter.

She and Mazur married after college, and spent the next two years in Greenville. Mazur worked in an electronic assembly shop and Majane started working in restaurants. At first, she waitressed, but then she developed an interest in what was going on in the kitchen. She got a job as a prep cook and quickly worked her way up to sous chef. She worked at a country club and several of Greenville's finest restaurants. She got pregnant and on February 4, 1987, gave birth to her daughter, Christine.

It was, her husband recalled, the best two years of their marriage.

But Majane Mazur began dabbling in drugs again. She found they were easy to come by in the restaurant world. It was an especially dangerous pastime for her. She'd been diagnosed as bipolar, a manic-depressive. When she stayed on her medication to treat it, she was fine. But then she'd start feeling like she didn't' really need her meds and would stop taking them. Her mother recalled that's when the trouble would start.

By August 1987, David Mazur said his wife had discovered crack cocaine, and their lives changed.

"When she was on crack, she wouldn't come around me," he said. *"She would always leave for three or four days."*

She once cashed his $1,500 tax refund and went

through it in two days. She quit her job too. Mazur thought of getting a divorce but didn't.

By the spring of 1991, David Mazur had had enough. While Majane and her mother were out doing grocery shopping, he loaded all of his and his daughter's belongings into black trash bags and dumped them into his car. He scooped up little Christine, who was just four then, and announced to his daughter that they were going on a trip. He explained that they were going leave her dog, Hilda, and her kitty, Knuckles, at a farm. He put her in his car and pointed his car north, driving all the way to his mother's home in Dunkirk.

Ten months later, his wife joined him there. She was pregnant, and he was not the father. Majane Mazur stayed off drugs during her pregnancy. In July, she gave birth at a Buffalo hospital and gave up the baby, a boy, for adoption.

She stayed in Buffalo, sometimes coming to live with her husband, but she returned to using crack and the destructive lifestyle that went with it.

A few months before her death, Majane Mazur disappeared with her husband's car, ending up in Lackawanna, the former steel-manufacturing city, just south of Buffalo. Her husband swore out a complaint accusing her of car theft, a charge that was dropped after she agreed to go through drug rehab, again.

Majane Mazur kept a journal during the twenty-eight-day stay at a Buffalo hospital.

> *Aug. 7—I feel like a little child who needs attention, or who is lost in the woods and doesn't know what path to take.*
> *Aug. 8—I realized I did not want to die today.*
> *Aug. 9—The men are still on my case making*

*comments, sexual comments. It's about to drive
me crazy.*

It was at rehab that Majane Mazur met the man police
later described as her pimp.

"I really don't want to say what I thought of him," her
husband said after her death. "He was a drug addict who
used my wife for his own convenience."

Majane and her pimp checked into the Hotel Huron in
downtown Buffalo on September 11, 1992. They paid
$24.95 a night for a room with a shower. Hotel employees
said she was seen in the company of many men. The staff
described the men as her customers. Her boyfriend, they
said, called them his "meal ticket."

Her husband had no idea what had happened to her. He
filed a missing person report with the Buffalo police, who
ran her name and found that she'd been arrested twice for
prostitution.

"I just went home after filing the report," he said. "It was
one of those things that I didn't really want to believe."

Throughout all of this, Majane kept in contact with her
mother. No matter how bad things got, she would call her
mother at least twice a week. She even called her when
she'd been arrested for prostitution. That had broken her
mother's heart, but Elizabeth Phillips told Majane she loved
her no matter what. She begged her to try to get some help.

Majane Mazur had come back to Greenville several times
already for three stints in rehab. She'd always emerged feeling hopeful that she'd kicked the habit once and for all, but
she'd beg her mother not to leave her alone. She knew what
she'd do if she had the chance. Her mother would watch her
as much as she could, but in an instant, Majane Mazur
would disappear, and the cycle would start again.

Even Christine remembered her mother's battle with drug

addiction. She revealed just two memories of her mother. One was watching her expertly carve an exquisite rose out of a tomato. The other was sitting down with her and asking her mother: "Why can't you stop using drugs?" Her mother replied: "I just can't stop. I'm sorry. I'm trying."

Mazur last saw his wife on October 24, 1992. She had called him, sounding scared, two days before. He traced the call to the Hotel Huron and drove there.

She was standing on the hotel steps and refused to talk to him. That was the last time he saw her.

Elizabeth Phillips recounted the last time she spoke with her daughter. It was a couple of days before she went missing. She seemed down about having given up her baby boy and she missed Christine terribly. She asked her mother if something should happen to her, that she take care of her little girl. Phillips had told her she would.

Then a week went by and she didn't hear from her daughter. Phillips first thought she'd gone on a drug binge. But in the pit of her stomach, she was horribly afraid that something bad had happened to Majane. She'd never gone more than three days without calling.

When police came to where the family had found Majane Mazur's body on November 22, 1992, they found it was covered by a black plastic garbage bag, with a piece of corrugated plastic covering it. When they pulled off the cover, they found her naked body. A plastic bag had been tied over her head. Her killer had also used a ligature to snuff the life out of her, leaving two long, red welts on her neck.

Even though she was just five, Christine could vividly recall the day she learned her mother was dead. She remembered seeing her father sitting on the edge of his bed. It was in the basement of his mother's home in Dunkirk.

His head was buried in his hands. "Your mother is not coming back," he told Christine.

She was already used to her mother not coming back, so she didn't know what he meant. She sat down next to him as he began watching a video of a television news report. There was footage of a body with a tarp over it and then of the body in a body bag being loaded up into an ambulance. Her father watched that video over and over again.

Police began an investigation into her murder. The double ligature mark on her neck was unmistakable. But Buffalo detectives never thought to connect her murder to the Bike Path Rapist cases. She didn't match his typical victim profile. They figured she was just another crack-addicted hooker, living a dangerous lifestyle.

The case became another unsolved murder. There was some speculation that it could have been connected to a Rochester serial killer who had been going after prostitutes, but that theory never went anywhere and the case went cold.

But then in 2004, the Erie County crime lab got a grant to test DNA from cold cases. The test results came back to show the same man had killed Linda Yalem and raped nine other women *and* had killed Majane Mazur—the Bike Path Rapist.

And now, with Joan Diver, he had killed a third time.

Elizabeth Phillips was lying in a hospital bed when Christine got the call from the 716 number. Elizabeth had colon cancer. She'd been diagnosed around the time of Diver's death.

Christine took the call outside and spoke briefly with the TV reporter. She ran back into the room and told her grandmother the news.

"Maybe they'll catch him before I die," Elizabeth said.

10

More Than a Rapist

Sheriff Howard's announcement sent shock waves across the region. It was a huge news story that had even caught the attention of the national media.

The newsroom at the *Buffalo News* was buzzing with excitement as reporters scrambled to put together a package for the front page.

Gene Warner, a veteran reporter who had been writing about the case since Linda Yalem's murder, wrote the main story.

The bike path rapist has returned, and authorities have the DNA to prove it, Warner wrote. *Now likely in his 40s or 50s, the man who terrorized Western New York women— sexually assaulting nine and killing two between 1986 and 1994—has been linked to a third killing, the late September beating and strangling death of Joan Diver of Clarence.*

Maki Becker, coauthor of this book, was a recent transplant to Buffalo from the *New York Daily News* and had covered the case since the murder of Joan Diver six weeks earlier. She tracked down one of the victims of the rapist. She was fourteen in 1989 when she survived being attacked by this sick and dangerous man, whom the police had so far failed to catch.

The survivor, now a grown woman with children, said

her husband had called her that morning to warn her about the news reports he'd been hearing on the case. She said she watched the TV news that morning and thought, *Hopefully, this time he'll be caught.*

Warner and Becker also worked together on a timeline listing each of the seven rapes and three murders now attributed to this one man. They noted that in seven of the cases, DNA evidence was found at the scene that positively linked the cases together. In the other three, the investigators had relied on his MO, the method of operation, or modus operandi. The timeline dated back to June 12, 1986.

As they worked on their stories, a copy editor approached deputy managing editor Stan Evans with a question that had been troubling him. Up until then, the paper—in fact, every media outlet—and the police had referred to this terrible man who had been attacking women in the region as the "Bike Path Rapist."

But it had become quite clear that he was more than a rapist. He was a murderer too. In fact, the slaying of Joan Diver made him a murderer three times over. It didn't make sense anymore to keep calling this predator merely a rapist.

Evans agreed and he walked over to Warner's and Becker's desks. He asked them what they thought of changing the moniker. They were on board. It sounded like the right thing to do, even though the task force was the Bike Path Rapist Task Force.

The next day, the man who had been terrorizing women for twenty years got his new name. DNA PROVES BIKE PATH KILLER IS BACK, read the front-page headline on November 17.

11

Task Force Starts Anew

Once the decision was made to form a task force, the heads of the law enforcement agencies that would form the task force began making calls to the detectives who would be on it.

Sheriff Howard made Scott Patronik his main point man on the task force.

Patronik, the chief of the sheriff's Special Services, was an unlikely cop. Raised in the Buffalo suburb of Orchard Park, he graduated from Buffalo State College with a degree in physics, then got a master's degree in computer science from James Madison University in Harrisonburg, Virginia.

"When I was a kid," Patronik said, "I never thought I'd want to be a cop. I always wanted to be an engineer."

After he graduated with his master's degree, Patronik came back to Western New York and went to work for Fisher-Price, the famous toy company in nearby East Aurora, where he had done a college internship.

But Fisher-Price was in the process of being bought out by Mattel, and Patronik saw the handwriting on the wall.

Longtime employees were being laid off, and he saw no future for him in the toy industry.

He had taken the state police test on a whim a few years back: "I don't even know why I took it." As he was wondering about his future, he got a letter in the mail from the state police offering him a job.

It took him two years to get it because of a hiring freeze, but once the state police began hiring again, Patronik's score of 100 on the entrance exam pushed his name to the top of the list.

Patronik was a road trooper in Auburn and Fishkill before his father had become ill with cancer in 1993, and Patronik got a hardship transfer to the barracks in nearby Boston, New York. He used his computer skills to work on a task force headed by U.S. Customs to root out child predators on the Internet.

In 1998, Patronik left the state police to work on the campaign of Pat Gallivan, a rising leader in the state police, when he ran for Erie County sheriff. To support himself, Patronik worked at Computer Task Group in Buffalo, and was a part-time police officer in the Village of Hamburg.

Once Gallivan won, he brought Patronik aboard as Special Services chief, in charge of the SWAT team, marine, aviation, and snowmobile divisions.

Although Patronik never worked as an investigator, he was not that surprised that Sheriff Howard had named him to the task force. He saw his role as more of a manager.

"I've had a lot of training in incident management," he said. "You hate to say it, but preparing for the big one."

He kept his sanity by hiking in the Adirondack Mountains in his spare time—he and his brother and friends had hiked twelve of the forty-six peaks over four thousand feet in recent years—and by scuba diving. He proposed to his wife underwater in Cozumel.

The day-to-day supervision would fall to Patronik and also to Steven Nigrelli, a lieutenant in the state police.

Neither man was a stickler on command hierarchy; they were both more managers than bosses. But as the task force developed, there was no question who its leaders were.

Nigrelli, assigned to State Police Bureau of Criminal Investigation, was driving back on the I-90 Thruway from Albany when he learned from his supervisor that he'd be on the Bike Path Rapist Task Force.

It was the assignment he'd been waiting for his entire career as a police officer.

Nigrelli came from a family of lawmen. "I like to say that in my family, we play follow the leader like no other family," Nigrelli said.

His maternal grandfather, Michael McCarthy, was a desk lieutenant with the Buffalo Police Department (BPD). His father, Joseph Nigrelli, was a detective sergeant in Buffalo. His oldest brother, Joseph, is a police dispatcher in Indianapolis. His older brother, Michael, is a captain in the state police Thruway detail, and their younger brother, Peter, is a patrolman in Buffalo. If that's not enough, he's got another fourteen relatives who are current or retired police officers.

At the time of Joan Diver's killing, Nigrelli had been in the state capital for a seminar on the BTK serial killer, Dennis Rader, who had been arrested the previous year. Rader had killed ten people in the Wichita, Kansas, area between 1974 and 1991. He had written taunting letters to the media following his slayings, signing them as "BTK," which stood for "bind, torture, and kill," a reference to his MO. He turned out to be a local dogcatcher. He was married, had a nice home, and was an active member of his church.

At the state police seminar, Nigrelli struck up a friendship with Otis Kelly, the Wichita detective who had addressed the panel. For five days, Nigrelli peppered Kelly with questions on how to set up such an investigation, the cold case files that need to be looked at, the old witnesses who needed to be tracked down and questioned again.

And now, Nigrelli was going to help lead the search for Buffalo's own BTK-type killer.

For years, Nigrelli had hoped to someday be involved in catching the Bike Path Rapist. It was not about the thrill or the glory of such a high-profile case, although there was no question he was energetic and ambitious. He aspired to head his own department someday, perhaps even becoming elected the sheriff of Erie County.

His emotional connection to the bike path case actually came before he even became a police officer.

In August of 1989, Nigrelli was twenty-three and working on the grounds crew of the Buffalo Bisons, the city's Triple-A baseball team. One evening at his job, he heard a woman screaming. It was a horrible sound. This was no joke. Something terrible was happening to the woman.

Nigrelli and three other groundskeepers ran toward the screaming. It was coming from a four-story parking ramp next door to Pilot Field. Nigrelli and a second grounds-keeper, Paul Britzalro, raced up the ramp to look for the woman. The two others, Michael Seltz and Jack Regan, were on the first floor when they saw a man coming out of the ramp with a bicycle on his shoulder, according to a *Buffalo News* article about the incident.

Seltz and Regan chased after the man and caught him. They held on to him until the police arrived. Nigrelli and Britzalro found the woman. She had wedged herself underneath one of the parked cars. They got down on their hands and knees to try to coax the woman out from under the car.

"We caught the guy," they told her. "It's okay now."

Nigrelli remembered how utterly terrified the woman looked. She seemed to be in shock. When she finally came out from under the car, he could see that the buttons on the Kelly green dress she was wearing had been ripped apart. He would later learn that she was from the same South Buffalo parish that he had grown up in.

The police came and took the assailant away. His name was Miguel Tiru.

The investigators on the case told Nigrelli that Tiru was a suspect in two other rapes. They were also looking into whether he could have been involved in two rapes that had happened in the Riverside area, and one that had happened in Amherst just four days earlier. He matched the description the victims had given.

Nigrelli had heard about those attacks. He remembered thinking that he might have helped catch a serial rapist.

He and the other groundskeepers were lauded by then-mayor Jimmy Griffin for saving the woman that day.

Tiru was soon ruled out as a suspect in the bike path cases. But he was convicted of second-degree robbery and first-degree attempted rape and spent twelve years in prison.

Ever since the day Nigrelli helped save that woman from being raped, he'd felt an emotional pull to sex assault cases. After graduating from Buffalo State College and joining the state police in 1990, he handled his share of rape cases as an investigator.

But finally, seventeen years after he thought he'd caught the Bike Path Rapist, he was getting another shot at it.

This time, Nigrelli, a marathon runner who knew the wisdom of staying in the race, thought he was going to catch him.

* * *

Buffalo's chief of detectives Dennis Richards was named by the city's police commissioner H. McCarthy Gipson to the task force, but Richards was far too busy dealing with the city's crime, so Buffalo had investigators on the unit, but no commander.

Amherst offered up Lieutenant Joseph LaCorte, who had worked on the Linda Yalem homicide and had been in charge of the Yalem investigation since 1991. LaCorte was at his home attempting to begin a long vacation when he got a phone call from his chief.

"Your vacation has been canceled," Chief Moslow informed him. LaCorte was then ordered to come in to the office immediately. It would be the first of forty-five straight days of working for him.

LaCorte, fifty-five, had been at the Amherst Police Department since 1979. He had two brothers who were also in law enforcement, but the tall and lanky lieutenant hadn't always aspired to be a cop. His first passion was music: the drums. When he graduated from high school in Buffalo, he left for Long Island, where he worked as a professional drummer. He played in a band with Bette Midler for a week.

But there was something inside him that drew him to the world of law enforcement. Had he had the gumption to go to college, LaCorte figured, he probably would have become a lawyer. Instead, he followed in his brothers' footsteps and became a police officer. He didn't consider himself a typical cop. His hero was Inspector Clouseau from the Pink Panther movies—no matter how bumbling he was, he always got his guy. And he never gave up. LaCorte's tidy office in Amherst was decorated with posters of the cartoon character.

* * *

The slaying of Linda Yalem and the two daytime rapes on Amherst's picturesque bike paths had been a black eye for the supposedly safe town, and it drove the department's detectives to be as methodical as humanly possible about pursuing the killer.

Since the trio of cases in 1989 and 1990 in their town, the Amherst police had accumulated a huge stack of documents related to the Bike Path Killer. They had, literally, thousands of pages of files and photographs, including a folder of one hundred 2-by-2 mug shots of possible suspects. They had giant poster boards with graphs and charts and presentation slides. They also had ten giant binder notebooks stuffed with well over one thousand pages of typewritten copies of detectives' worksheets.

The binders had been started shortly after the Yalem murder. They were ordered by Thomas Gould, who, at the time of the Yalem case, was a detective lieutenant, the position LaCorte held. Back in 1990, computers were only just starting to be used. All police reports were still typewritten at the time and they were kept in files. This meant keeping track of them was often a tricky feat. Gould wanted to be sure that every tip, lead, and shred of information was saved, catalogued, and easily retrieved, so he created a system for his detectives' work.

Every time a detective followed a tip or a lead on the bike path case, the detective was under strict orders to dictate his notes into a tape recorder. That, in turn, would be handed to a secretary who typed them. She would file each document in the binders and then make a reference to them in the index by placing the page numbers of whatever documents contained the subject's name next to the name listed.

By 2006, it contained the names of hundreds of people—anyone the Amherst police had ever gotten a tip on or had questioned over the last two decades that had any kind of connection to the bike path case. The indexing made it easy for someone to look up information on any past suspect.

The binders were kept on a counter at the back. It was the kind of methodical, exhaustive work that Amherst police officers prided themselves on.

For six months after Yalem's murder, Gould had eight detectives working the case. After that, the crew had been whittled down to three. But it was always Gould's priority. Until he retired as captain and chief of detectives in 1997, Gould would hold sessions every couple of months at which he'd split up all the paperwork in the binders among his detectives and they would read through the documents, looking for any missed clues or opportunities. But over all those years, the painstaking cataloguing and review sessions never yielded anything.

When Ed Monan was named Amherst's chief investigator on the Bike Path Rapist cases, he took the assignment to heart. Two years into the assignment, Monan was focused on the Suzi Coggins case. From poring over her case file, he got the impression that the man who had raped her seemed very familiar with the area. The bike path by the high school wasn't the sort of place that was well known to people outside of Hamburg. He had the feeling that the suspect might live in that town.

As he searched through the binders of all the old tips and leads, Monan came across a file that named a potential suspect who lived in Hamburg, but then had ruled him out. Later on in the stack, there was another tip that included the same name, but with a slightly different spelling. Monan looked up the names and got two hits. One was a man that just didn't fit in description or age. The other was a convicted rapist who lived in Hamburg. He retrieved a photo of him and noticed that he fit the description of the Bike Path Killer. He was on the short side, had dark hair and olive-colored skin.

His name was David E. Oliveri.

The fact that his name was David was significant. He knew from his research over the years that one of the victims from Buffalo had told investigators that her attacker had said his name was "Dave."

Monan showed LaCorte what he had found and they took it to their chief of police. It sure looked like this was their suspect. They looked into Oliveri and learned he had just recently moved to North Carolina.

The APD was under tight budget restrictions that year, but the police chief ignored that. He sent Monan, LaCorte, and a third detective, Michael Moore, on a plane to Charlotte, North Carolina. They were given one task: to get this man's DNA whatever way they could, and they weren't to come back without it.

Monan and LaCorte knew this would not be an easy task. Bosses always think perps spit everywhere they go, spreading their DNA. They don't. Following them around can often be a frustrating, futile task, but the men knew they had to do it. Everyone in the Amherst Police Department was betting their paychecks that this was the guy they'd been looking for.

They went through the garbage at Oliveri's home in Indian Trail, a suburb of Charlotte, but found nothing. They began following him around, wherever he drove. They found out he worked at a Harley-Davidson dealership. They watched him there and saw he took frequent outdoors smoke breaks. When he'd go back in, they grabbed his cigarette butts. They Express Mailed the butts back to Amherst for analysis, but there was no DNA to be found on them.

On one occasion, Oliveri suddenly started driving very fast and very erratically. Monan, LaCorte, and Moore thought they'd been made. But they stayed on him, tailing him in their rental car, as Oliveri drove close to one hundred miles per hour and then suddenly calmed down. It sure seemed weird and it only confirmed the suspicions the detectives had about this man.

After several more days of these dead ends, the men realized they weren't going to get his DNA just by following him. They needed to get more proactive. They came up with a plan. It happened to be Race Week at the Lowe's Motor Speedway and there were two hundred thousand people expected to descend on the Charlotte area to take in the NASCAR event.

LaCorte, Monan, and Moore decided they were going to pose as representatives of a children's dental charity who were doing a fund-raiser connected to Race Week. The plan was to say they were collecting old toothbrushes. For every old toothbrush that was donated, a certain amount of money would be given to their charity and the donors would be given a new toothbrush in return. They made fake name tags for themselves, drew up a big flyer touting their phony charity, and knocked on Oliveri's door.

A kid answered the door and LaCorte launched into the charade. The kid went for it and went and got every family member's toothbrush. The detectives were psyched. Their scheme had worked. They raced back to their hotel room and gave their boss the good news. A few minutes later, they got a call back. The district attorney's office wasn't going for it. A seizure like that just wasn't going to stand up in court. They were told they needed to go back and get someone's signature for the toothbrushes.

The detectives were crushed. They thought they had just pulled off a brilliant maneuver, but they decided they'd give it another shot and went back to the house. They rang the doorbell and this time Oliveri himself opened the door. "I wondered what happened to our toothbrushes," he said as he signed the waiver that was handed to him.

The detectives were deeply relieved. They sent the toothbrushes to Buffalo and waited in their hotel room to hear about the DNA test results—and for the go-ahead to arrest Oliveri. Monan had begun contemplating retiring. He thought this would be such a wonderful way to end his career.

The next day, the results were in. Oliveri was not the Bike Path Killer. LaCorte, Monan, and Moore were flabbergasted. They thought for sure they had their man. They couldn't believe they'd been wrong. They were so upset that they got in their rental car and started driving back to New York. They couldn't stand the idea of sitting around until the next day to catch a flight to Buffalo.

However, there was a silver lining. A few days after they returned, they learned that the DNA was a hit on another unsolved rape. On July 26, 1995, a fourteen-year-old girl had been lured into the woods behind McKinley Mall, which straddles South Buffalo and Hamburg, and was raped. Shortly after that incident, another man, a mentally disabled former steelworker, was arrested and blamed for the rape. He was freed after he had spent five months in jail. Now the real rapist had been found.

Captain Daniel Shea from Hamburg, Monan, and a third detective flew down to North Carolina and picked up Oliveri. He was convicted of first-degree rape and was sentenced to fifteen years in prison.

And the bike path case remained unsolved.

12

The Investigators

It was no surprise to Alan Rozansky when he got the call from Patronik that he'd be the sheriff's man on the task force. As the lead investigator in the Diver homicide, and one of the sheriff's senior detectives, he expected the call. It was still an honor. He was itching to find the man who had killed Joan Diver.

Rozansky joined the sheriff's department in 1970 when he was just nineteen years old. At the time, he was finishing up his first year at the University at Buffalo. He was majoring in sociology. He was in school as part of the Law Enforcement Education Program (LEEP): his tuition was covered, but he had to commit to working in law enforcement for four years after graduating.

At UB, Rozansky ran into a friend of his from high school and found out he'd been working undercover for the sheriff monitoring subversive activities on campus. There'd been widespread demonstrations on campus the previous academic year, touched off by a protest over racial inequalities in UB's athletic department. It had escalated as the campus called in Buffalo police to quell the unrest. Thousands of students were involved in protests, which sometimes grew ugly. In one case, a firebomb was thrown into a library destroying hundreds of books. At another demonstration, students roasted a pig in effigy.

Rozansky was eager to sign up. He needed the extra money and it was a way for him to get some law enforcement experience. He went to school full-time as he kept tabs on the students for the sheriff's office. He soon was assigned other undercover work, mainly in narcotics. After graduating, Rozansky stuck with the sheriff's department, even past his four years, working an assortment of beats. One year, he and his friend from UB were on DWI detail. They racked up five hundred arrests. He eventually worked his way up to detective. He worked in the warrant squad and also in narcotics.

In a city of mostly Catholics, Rozansky stood out as one of the few Jewish detectives in the area. He knew of one Jewish cop in Amherst and there was a Jewish FBI agent who worked out of Buffalo. But that was it. In New York City, there are plenty of Jewish cops. But in Buffalo—not so. That never was a problem for Rozansky. He never got any flak about it. Generally, it meant always volunteering to work Sundays, Christmas, and other Christian holidays.

Fellow investigators say he reminded them of the old TV detective Columbo because of his sometimes rumpled clothes and the roundabout ways he used to get his suspect.

Rozansky was joined on the task force from the sheriff's department by Greg Savage, a detective sergeant, and Greg McCarthy, a narcotics detective who was first cousins with Nigrelli.

Nigrelli decided to bring on Josh Keats to work with him. He knew Keats, from the Violent Crime Task Force and knew him to be a top-notch investigator.

Keats still looked like the three-sport athlete he was at Orchard Park High School, a suburb to the east of Buffalo, and the home of the Buffalo Bills. He had taken an unlikely route to police work.

He graduated from Allegheny College, a high-achieving small liberal-arts school in Meadville, Pennsylvania. While classmates headed off to law school, medical school, or Wall Street, Keats went back home and started taking police tests.

"I always wanted to be a cop," Keats said. "No question about it."

He joined the state police in 1994, and before he was picked for the task force, he'd worked his way up from a uniformed trooper to the Bureau of Criminal Investigations. Keats investigated homicides with his partner, Chris Weber, a late addition to the task force.

Dennis Richards, the Buffalo chief of detectives, had an easy decision picking Buffalo's representative. He chose Dennis Delano, a gruff, old-school detective who bore a passing resemblance to Dennis Franz's Andy Sipowicz character on the ABC police drama *NYPD Blue*. He spent years in the department's auto theft squad, was the department's cold-case detective, and had been given the Majane Mazur case.

Delano came from a family of cops. His brother Paul was a retired Buffalo detective, and Paul's son was now a detective. So, too, were the children of their brother Bob on the Buffalo Police Department. Bob Delano was a former Buffalo parks commissioner, who had gone to prison after a celebrated trial in Buffalo on charges that his workers did favors for him and other top city leaders.

LaCorte, too, had an easy decision to make on Amherst's representative. He chose Ed Monan, the veteran detective he had gone to North Carolina with, who had become the department's lead investigator in Linda Yalem's unsolved killing and the town's two other bike path rapes.

Monan took on that role when Ray Klimczak retired in 2002. Even before that, Monan had been interested in working on the case. As a patrolman, he had been part of the search party that had found Linda Yalem's body. He had volunteered to Lieutenant Gould to help out in the case in any way that he could. Gould assigned him to surveillance duty. Like Klimczak had before Yalem's murder, Monan spent hours out on the bike paths dressed in camouflage looking for potential suspects. It was only natural that Monan would be put on the task force.

13

Ten Known Cases

Before the task force members left for the weekend, LaCorte pulled out all the paperwork that Amherst had collected over the years on the Bike Path Killer case and brought it all into the task force office. He also showed them where the binders from the Yalem case were kept: on the counter in the detective bureau.

All the task force members needed to get familiar with all ten cases that had been linked to the Bike Path Killer, either through DNA or by MO. Over the span of twenty years, he had committed seven rapes and three murders, the last being Joan Diver. Among the paperwork they would look at was a booklet that Lieutenant Gould had written up over a decade ago. In it, he had laid out all the details in the first seven cases, up to the Linda Yalem homicide. Gould had made one thousand copies of this packet and distributed them to every law enforcement agency he could think of. He was hoping that someone from another jurisdiction would notice that the cases matched the MO of one of their own or would somehow jog the memory of some investigator.

Now all of this information was in the hands of the people given the sole task of finding the killer.

* * *

The task force members saw how this rapist/killer that they were hunting had struck all over Erie County. There had been five cases in Buffalo, three in Amherst, and one each in Hamburg and Clarence.

His victims ranged in age from fourteen to forty-five. They were all white women, but didn't fit any one profile. He didn't seem to have a "type." The one thing they shared was that they were alone on a bike path or some sort of isolated shortcut when they were attacked.

The MO in each case was eerily similar. Each victim was choked with a garrote, a bit of rope or wire he looped around their necks. The rapist used the garrote to control his victims and often forced them to walk long distances to a preselected location for his rapes. He gave direct orders to his victims, and before he would flee, he always told them to wait a period of time before moving.

Every cop in town knew at least a little something about these cases. In fact, it seemed everyone in the county did. The list of incidents had been printed over and over in the *Buffalo News* and shown in graphics on the TV news through the years as investigators pleaded with the public for help in catching the culprit.

Over the years, the case had been featured on *Unsolved Mysteries*. A chance to run it on *America's Most Wanted* (*AMW*), before the Joan Diver murder, ended after the Amherst police objected to the show's sharing of a telephone number of a rape victim with the press. However, *America's Most Wanted* eventually did produce an episode about the case later on. Each time those shows were re-aired, even if it was in the middle of the night, tips would suddenly start pouring in from all across the country. The killer remained free, though.

Now, with the task force members assembling with the sole goal of finally catching this elusive predator that had hurt so many women over so many years, it was time for them to take a good hard look at these cases with their fresh eyes.

They started with the first case. The first case that they knew of.

June 12, 1986—It was a little after 9:00 A.M. on a Thursday when a forty-four-year-old well-to-do woman went out for a morning jog in Delaware Park. The park is beloved by the people of Buffalo, a remnant of the city's golden era when money from steel and shipping transformed it into a world-class metropolis. The park had been designed by Frederick Law Olmsted, the designer of New York's Central Park, and featured a man-made body of water known as Hoyt Lake, gently sloping hills, lush trees, a golf course, and two popular exercise paths.

She was running on the path that encircled Hoyt Lake, a one-mile-loop popular with joggers and dog walkers. At about 9:25 A.M., she came to a split in the path near a life-size replica of *David,* a bronze casting of the original Michelangelo masterpiece. The statue sits on top of a hill and looks on one side to the park and to the other at the Scajaquada Expressway, a well-traveled highway.

A runner in a gray jogging suit, wearing what the woman thought was a whistle on a cord around his neck, was coming toward her. Just as he passed, the woman would later tell police, she felt something go around her neck. She then felt it tighten. She struggled to get her hand underneath whatever it was that was strangling her. She believed it was some sort of a cord. As she fought, the cord got tighter and tighter.

"Shut up and walk," she heard the man say. "Don't resist and you won't get hurt." Pulling on the garrote, he forced her into some underbrush. "No talking," he commanded. Then he demanded: "Stop."

The man was not tall, certainly not more than five-nine,

she noticed. He was of medium build, possibly Italian. He had short, dark hair and dark mustache. The man then said in his smooth, baritone voice: "Remove your shorts and panties."

She complied.

"Put your shorts over your head." The man then lifted up her shirt, pulled down her bra, and fondled her.

"Lie down," he demanded. She lay down on the ground. He got on top of her and raped her. When he was done, he got up and told the woman: "Give me ten minutes."

But before leaving, he had one more act of cruelty in store for the woman. He tightened the garrote that was still around her neck one more time. He pulled and pulled until she passed out.

He was long gone by the time she regained consciousness.

The rape stirred fear among the people of Buffalo. It prompted the head of the police sex offense squad (SOS) at the time to issue a warning to women joggers. *"It is only common sense to stay away from isolated and wooded areas of the park,"* Assistant Chief of Detectives Gregory Simonian told the *Buffalo News*.

The rape was all the more shocking because it had taken place in roughly the same area where a series of rapes had occurred a couple of years earlier. A suspect had been arrested in those rapes and was about to go on trial for them. Runners had just begun to let their guard down again when this woman was attacked.

The next case police knew of was the July 14, 1986, rape of Suzi Coggins, seventeen, in Hamburg. She was taking a shortcut through a wooded area on her way to summer school at Frontier Central High School when she was attacked. He used a rope to choke her and control her.

June 10, 1988—There were just a couple of weeks left of school as a sixteen-year-old student at Riverside High School took a shortcut to school along a set of old railroad tracks. The neighborhood, in the northwest section of Buffalo, abuts the bank of the Niagara River, which is actually a strait that flows north and empties Lake Erie into the world-famous Niagara Falls. Riverside is a working-class community dotted with modest homes and a large steel plant.

It was about 9:00 A.M. when the girl saw a man walking toward her. She thought he was short, about five-five, and maybe 170 pounds. He had brown hair and had a lot of stubble on his face. He was wearing a plaid shirt, blue workman's pants, and a blue baseball cap.

Just as she walked past him, he suddenly turned around and wrapped a cord around her neck.

"Shut up till we get there," he ordered her.

Pulling hard on the cord, he pushed the teenager, forcing her to walk six hundred feet to a junkyard. He stopped next to a junked car.

"I just got out of prison for raping and killing a girl," the man taunted her.

He then ordered her to take off all her clothes, or "I will strangle you."

The girl did as she was told.

He then gestured to pieces of gray duct tape that were lined up on the junked car.

"Tape your eyes," he told the girl. She did. Then she felt him put more duct tape over her mouth.

"I'm going to play with myself for a while," he informed her.

The teenager was terrified. And she tried to scream through the tape over her mouth. "Shut up!" he barked.

"You're giving me trouble. I'll kill you if you keep giving me trouble."

He raped her on the ground.

"Lie here for twenty minutes," he ordered the girl before running away.

May 1, 1989—Another Riverside High School student was taking the railroad shortcut, despite what had happened there a year earlier. It's not clear if she had known about the other attack. It was 7:45 A.M. and the fifteen-year-old girl was on her way to school.

As she was walking along the tracks, she saw a white man in a navy blue jogging suit, a shiny silky jacket, and a blue baseball cap come toward her. He flashed a smile. After walking past him, she turned around and saw that he was suddenly running toward her with what looked like a rope in his hand.

The student turned to run, but the man caught up with her. He quickly wrapped the rope around her neck and tightened it.

"My name is Dave," he told her. "Shut up or I'll kill you."

The man forced the girl to walk behind an abandoned building. The junkyard where the other student had been raped the previous year was visible from the building.

"I want a piece of ass," the man told the teenager. He handed her white surgical tape and ordered her to tape her eyes closed. He then pulled down her pants and raped her from the front and from behind. "Do it doggie-style," he had crassly demanded of her.

When he was done raping her, he told the girl: "Take off your shirt to give me more time to get away. Stay here for ten minutes."

Buffalo police investigating her case began looking at whether her rape might be related to the one from June 1988.

The next three times, he struck on Amherst's bike paths.

* * *

August 24, 1989—A fourteen-year-old girl had just spent the night at a girlfriend's house and was on her way to cheerleading practice at Sweet Home High School. It was about 9:00 A.M., and the girl set out on the Willow Ridge bike path, which runs from Ellicott Creek to behind the Willow Ridge subdivision, along Interstate 990. She wasn't all that familiar with the route.

She was walking down the path when she was suddenly attacked from behind. She felt what seemed like a rope around her neck. Someone was pulling on it backward. Hard.

"You scream and you die," she heard a man's voice tell her.

The girl asked him what he was doing.

"I'm a little horny," he replied.

The man pushed her along the path until they got to a three-foot-high wire mesh fence. The girl stood face-to-face with the man. She stared straight ahead, right into his eyes. He had dark brown hair and a mustache. She thought he might be of Mexican, or at least some type of Hispanic, descent.

The man then picked the girl up and carried her effortlessly over the fence and took her to a clearing in the woods off the path. He then told her to sit down.

The man ripped the cheerleader's bra and pulled off her pants. He pulled the laces out of her sneakers and used them to tie her hands behind her back. He took a roll of medical adhesive tape and wrapped tape around her wrists. He also put pieces of tape over her eyes and her mouth.

All the while he kept the rope around her neck, tightening it to make her comply with his commands. He stood above her as she lay on the ground, asking her questions, about where she lived, and such. As she would answer, he'd pull on the rope and she'd briefly lose consciousness.

"What's the matter?" he asked her at one point.

"You're my third," he also told her.

The man raped her there on the ground. When he finished, he told her to "stay put." He then pulled on the rope again until she passed out.

At least an hour passed before the girl awoke and stumbled out onto the path, where some joggers found her.

The entire Amherst Police Department was in shock. None of the cops could ever remember a rape in broad daylight by a stranger happening in the town of Amherst.

The next victim was the secretary who was trying to keep fit for ice-skating by walking each morning on the Ellicott Creek bike path. She was raped on May 31, 1990.

His last victim in Amherst marked his first murder—Linda Yalem, on September 29, 1990.

He killed Majane Mazur two years later, on or about October 30, 1992. Her body was found three weeks later.

October 19, 1994—Another Riverside High School student was walking to school that morning. It had been many years since other girls at her high school had been raped on their way to the high school using the very shortcut she was on. The fourteen-year-old either didn't know about those rapes or had figured it had happened so long ago, it wasn't going to happen again.

She was walking along the railroad tracks when a man approached her from behind, at about 7:45 A.M.

"If you move or scream, I'll kill you," he threatened her. She did exactly as she was told.

He ripped her clothes off and made her lie down on the ground.

"How old are you?" he demanded of her. "Did you ever have sex before?"

The man put tape over her eyes and bound her wrists together behind her. He put her pants over her head.

He raped her, but he let her live, unlike his previous two victims.

"You can leave in a half hour," he told her before scurrying away.

And then, it was as if he had vanished. For twelve long years, he went dormant. That was until Joan Diver.

Chapter 14

Task Force
Goes to Amherst

Howard and the other police brass came to an agreement that the task force would be headquartered in Amherst. Part of the reasoning was that it happened to be fairly close to Clarence. The state police did have barracks in Clarence, but it was very small.

It was also understood that Amherst police had compiled the most data about the entire Bike Path Rapist case over the years. Up until 2004, when DNA tests showed Mazur was a victim of the Bike Path Rapist, it had been assumed that Linda Yalem was his only homicide. That had only put more pressure on the Amherst police to try to do everything they could possibly do to crack the case.

The Amherst police also felt that they had a more vested interest in it. Some of the detectives had truly taken these attacks in their town personally. Homicides and rapes weren't totally unusual in places like Buffalo, with its sad but typical big-city problems: poverty, drugs, gangs, and the like. But they so rarely happened in Amherst. Murders and rapes tended to be the result of disputes between two people who knew each other. Crimes of passion. But women being targeted in broad daylight? That was totally unheard of.

Amherst, the largest town in Erie County, with its 116,500 residents, is a largely white suburb to the northeast of Buffalo. While blacks and Hispanics make up more than a third of Buffalo's nearly three hundred thousand citizens, and the city is ranked as the nation's second poorest big city (as of the 2000 census), Amherst is nearly 90 percent white, and largely affluent, according to the 2000 census.

After the decision was made in Albany to build the new campus of the state University at Buffalo in Amherst, the largest university in the state system, Amherst became the fastest-growing town in the state by the late 1980s.

Its police department had been formed a year after the town began in 1818, when Joseph Hershey and Palmer Cleveland were appointed its first two constables. The department's 154 sworn officers patrol the town's fifty-four-square miles and for the past half-dozen years have made Amherst among the top two to three safest municipalities in America.

Headquarters for the department, where the task force reported on Friday, November 17, 2006, is located in the center of the Audubon New Community, one of three planned communities set up by the state's Urban Development Corporation in the 1970s to coincide with the state's plans for the new university campus. "Live, work, play" was the development's motto, as government offices, business parks, recreation areas, and a mix of private housing, senior citizen apartments, and subsidized housing, were built on what had been fields and forests.

Amherst Police headquarters, named in 2006 for longtime chief Herbert E. Zimmerman, is a low-slung brick building with plenty of space. Which is what struck the Bike Path Rapist Task Force investigators who reported that first day as a bit odd. They were taken to a windowless beige interview room, no bigger than ten by ten feet, with two desks shoved together in the middle of the room, a few chairs scattered around the walls, phones, a computer and table, some filing cabinets, and a closed-circuit television (CCTV) camera normally used during interrogations. There was one door. A corrugated wall set it off from an identical room on the other side. This would be their new home.

By the time the task force members began arriving on November 17, fresh tips from the public were already pouring in. They were coming in so fast that the voice mail box on the tip line would fill up, and the calls were being bounced down to the Amherst dispatchers.

LaCorte was in charge of cataloguing all of these tips, ranking them by importance and usability, and then dividing them up among the investigators on the task force. It was a system he had learned back in 1998 from the FBI after the shooting death of Dr. Barnett Slepian, an Amherst gynecologist who performed abortions. It would turn out that he'd been targeted by James Charles Kopp, a militant antiabortion activist. Thousands of tips streamed into the APD then too. The FBI set the department up with a computer program that organized the tips into various categories, from name and date to specific description details. For instance, if a detective wanted to see any tip involving a red car seen at a crime scene, he could input "red car" and get a list of all of them.

LaCorte knew from experience how tips can range from the totally pointless to the absolutely bizarre. He'd seen tips from people saying they saw a person who matched the description of the Bike Path Killer walking on a street a few years before, and leave it at that. People called in famous Buffalo personalities as potential suspects. LaCorte recalled the day years earlier when a woman walked into the Amherst Police Department, asking to talk to detectives. She told the receptionist at the front that she believed her husband was the Bike Path Rapist. She was immediately escorted upstairs. LaCorte and Klimczak, who had not yet retired, sat down with her. They were very curious about what this woman had to say.

"I think it's my husband," the woman said.

LaCorte asked her: "Why do you think that?"

The woman had a deadly serious look on her face. She leaned in and said quietly, "He touches me when I'm sleeping."

LaCorte remembered how he and Klimczak refused to look at each other because they knew they'd bust up laughing. They told the woman they'd look into her situation and escorted her out.

With the bike path case reopened, the hotline was receiving a lot of the same types of calls. It seemed everyone with a grudge against someone was turning them in. But LaCorte believed there was a chance that one of those tips could turn out to be the key to solving the case. He had his tip program back up and running to deal with all of the incoming information. A secretary was busy inputting each tip that had come in, and he began ranking them as one, two, or three, based on how good the tip seemed to be.

As the detectives filed into the office, he began dividing them among the detectives, but they weren't sure what to make of this. Keats, the state police homicide investigator, had been under the impression that he should be delving into the old cases and the Diver homicide. But everyone tried to make the best of it. They knew they certainly couldn't ignore the tips.

Rozansky let his fellow task force members know that the sheriff's office would be working with the state probation office that weekend to try to round up as many parolees as possible who had failed to give a DNA sample. A state law had passed the previous summer mandating anyone on probation to submit to DNA tests as a condition of their release. Those not in compliance could be picked up and forced to comply. The hope was that maybe the killer was on probation for some unrelated crime and could finally be forced to give his DNA.

The task force members all agreed that the following Monday, they would hold a press conference to introduce the task force. Amherst police pushed the idea of having one every day, to try to keep the tips coming, which some of the others thought might be a little over-the-top. But they agreed.

15

Lots of Leads

The news about the DNA did not surprise retired Amherst detective Ray Klimczak one bit.

As the investigation into the Joan Diver murder had stretched on, he hadn't been able to stop himself from checking in with his old comrades at the Amherst Police Department. He would call Moslow and LaCorte to check in with them on any news.

He couldn't understand how any investigator could think that this was the work of anyone but the Bike Path Rapist.

This poor woman had been strangled to death on a bike path—on the anniversary of the Linda Yalem murder. There was a double ligature mark on her neck. How could it be anyone else?

The year had already been a difficult one for the retired detective. That spring, one of his sisters, a nun, had been murdered by an ex-con. Sister Karen Klimczak had been a fixture in Buffalo. She was fiercely devoted to nonviolence. She designed and distributed lawn signs that read NONVIOLENCE BEGINS WITH ME, which had become quite popular in the Buffalo area. She was also famous for a giant dove-shaped sign that she maintained that tracked the number of days between homicides in Buffalo.

Sister Karen ran a halfway house in a church building, where her dear friend and colleague, Father John Bissonette, had been beaten to death during a robbery. She felt it would be a fitting tribute to his pursuit of peace to bring ex-convicts to the house to help them with their transition from prison to life outside. One of those ex-cons, Craig Lynch, decided to steal Klimczak's cell phone so he could sell it to get some money to buy crack cocaine. He was in her room when she came in. He grabbed her and beat her until she was dead. It was the night of Good Friday, 2006. He took her body and buried it in the earthen floor of a dilapidated garage, across the street from his own mother's home. He soon confessed to the killing, saying it was an accident.

Klimczak had been devastated by his sister's death.

And now, with this latest bike path murder, he couldn't stop thinking about the bike path cases. Diver's brutal murder, so close to his own home, had brought back a flood of memories from all those years he had spent chasing the Bike Path Rapist.

There were so many times that the Amherst police had thought they had the guy.

Even before he was put on the case, there had been a false alarm.

Shortly after the rape of the teenage cheerleader, Buffalo police had alerted Amherst that they had just put a man in jail with a prior history of rapes. The Amherst police went down to the holding center to interview the inmate. The man acknowledged he had raped in the past, but he was adamant that he had nothing to do with the Amherst teenager's rape. The Amherst cops took his photo and put it in a photo array for the Amherst girl to take a look at. She picked the man out right away and the Amherst police went back to the man sitting in jail. This time, the suspect voluntarily gave his blood to prove his innocence. The blood was sent to the FBI lab for testing. About six months later, the tests came back. No match.

Klimczak recalled another false alarm.

It happened during one of his early-morning camouflage details on the Ellicott Creek bike path. At about five-thirty, Klimczak, crouched down in the brush, saw a man walking back and forth on the path. He kept turning his head back nervously. He was on the short side. He had dark hair and a dark mustache. Klimczak radioed in his information. A patrol officer stopped him and found out his first name was David. That was a red flag: one of the girls raped in Buffalo had told investigators that the rapist said his name was "Dave."

Klimczak and another detective, Michael Dailey, began investigating the man. They found out that he used to live near where the two Buffalo high-school girls were raped and that he had recently moved to Amherst. He had just gotten a job doing maintenance at UB's north campus. He lived with his mother, and people who knew him said he had problems dealing with women.

He looked like a possible candidate.

Klimczak and Dailey approached this man and asked him to submit to a blood test for DNA. He refused, so they kept asking. They would find him at his home and at campus and continued to pressure him until he finally relented. "Enough is enough!" he yelled at them, and let them take him to a phlebotomist. His blood was sent to the FBI lab.

It came back negative. No match. Again.

The investigation continued as such. Hot leads that turned out to be nothing.

There were times when it seemed almost comical—if it hadn't been that the suspect was a sadistic rapist and killer.

Someone had phoned in a tip that the rapist was a man who played bingo every Wednesday night at a Catholic church in the Riverside area of Buffalo. The tipster said the man had dark hair, a mustache, and might be a priest.

Klimczak paired up with his partner at the time, Detective Robert Brown, a huge man, about six-three. They went to their captain and told him they wanted to pursue this lead. They planned to go undercover and blend in with the bingo players while they tried to find the mustachioed priest. They asked if they could have some cash to play bingo, but the captain balked. He told them to use their own money and they'd be reimbursed for any expenses.

On the following Wednesday night, Klimczak and Brown headed to the Riverside church. They watched as a steady flow of older women made their way into the church. They followed them in.

A young woman was working the front desk. "Can I help you?" she asked sweetly.

Klimczak said: "We want to play bingo tonight. How much is it?"

"How many cards would you like to play?" the woman asked.

Klimczak and Brown had no idea. They'd never played bingo before.

Brown hedged: "Whatever is like the normal amount?"

The woman replied: "It's three cards for five dollars."

Klimczak and Brown figured that sounded reasonable. "Okay, we'll take three cards," Brown said.

"Well, you want three cards each, right?" the girl asked.

"Oh yeah. We each want that," Klimczak said.

They walked into the bingo room and found the entire crowd staring straight at them. They were the only men in the room, and all the women there appeared to be regulars. Many of the players had arranged their lucky troll dolls and other trinkets on the tables in front of them.

Klimczak and Brown, trying to be as inconspicuous as

possible, took a seat at a table toward the back. The ladies at the table were very curious about them. The detectives were determined to wait around for their suspect so they began to play bingo.

The bingo caller yelled out "B-3," and suddenly the woman sitting next to Detective Brown jumped up. "He's got bingo! He's got bingo!"

Brown was mortified. So much for the undercover surveillance they had hoped to do. Brown was handed $40 for his bingo achievement.

Klimczak and Brown realized that the bingo mission was a bust, so they asked the ladies sitting by them what time bingo ended. They said refreshments would be served during the break. The new plan was to just sneak out then.

Break time soon came and Klimczak and Brown began walking out. "How come you're leaving?" the ladies screamed at them. "You've got a lucky card!"

Brown handed over his cards to their new friends at the table and told them to enjoy the rest of the game.

As they were walking away, Klimczak overheard one of the ladies whispering to another: "I think they're gay."

The detectives had to laugh. But then they realized they were back to square one. The lead on the priest at bingo was a dud. And tomorrow they'd chase down another one.

Klimczak had pursued dozens of leads like that up until the day he retired in 2004. None of them had ever amounted to anything. He hoped that this new task force would have better luck, but he also knew they'd probably face a lot of dead ends as well.

16

The Prosecutors

Kenneth Case always knew he wanted to be a lawyer. It took him a while to realize he wanted to be a prosecutor.

Case followed his father into a large firm representing insurance companies in Albany, New York, following his graduation from law school at Western New England College in 1987.

But being the son of a senior partner in a forty-member firm was not why he went into law, so he moved with his wife to her hometown of Buffalo, where he took a job with John Condon, one of the better criminal-defense trial lawyers in town. Condon died in 2008.

It was during Condon's defense of Edward Beaufort-Cutner, a reserve sheriff's deputy involved in a vicious attack on a local female real estate agent, that Case realized the good guys were sitting on the other side of the courtroom.

He interviewed with a former partner at Condon's firm, Kevin Dillon, then the district attorney, and was all but hired until Dillon realized there were years of appeals coming in the Cutner case. It wouldn't look right to hire a member of Cutner's defense team, so Case went to work for a legal publisher, Westlaw Publishing, for three years to wait out the appeals.

He became an ADA in 1993, and six years later, he joined the DA's homicide bureau. By the time Joan Diver was killed in September 2006, Case had prosecuted one hundred homicides, taking twenty-five of them to trial. He had won every one.

But Case was not the bureau chief, and many of the glamour, high-publicity homicides over the years had gone to more senior prosecutors.

That was the situation again when Joan Diver was killed. As homicide bureau chief, Frank A. Sedita III, the DDA, was called on by his boss, District Attorney Frank J. Clark, to handle it.

Sedita is the scion of a powerful political family in Buffalo. His grandfather Frank A. Sedita was mayor of Buffalo during the 1960s, a time when Buffalo began its slide as a Rust Belt city, and much of downtown and its surrounding neighborhoods were demolished under the guise of urban renewal. He remained a beloved figure among the area's many Italian-Americans. His father, Frank A. Sedita Jr., or "Chickie," a boyhood nickname that stuck, is a state supreme court justice.

Frank III is a career prosecutor, who was being groomed to take over Frank Clark's job as district attorney when he retired.

But Sedita, an experienced homicide prosecutor who had tried some of the office's major cases, was busy getting ready to try a complicated homicide, and he was butting heads with some of the sheriff's detectives investigating the Diver homicide and another killing in Clarence, the shooting of Thomas Montgomery in a factory parking lot.

So Clark assigned Case to handle both the Diver homicide, as well as the shooting of Thomas Montgomery.

Case discovered the sheriff's department was looking at two people in the Diver homicide: her husband, Steven, the university chemistry professor whose behavior after the homicide baffled the investigators, and the so-called Thong

Man who had been seen running on the bike path in strange attire near the time of the Diver homicide.

Both Case and Sedita had their doubts about whether the Diver homicide would be solved.

Sedita said he told Frank Clark when Diver was first killed, there were two possible suspects: her husband or the Bike Path Rapist.

"And I didn't think it was her husband," he said.

The signature double-ligature mark on Joan Diver's neck, the coincidence of her murder occurring sixteen years to the day after Linda Yalem's killing, and the fact the crime happened on a bike path convinced him the killer had struck again.

Like Case, Sedita is both book- and street-smart. He had eight years of education from the Jesuits, first at Canisius High School, then Canisius College, graduating in 1983, magna cum laude.

He was a Frank Raiche Pre-Law Scholarship student at Canisius, a program named after a famed Buffalo defense attorney, and he graduated from the University at Buffalo Law School.

Since coming to the district attorney's office in 1988, he had risen quickly, and in 2002, he was named one of Frank Clark's top deputies and chief of the homicide bureau.

Both he and Case were concerned about the sheriff's investigators' preoccupation with Steven Diver.

"Not that Steve did it intentionally, but I think it was just a result of circumstance, he ended up making himself a pretty good suspect," Case said.

"Again, not intentionally, the sheriffs weren't the most experienced in homicides, it was a clash of personalities. Diver was mad at the search being given up, which made him pull back, and when he pulled back, that made them more suspicious. He hired a lawyer, he had a family spokesman. So we wasted a lot of time looking at him, a lot of that was before I was involved."

17

Pleas to the Public

Over the first weekend after the task force was formed, the parolee sweep began. Sheriff's deputies arrested one man, a white man in his forties who had skipped out on a court appearance just a couple of days earlier when he was scheduled to submit to a DNA swab of his cheek. They were especially intrigued to learn that his birthday happened to fall on September 29.

But they all had a gut feeling that was just far too easy. It would take far more to catch the killer.

Monday started off with the big press conference. It was packed with local print, TV, and radio reporters, as well as crews from both *America's Most Wanted* and Fox News' *Geraldo Rivera*.

The heads of the police agencies on the task force introduced themselves and handed out a case summary of the ten attacks that had been linked to the Bike Path Rapist. The list was succinct and lacked much of the detail that had been given out to the task force members. Over the years, both Amherst and Buffalo police had been criticized for putting out too much information to the public. It had led to too many false leads.

The task force members told the reporters that their agencies were working with the FBI to come up with a new composite sketch of the killer. And they asked the public to call in tips. By the time the press conference had started, they had received three hundred calls with information.

The task force members would be busy sifting through them all for the next couple of weeks.

LaCorte divvied them up, and the detectives would go through each one, trying to determine whether they were useful in any way or could be ruled out. He followed his predecessor Tom Gould's model for keeping track of information. He handed out tape recorders to each of the task force members so they could give their notes orally. The notes were then transcribed by Amherst clerks, and then the paperwork would be sent back to LaCorte. After he signed off on it, his boss, Captain Timothy Green, would look over them as well, before determining what to do with each mini-investigation.

Not everyone knew each other at first, but with the close quarters, that changed in a hurry. "There were only two desks," said Nigrelli, who was in Albany at a conference when the task force was announced and got there a few days later. "So when you walked in the room, it was Alan (Rozansky) and Josh (Keats) on one side of the desk, Ed Monan was on the other side. And I sat in a chair, just a regular chair, and Dennis Delano sat in a chair."

"They gave us each a little spot on the desk," Keats remembered. "Basically, if you wanted to read something, you needed to go in the corner."

Delano got a board and put it across his lap to use as a desk.

"So we had files in our laps," said Nigrelli. "It just wasn't the setup for a long-term investigation. We told them that, we expressed this at the beginning."

Nigrelli and Patronik talked to LaCorte and Tim Green, a captain who was Amherst chief of detectives, and told them they needed more room. Amherst offered a larger room, with computers, phone lines, and a white board, but said it would be needed soon for police training.

That day, Rozansky, along with Greg McCarthy and Jack Graham, gave a presentation on their investigation into Joan Diver's murder to the other task force members. They believed the key to cracking the case could very well lie in Joan Diver's death. Here they had the freshest evidence. They also had an intriguing anomaly to work with. They knew their killer had driven Diver's car. It was something he had never been known to do before. And it was how he tripped up and left his DNA behind. It appeared he had gone to great lengths to avoid leaving any trace of himself, other than his trademark garrote scars, at the crime scene. But here he had tripped up. It meant he had made a mistake. It meant he could be caught.

The next day, another press conference was held.

Already, it seemed the task force members were running out of fresh information to give out.

Once again, they talked about their plans for a new composite sketch. Several had been done over the years and they all looked relatively similar. The last one had been made in 1994, based on the description given by the fourteen-year-old Riverside High School student who had survived her attack. She had said the rapist had thick dark hair with some gray in it and that his hairline was starting to recede. He had thick eyebrows and a just-graying mustache. The task force was hoping to get a new sketch that would factor in twelve years of aging.

They did have one piece of news: they gave out the number of their new toll-free tip line. The number was 277-1990. The 277 stood for BPR as in Bike Path Rapist. 1990 was the year Linda Yalem was murdered. The phone number was LaCorte's idea.

They then announced that there would be no more

press conferences until the following Monday. Thursday, November 23, was Thanksgiving and they figured everyone would be heading out of town shortly.

But it would not be a restful four-day holiday for the task force members. They kept working.

LaCorte came in every morning to record all of the overnight tips that had come in and input them into his computer program.

Rozansky interviewed two Town of Clarence workers who said they had seen a white Ford truck that Steven Diver had seen next to his wife's the day she went missing. He was hoping that they had seen something, possibly even the killer getting into Diver's car, but they had no helpful information.

The Monday after Thanksgiving, LaCorte decided to try another approach at getting tips. He made an appeal to the woman or women in the killer's life to step forward.

He said the investigators believed that the man they were looking for may very well be hiding in plain sight. They believed he could be married, have a girlfriend, or could be living in the basement of his mother's house.

He asked all women who may have had a suspicion about a man in their lives to think about the dates when the Bike Path Killer was known to have attacked and try to figure out whether they had seen their loved one that day. Perhaps he had disappeared and didn't have a good explanation. Or maybe he was acting strangely.

"They know this man," LaCorte told reporters. "They've lived with him from Day One."

In addition, the task force put out a renewed call to the public for anyone who may have seen the white truck in the Salt Road lot to call the tip line.

They also announced that the daily briefings would stop.

18

America's Most Wanted

The task force members believed there was a good chance that their killer had left the Western New York area sometime after 1994, before returning to kill Joan Diver. This twelve-year gap just didn't make sense. They found it hard to believe that a serial killer, who seemed to be becoming progressively more violent and deadly, simply stopped raping and killing for more than a decade.

They believed he may have been attacking women somewhere else. That meant they needed to take their investigation nationally, even internationally.

One of their first calls was to another task force that had been formed just across the Canadian Border in Niagara Falls, Ontario, where five prostitutes had been found murdered over a decade. One of the victims' bodies had been discovered in early 2006. The MOs were different, a couple of the women had been shot, but the task force wanted to cover all bases.

They then met up with the producers of *America's Most Wanted*. The Amherst police had worked with the FOX-TV show before, although they ran into problems when the show's producers gave out the phone number of one of the victims Amherst had provided to another news outlet without the victim's permission. That had caused major friction.

But the show's producers came back, and the task force was eager to work with them. They needed the national exposure.

The crew spent a week in Western New York, interviewing detectives and revisiting the locations where the rapes had occurred.

They also did an interview with the victim of the 1994 rape in Riverside. She spoke on camera, but with her face obscured so she could not be identified.

An adult now, the woman described the attack in a vacant lot behind a junkyard.

"I saw him," she told the *AMW* interviewer. "He grabbed me from behind. It was like a white electrical cord, like the ones that run in the walls. I could see it as it went across. It didn't go across my neck at first. Went across my mouth and neck. . . . He was a bigger man. He took over and was dragging me and pushing me to this spot."

The woman recounted how her attacker told her not to fight. "It'll be worse if I do more," she said the man told her.

She continued: "Eventually he was able to get [the cord] down around my throat. I didn't have control. He pushed me back. He taped me. He wanted to tape my eyes. I didn't want him to tape my eyes. I didn't want to not know what was going to happen. He didn't.

"He put me on my stomach. He taped my arms behind my back, flipped me over, and proceeded. He cut my underwear and my bra. But because I was fourteen, and I hadn't had any sexual experience, it was a lot tougher for him."

The woman was asked why she believed her life was spared. The two women he had attacked before her had both been killed, as was the victim after her.

"I think he didn't kill me because I did what he wanted to do," she said. "I couldn't fight as much as grown women could fight. . . . I think he might have gotten frustrated with me—the fact that I was a virgin, and I don't think he could perform everything he wanted to do."

Al Rozansky, Ed Monan, and Dennis Delano all flew on the weekend of December 2 to Washington, D.C., to participate in the live segment of the show. As the show progressed, tips were coming in from across the country and the detectives were there to assess them.

There were tips from everywhere, from Georgia to Ottawa.

"We received numerous tips," Rozansky said on air. "We appreciate everybody's help. We expect to go back home, go over them and evaluate them, and do our research. Hopefully, it'll lead us to something that can help us arrest this. . . ."

Delano added: "Hopefully, that one tip is in there."

Late that night, the three detectives flew back to Buffalo to continue their search.

19

Tempers Fly

John Simich, the head of the country's forensic police lab, and Paul Mazure came to the task force office in Amherst on December 4 to do a presentation on the DNA evidence.

DNA had linked this serial rapist to three murders and a half-dozen rapes. They wanted to know what more could science tell the investigators about who their suspect was. What clues did his DNA reveal?

The task force members had learned from tests on the DNA over the years that the Bike Path Killer was either Hispanic or part Native American. They had read reports in the *Buffalo News* about this. They wanted to know just how certain that information was. The victims had given a variety of descriptions. A couple had said he had a Spanish accent. Several had said they thought he was Italian. At least one was certain he was Mexican or of some other Hispanic origin.

Knowing that he wasn't white would help the task force rule out a lot of suspects. Being able to say definitively that he was Hispanic would be of even greater use.

Simich and Mazure broke down what the DNA analysis had told them. They explained the percentages and odds of what the testing had shown. The forensic scientists displayed photographs of people who had similar DNA profiles. Simich explained that, genetically speaking, the rapist matched most closely a woman from Acapulco, Mexico.

The upshot: there was a high probability that the person they were looking for was Hispanic.

It was interesting information, but what would they do with it?

Back in the cramped interview room, tempers were beginning to show themselves. And chasing down tip after tip after tip was getting to some of the task force members.

"We were so inundated with leads and tips, from people being on the bike path and seeing a suspicious guy, to knowing this guy who might have been the killer twenty years ago and is still alive," Keats said.

Some were beginning to feel they were so bogged down with tips that they weren't paying enough attention to the actual investigation.

Keats remembered thinking: "We've got to do something, we don't have the manpower to do both."

LaCorte tried to smooth things over. He started giving the tips out to his own sixteen detectives and had them do all the nitty-gritty background work on each tip. That information was then handed to the task force members to chase down, but that didn't seem to solve the problem either.

After Simich's presentation, Rozansky pulled out a pile of tips from *America's Most Wanted*. He and Delano planned to start going through them.

"I got talking to Dennis about something, and when I turned around, the tips were gone," Rozansky said.

Rozansky turned to LaCorte. "Joe, did you take those tips that were here? I just put them down."

It turned out that LaCorte had taken them to input into his tip program. But Rozansky got them back.

A few minutes later, he said, the tips were missing again. It was obvious that LaCorte wanted them.

"Joe, don't even tell me you took those tips back from me again," Rozansky said. Now Delano got into it as well. He was a homicide detective schooled in cold cases. He believed that chasing down tips was preventing him from doing what he had been assigned to do: look at the old cases. They began accusing LaCorte of saving the best tips for his department. He denied it.

They began to argue. Fed up, Delano announced that he was going back to Buffalo to work there. As Delano and La-Corte shouted at each other, Delano headed through the department toward the door, with Rozansky right behind him. Heads popped up from the cubicles, where other Amherst detectives were quietly working.

The task force had only been formed for two weeks, and already it was falling apart. Something needed to be done.

After the dustup, the task force members from the sheriff's department and the state police met at a Tim Hortons coffee shop in Amherst. They decided that they needed a new place to work, and they needed more investigators to look at both the tips coming in that Amherst wanted covered and the old cases they wanted to work on.

"So there you have Delano, with all the years he's got on, you've got Monan with twenty-six, Rozansky, twenty-nine or thirty years at this point," said Keats. "They come here expecting to work the case, but that's not what we were doing. We were sitting there running tips down, some of which could have been the tip that brought the case, but literally we'd start the day with fifty or sixty of these tips in our little cubby and that's when we said, 'Look, the four of us can't work these old cases and Diver with fresh eyes, and do all these tips.' It was impossible, we'd be here six months before we'd get to all these tips, and then six months later, Diver would be all that much colder."

There was also the fear that the Bike Path Killer could strike again. All of his attacks had taken place during the warmer months—always between June and October. Those were the months that people in Western New York were most likely to be outside. Winter was fast approaching by the time the task force had formed. That meant they had just over six months—tops—before their killer might start thinking of finding another victim.

After Sheriff Howard was briefed, he ruled out using any sheriff's department offices, and Buffalo's detective chief Dennis Richards said the same about using Buffalo Police Department offices because it would raise the same problem. The task force needed its own place, independent of any department, and it needed more members.

"Some of our people tried to get me to host it at one of our unused office spaces, and I said absolutely not," Howard said. "If you want to find another place, if you can't find a government building, a vacant school, or other office space, I'll reach out to the business community, but see what you can find first."

Scott Patronik, the sheriff's chief, had a great idea for a new location. Directly across the street from the newly built Central Police Services building, where his own office was located, was a vacant, one-story building. The county had recently bought it. It had once held a legal publishing company, and then a collection agency, but was currently empty. He got the sheriff's okay, and started setting up shop at the Oak Street address.

The task force had found a new home.

20

Back at Amherst

Despite all of the bickering, the task force members were making some progress on the case at Amherst.

The DNA from the Joan Diver's ignition switch had shown that the Bike Path Rapist was the killer. But there were some members of the task force who had lingering suspicions about Steven Diver, even with the overwhelming evidence that someone else had been involved. They were convinced that he had been trying to hide something from them.

But others felt the Steven Diver factor was becoming a distraction. They didn't believe he had anything to do with his wife's death whatsoever, and they were wasting their time focusing so much attention on him.

They decided they needed to talk to Diver one more time, to erase any doubts about him.

Diver came into the Amherst office and sat down with Ed Monan and Josh Keats. It was clear just by looking at him that there was no way whatsoever that this guy was the Bike Path Killer. He was too young, too blond, and too slight to be the killer. The detectives came away from the interview believing that Steven Diver's behavior had been badly misinterpreted. The stress of his wife going missing and then turning up murdered had made him act irrationally. They thanked him for coming in and assured him that he was cleared of any suspicion.

Although Steven Diver was no longer being looked at, his wife's murder was still a critical piece of the puzzle and the task force members believed there were clues to be gleaned from investigating it further.

They decided they wanted to try to find any surveillance camera footage in the areas around Clarence where Diver's body and her SUV had been found.

Chris Weber was Josh Keats's partner in the State Police Bureau of Criminal Investigation, who usually handled homicides. He was brought in when the task force decided they needed someone to work with Amherst police on the tips coming in.

Weber, who had a degree in sociology from Buffalo State College, had been a trooper for the past eleven years, and as sergeant, he outranked Keats. He was given the assignment of seeing if there were any video surveillance cameras in Clarence near the bike path. It was a suggestion Steven Diver had made to the sheriff's investigators at the time of his wife's disappearance, but it had never been followed up on.

Weber went from store to store and eventually got to a Mobil gas station on the corner of Main Street and Salt Road, right next to the parking lot where Joan Diver had left her car, and where her husband had spotted it. The gas station owner just happened to have saved the video from September 29. Weber also found surveillance camera footage at an M&T Bank on Main Street.

Weber brought the tapes back and spent hours and hours watching the footage. He even ate his lunch as he watched images of cars pulling in and out of the gas station and driving past the bank.

Weber eventually found something he thought could help. A blue Ford Explorer SUV that exactly matched Joan Diver's car pulled into the gas station, looped around, and then made a turn onto Main Street. He couldn't make out the license plate number, but it was the exact make, model, and year of Joan Diver's car. He also couldn't make out who was driving. From the timing, it was evident that the killer was behind the wheel, but there was no way to enhance the images enough to show his face.

At roughly the same time, the Amherst Police Department got a tip about the white truck that Steven Diver had seen parked by his wife's car in the Salt Road lot.

A man said he had snapped a photo of a white pickup truck that had been parked in that lot on another day. He also got the truck's license plate number.

Ed Monan tracked down that lead. The belief was that the man in the white truck probably wasn't the killer, but maybe he saw him. Maybe he could give a good description or had seen something that could help identify him.

Monan ran the plate number and learned that the man worked at the chicken-processing plant, right near where Joan Diver's body had been found. The man told Monan that he did indeed park in the Salt Road lot quite often. He would do it while waiting for his shift to begin at the chicken plant. He also said he didn't remember seeing anything suspicious on September 29.

It was another lead that turned out to be useless.

21

No Longer
Under Suspicion

For the first time since his wife's body was found alongside the Clarence bike path, Steven Diver had been told he was no longer under suspicion.

Diver was still reeling from the loss of his wife, the mother of his four children. He was now a widower, and though he never underestimated how much Joan had done for the family, he now was finding out firsthand just how hard she had worked.

Diver had never spoken to the media. A friend in the university chemistry department, Huw Davies, had handled all the questions from reporters. Diver had hired a lawyer to deal with the police and prosecutors.

He had reasons for his coolness toward the press and the Erie County Sheriff's Office. He had been labeled uncooperative by unnamed sheriff's investigators and that was reported in the media.

The sheriff's department had bungled the search for his wife's body, refused to concentrate their search in the daylight hours to the section where she always ran, and called it off after two days. It took the community search by friends of the Diver family to finally find her. By that time, two days of steady rain had washed away any crime scene evidence.

"Our kids had just lost their mother," Diver told the authors of this book. "If there was a mistake in the investigation, it could have resulted in my arrest. Then the kids would be parentless."

Diver, a scientist who never published his research until everything was proven or explained, could not understand how the media could give the impression he was somehow involved in his wife's killing without some kind of proof.

"I don't think the media ever considered how I might behave in my situation, assuming that I was innocent," he said. "That just isn't as interesting—a grieving husband is a dime a dozen."

There were no lesson plans for what would happen when a murderer suddenly snatched away the person whom you care about the most in the world—a woman Diver used to study with in Utah's Millcreek Canyon while they were both students at the University of Utah.

"What should victims' families do?" Diver asked. "Should they get on TV and try to convince the public that they are innocent? Should they really have to? Should they fight a war of words in a time of the worst imaginable woe?"

Despite his misgivings about the sheriff's department, Diver had done everything asked of him by the district attorney's office as the hunt continued for his wife's killer. He voluntarily submitted a DNA sample, and he continued to talk to prosecutors.

He was called to the DA's office the day the DNA test came back to the Bike Path Rapist, and learned firsthand about the drop of sweat found on the steering column of his wife's car.

"I was completely taken off guard," he said of learning that his wife had been a victim of the serial killer. "This seemed unreal. I was shocked by their news that they knew it was the Bike Path Killer.

"I kept asking questions to stave off the shock waves. I was also shocked by how much the DA seemed to know about this person. I went from feeling that the weight of the investigation was directed to me to this killer, who apparently had quite a history of raping and killing in Western New York. I knew about Linda Yalem's murder, but had no idea how extensive his crimes were and over such a long period of time. It seemed absurd that the investigation was ever directed toward me."

On November 27, the same day Lieutenant LaCorte put out the public plea to any woman who might suspect her husband of being the Bike Path Killer, Diver came in to the Amherst Police Department to meet with Ed Monan and Josh Keats.

Diver came accompanied with a lawyer. They asked him more about Joan's life, wondering whether there was a UB connection, because Yalem was a student, and she a professor's wife. Diver had a lot of questions for them about Yalem's killing and the Bike Path Rapist. He found the two detectives to be polite, certainly more cordial than the sheriff's deputies had been. They told him he was no longer considered a suspect, but they asked him to undergo a lie detector test. Diver refused.

Lieutenant Steven Nigrelli, one of the co-leaders of the task force, said he told everyone in the group to forget about Steven Diver, as well as the Thong Man, whose car and apartment had been searched by the sheriff's detectives under a court order.

"There is one person responsible for these rapes and murders and that's the Bike Path Rapist," Nigrelli told the task force members. "I don't want to hear anything more about Diver and [Thong Man]."

22

Waiting

The weeks after the DNA on Joan Diver's car had come back and the task force had formed should have been exciting ones for Christine Mazur. Finally, after all these years, it seemed like the police had a real chance at finding the man who had murdered her mother.

But Christine Mazur had a lot on her mind.

She was worried sick over her grandmother Elizabeth Phillips, the woman who had, for all intents and purposes, raised her as her own daughter. Phillips, who had colon cancer, was in the midst of what seemed like endless rounds of chemotherapy and radiation. The treatments were wearing her down, and everyone was worried that she wouldn't live much longer.

Christine was worried that she was about to lose another mother.

Shortly after Majane Mazur's death, Christine and her father had come back down to Greenville. They lived near Phillips, who had watched after Christine. She would pick her up from school and take her to her dentist or the eye doctor. The two grew close, the same way she and Majane had been. They talked every day, even when Christine became a teenager. For Phillips, it was like watching Majane grow up all over again.

Over the years, Christine's memories of her mother had faded, but she still missed her terribly. Often her family members would find her crying. They'd ask her what was wrong. "I miss my mom," she'd say.

Phillips had dreaded the day Christine would ask her what had happened to her mother. When Christine was little, they would tell her that her mother was in heaven, and left it at that. How could a little girl understand something as horrific as murder? they thought. But Phillips had made a promise to herself that if Christine asked, she'd tell her the truth.

That moment came one day and Phillips told her the whole terrible truth. She said her mother had been murdered in New York and that it took almost a month to find her body. She told her about the drugs and that her mother had been arrested for prostitution.

The drugs and the arrests had always been difficult for Phillips to accept. She knew her daughter's addiction was a disease, but it didn't make it any easier to think of things her daughter had done because of it.

Back around the time after Majane was killed, Phillips made it a point to be very involved with the investigation and to find out how her daughter had ended up the way she did. She asked the police exactly what Majane had been arrested doing. They told her she was standing on a street corner.

She also called the morgue. She asked the coroner how much drugs were in Majane's system. It was the only time she was hoping to hear that Majane had been high. She hoped that if Majane had been drugging, maybe she hadn't suffered so much when she died. The coroner reported that there were very little drugs in her body when she was killed. Perhaps she was trying to sober up when it happened, Phillips thought.

But at the end of 2006, Phillips was far too sick to keep

tabs on the Bike Path Rapist Task Force's progress. She relied on Christine for that.

Christine scoured the Internet constantly for updates. She was in her second year of college at Tri-County Tech. She was studying to be a veterinary technician and was busy with that, but she always tried to take time out to see what was going on in Buffalo. A friend videotaped the episode of *America's Most Wanted* for her.

A little before Christmas, Christine learned she was pregnant. It wasn't how she had planned her life to go, but she was still happy. Two days before Christmas, she and her boyfriend went to Majane's sister's house for a family gathering. Gifts were exchanged and people were sitting around talking when her boyfriend handed her a box.

"You forgot this present," he said.

Everyone in the room was staring at Christine. She wondered what was going on.

He handed her a little box and got down on his knee.

Christine said yes.

It was a beautiful moment, there in front of all the family. She was so happy. But it was yet another moment in her life that she wouldn't be able to share with her mother because some cold-blooded serial killer decided to murder her.

There had been so many moments like that over the years. The day she went on her first date. Getting ready for the prom. Graduating from high school. The day she learned she was going to be a mom too. And now there'd be so many more. Her wedding day and the birth of the baby growing in her belly.

It made Christine hate the Bike Path Killer all the more. She prayed he'd be caught. He needed to pay for taking so much away from her.

23

December 11
Through 12

As the task force members began settling into their new space in downtown Buffalo, two criminal profilers from the FBI, Agents Bob Morton and Kirk Mellecker, came to town to assist the task force. They were there to review the bike path cases and give the task force members some suggestions on what they should be concentrating on.

They were to be in town for just two days: December 11 and 12. The profilers asked to meet with any officers who had extensive knowledge of the old cases.

Patronik, Rozansky, and Savage sat down with the profilers back at the sheriff's office to give them the details on the Diver murder. They showed them the case file, including all of the crime scene photographs.

The Amherst cops briefed the agents on the Yalem case and the two rapes in their jurisdiction. They took the profilers to the places where the attacks had taken place and showed them how they believed each attack had gone down.

Detective Dennis Delano, being a homicide detective specializing in cold cases, was the expert on the Mazur murder. It was on the top of his list of cases to solve. But he didn't know much about the four rapes that had taken place in Buffalo: the one in Delaware Park and the three in the Riverside and Black Rock areas.

The day the profilers arrived, Delano made a call to a colleague in the BPD, Detective Lissa Redmond. She was a member of the police department's well-respected sex offense squad, or SOS, Buffalo's version of a special victims unit (SVU), like on the hit TV show.

Redmond was sitting at home in her pajamas when Delano called. Diagnosed with multiple sclerosis, she had gone on medical leave the week that Joan Diver had been killed. Delano knew that there was probably no one better acquainted with all of the details of the Buffalo rapes than Redmond. The first day of her assignment to the SOS unit, Redmond's boss, Lieutenant David Mann, had walked up to her and handed her a blue notebook crammed with information about the unsolved bike path cases.

"Would you be interested in working on this?" Mann asked her. Full of passion for her work, she had enthusiastically replied, "Yeah!" It was the sort of case any good cop strives to take on—and solve. As she studied the cases, she learned she had a personal connection to the case. Redmond had gone to high school with Suzi Coggins.

Over the years, the Buffalo SOS had devoted whatever spare time they had to the bike path case. They even had a room devoted to the case, piled high with old files and adorned with charts and timelines. From time to time, they'd turn up a potential clue, sometimes a suspect. At the same time, Amherst investigators, still bristling that they had never caught Linda Yalem's killer, were also continuing their search for the killer.

Sometimes the departments would reach out to each other to share information. When the Majane Mazur case turned up, for instance, Buffalo handed over copies of all the paperwork from the case. Amherst police had provided some information they came up with following the 1994 rape in Buffalo's Riverside neighborhood. It wasn't even their turf, but they had insisted on helping out anyway.

But over the years some Buffalo detectives had grumbled about how Amherst seemed to be secretive about their files. It had become something of a sore point that built some resentment for the Buffalo cops.

And all the while, the killer remained free.

The formation of the task force was a chance to put that all aside. This was to be the first real opportunity for both police forces, and other agencies, to actually work side by side and share all of their information.

Delano knew that and told Redmond she needed to come meet with the profilers. Redmond wasn't supposed to go back to work until January, but she agreed. She hastily threw on a suit and drove down to the new task force office on Oak Street.

That day turned out to be a tense one for the Buffalo Police Department. On the other side of downtown, a teenager who had shot two Buffalo officers—leaving one paralyzed from the neck down—had a court appearance. Just about every cop wanted to be in the courtroom to show their support for their fellow officers. Among them was Redmond.

The profilers had wanted Redmond to go out to lunch with them to discuss the Buffalo rape cases, but she asked to meet them later, after the arraignment. They understood.

At the Oak Street office, Redmond, Delano, and Scott Patronik, the sheriff's chief, sat down with the profilers and went over the four Buffalo sex assaults that had been linked to the Bike Path Killer. She showed them a timeline that she and her colleagues on the sex offense squad had put together.

The profilers peppered Redmond with questions about the rapes in the Riverside area. They didn't have a good grasp of what kind of terrain it was. "Was it parklike?" one asked Redmond.

Redmond explained that it was anything but. The area was an open field near an industrial zone, with old defunct train tracks running through it. A giant factory was nearby. Redmond explained to the profilers that it's the sort of place only locals would know about. "The average citizen who was not from the neighborhood would not be on those 'paths,'" Redmond told them.

She also discussed with them some intriguing clues that had been gleaned from some recent analysis that had been done on the DNA samples taken from the victims.

In 2004, after DNA tests had linked Majane Mazur's murder to the Bike Path Killer, members of the Buffalo SOS decided to have samples taken for the 1994 Riverside victim's rape kit retested. Back then, forensic scientists weren't able to get a DNA match from the kit because they couldn't find any sperm.

But in the years since, DNA analysis had become so sophisticated that scientists were able to determine a genetic match without sperm or blood. All they needed was a Y chromosome. The sample was rechecked and this time the forensic scientists were able to get a positive DNA match. The girl had most definitely been raped by the Bike Path Killer.

The finding also provided another piece of potentially important information. The killer had lost his ability to make sperm between the time he killed Majane Mazur and when he raped the Riverside High School student. That meant he had either had a vasectomy, had suffered testicular cancer, or had some other serious ailment that had affected his fertility.

Back in January 2005, the sex offense squad released that information to the public, in the hopes of jogging someone's memory. *"Anybody who may know about a person who seemed suspicious and had a vasectomy or an infertility problem should call us, or they could leave an anonymous tip,"* Detective Salvatore A. Valvo told the *Buffalo News*.

At the end of Redmond's sit-down with the FBI, Patronik approached Redmond.

They were old friends. They'd actually known each other since high school. Their best friends had dated each other back then.

Patronik asked Redmond if she'd be joining the task force when she came to work in January.

"I don't know," she said coyly. "You'll have to ask [Buffalo police commissioner] Gipson."

Patronik said he planned to do just that.

On December 12, after meeting with all of the investigators and sifting through their paperwork, the profilers gave a presentation based on what they had learned.

They had come to three intriguing conclusions:

Number one—The 1986 rape of a woman in Delaware Park was more than likely *not* the first time the killer had attacked a woman.

The profilers pointed to the sophistication of the attack. They said it seemed well planned and well executed. The assailant knew exactly what he was doing when he pounced on the woman, wrapped the rope around her neck, and dragged her into a clearing.

They urged the task force members to look further back in their records to see if there might be other unsolved rapes that might bear some sort of resemblance to the 1986 case.

Number two—The Bike Path Killer probably patronized prostitutes. They based that on the murder and rape of Majane Mazur in 1992. Up until then, Mazur's killing had been considered something of an anomaly. She was a crack-addicted prostitute and seemed to have nothing in common with the middle-class girls and women who had been identified as victims of the Bike Path Killer. That was the main reason Mazur's murder went unconnected to the bike path case. Of course, that was until Dr. John Simich got his grant in 2004 to run DNA tests from cold cases.

The profilers told the task force members that there was a very good chance that their killer had sought out the services of prostitutes before. They urged the task force members to look at files of Buffalo-area johns.

Number three—Finally, the killer may not have always used the same MO. The Bike Path Killer was infamous for his use of his garrote device. The trademark double-ligature mark had been on all of the victims, and it was considered his calling card.

But the profilers said the garrote showed a level of expertise attained, most likely, from experience. From trial and error. They urged the task force members to once again go back to cold rape and murder cases throughout the region without discounting those not involving a garrote.

Armed with the new information, the task force members split up the work. A call was made to CPS for a list of anyone in Erie County, especially Buffalo, who had been arrested for patronizing a prostitute between 1990 and 2000. They picked Buffalo because, being a city, it had the biggest prostitution problem in the area.

As the lone Buffalo representative on the task force for the time being, Delano decided to start looking at old rape cases from the city. He knew he couldn't do it without help from Redmond, who was familiar with a lot of the files he wanted to see.

The case files, in fact, had been packed away recently. The SOS unit had moved in the spring of 2006 from its bare-bones offices in police headquarters—where victims coming in to give statements often found themselves elbow to elbow with violent criminals—to the Family Justice Center, a less intimidating office in a downtown office building where victims of rape, domestic violence, and child abuse were interviewed and counseled. The files had yet to be unpacked.

Delano had the files carted over to the new task force headquarters. Redmond, who was hoping the police commissioner would assign her to the task force, agreed to help Delano. Even though she wasn't supposed to start working again until the new year, she started showing up at the task force office to sort through the boxes.

Those boxes were filled with cases of high-profile, serial crimes. They came to the task force in a large metal file cabinet. It had wheels and a lid on top. She brought it into Delano's office. The box would sit unopened for about a week.

24

Coping

Every time Suzi Coggins turned on the TV, picked up a newspaper, or clicked on the radio in her car, it seemed all anyone was talking about was the Bike Path Killer. There was so much talk about with the DNA test results, the formation of the task force, the tip line, composite sketches—everyone Coggins knew also knew she had been one of his victims. There had been no keeping the rape secret in her tight-knit community. It seemed anyone she'd ever met was calling her all of a sudden. "Are you okay?" they'd ask. "How are you feeling?"

"I'm fine, I'm fine, I'm fine," she'd tell them, wishing they'd stop prying.

It was driving her crazy.

She thought she had put that awful episode of her life behind her. It had happened two decades ago. She was an adult now. She was a mother of two children, a twelve-year-old girl and a ten-year-old boy. She was separated from her husband and had been seeing a wonderful man for the last two years.

But with the Bike Path Killer emerging from the shadows, the peace she thought she'd achieved was shattered. It was especially hard for Coggins to hear about Joan Diver. She had read in the news that Diver was a mother of four young children. Since Suzi was a mother herself, it broke her heart.

She had told her daughter about the rape, but not her son. He was too young to understand. She told her daughter, not to scare her, but to teach her daughter about how to avoid dangerous situations.

From the time both of her children were little, she would encourage them to approach strangers while she watched. She would send one of her children to someone to make change for $1 or to get directions. When they'd come back, she'd ask them how that stranger made them feel. If her children would tell her that the person made them feel scary or yucky or somehow uncomfortable, she would tell them to trust their gut feeling. She wanted them to hone their instincts so that if they ever encountered someone who might not seem quite right, they'd know to run away. She wanted to make sure her children never went through what she had.

Shortly after the announcement about the DNA in Joan Diver's car, Coggins called up Danny Shea. He was now a captain at the Hamburg Police Department. She asked him about what was going on and he filled her in on the latest developments. He also had her come in and give a description of the killer again. He pointed out to her that she was the only one of the victims who had mentioned that he had pockmarked skin. She didn't know why he needed her to describe the man again, but she was happy to do anything to help. Shea had always been so nice to her over the years.

In the weeks after the announcement, Coggins began sinking into a depression. She'd sit on the couch for hours on end, unable to move. Her boyfriend, Ken Barnes, whom everyone called "Barnesy," would find her in that state on the couch and sit down next to her. He was a big, burly guy that Coggins had met at her parents' bar about fifteen years earlier. Despite his stocky build, he had always been very gentle with Coggins.

"How are you doing?" he would ask her as she cried on the couch.

She'd say, "Okay." Barnesy knew she wasn't, but he knew not to push it. He would look after her as she tried to cope with this wall of emotion that was building up inside her. But he gave her space, allowing her all the time she needed to work through all of her feelings.

Coggins loved him for that. She'd never been with anyone who was willing to be so patient and compassionate.

But even with her big strong man, Coggins had stopped feeling safe. She had a dog too, and that didn't work either. Not even locking all of the doors and then checking them one more time made her feel at ease knowing that the Bike Path Rapist was still out there.

25

The Box

About a week before Christmas, Steve Nigrelli, the state police lieutenant and co-leader of the task force, and Josh Keats, the young state police homicide investigator, ate their lunch at the task force headquarters. The task force members had been following some promising leads, but as of yet they had nothing. They felt they were no closer to finding the Bike Path Killer than they had been the day the task force started. With the holiday season in full gear, it seemed the case would drag well into the next year.

Nigrelli and Keats were both on a tuna fish diet. Both were fit, but they were looking to take some weight off before the coming big meals during the holiday. They were eating in Keats's cubicle when the phone rang. When another line rang in Dennis Delano's nearby office, Nigrelli went to answer it.

"After I took the phone call, I started looking at his desk because it had so much shit on it," Nigrelli said of Delano, whose office looked much like the rumpled detective. "It was like a bomb dropped in there."

Keats came into Delano's office and pulled a big metal file cabinet over to his chair.

"What's that?" Nigrelli asked.

"Those are the files you asked for a couple of weeks ago," Keats told him.

Keats put a big wad of chewing tobacco in his lip, opened the lid of the file cabinet, and began reading through the old cases as Nigrelli swung a golf club he had found weeks ago in the building. Nigrelli often swung the club as he tried to think like the killer and how he could trip him up.

A few minutes had passed when Keats found a file that caught his attention.

On top was a memo written up by Angelo Alessandro, who had been chief of detectives for the Buffalo Police Department in the 1980s. It was a request for a list of all sexual assaults that had taken place in or near Delaware Park from 1980 to 1984. Under the memo was a typewritten spreadsheet. There were six incidents listed, five rapes and one attempted rape:

> *Victim 1*
> *Victim: Age 21*
> *Date: April 14, 1981*
> *Time: 9:45 a.m.*
> *Location: Delaware Park statue of David woods*
> *First contact: Suspect passes victim attacks from behind*
> *Weapon: Knife*
> *Detail: Tells victim to remove clothes*
> *Actions: Rapes victim on ground*
> *Verbiage used: "Come with me or I'll cut your fuckin' face." "Let's run for a while." "Give me 30 seconds."*
> *Suspect Actions: Made victim lay on ground. Made victim run with him. Held knife near vagina.*
>
> *Victim 2*
> *Victim: Age 21*
> *Date: Nov. 19, 1983*
> *Time: 4:30 p.m.*

Location: Delaware Park statue of David woods
*First contact: Suspect passes victim attacks while
passing*
Weapon: Gun
Detail: Pulls victim's pants down
Actions: Rapes victim on ground
*Verbiage used: "You better come with me or
I'll blow your head off." "Don't look at me." "Don't
scream." "Give me 20 seconds."*
*Suspect Actions: Made victim lay on ground.
Pulled cap over victim's face.*

Victim 3
Victim: Age 20
Date: Dec. 19, 1983
Time: 5 p.m.
Location: Delaware Park statue of David woods
*First contact: Suspect passes victim attacks from
behind*
Weapon: Gun
Detail: Tells victim to remove clothes
Actions: Rapes victim on ground
*Verbiage used: "If you scream, I'll blow your
head off." "Don't look at me or I'll kill you." "Wait
10 minutes."*
*Suspect Actions: Made victim lie on ground. Pulled
knitted tube over head. Removed tube [top] and put
victim's shirt over her face.*

Victim 4
Victim: Age 28
Date: Dec. 22, 1983
Time: 5:15 p.m.
Location: Delaware Park statue of David woods
First contact: Suspect passes victim from behind
Weapon: Gun

Detail: Puts hands under victim's clothes
Actions: Fondled victim from behind while standing
Verbiage used: "Don't move or I'll blow your head off." "Don't look at my face." "How old are you?" "Don't look at my face, lady."

Suspect Actions: Placed hands under victim's clothes. Fondles vicitim from behind. Was forced to release victim before rape.

Victim 5
Victim: Age 22
Date: April 3, 1984
Time: 11 p.m.
Location: 1700 Elmwood Ave. Railroad Overpass
First contact: Suspect passes victim attacks from behind
Weapon: Gun
Detail: Removes victim's clothes
Actions: Rapes victim on ground/RR stairs
Verbiage used: "Shut up." "I've killed girls before." "Put your coat over your head." "Wait 10 minutes."
Suspect Actions: Made victim lie on ground. Fondled victim from behind. Pulled ski mask over her face. Removed ski mask and put victim's coat over her face.

Victim 6
Victim: Age 21
Date: July 8, 1984
Time: 7:50 a.m.
Location: Delaware Park statue of David woods
First contact: Suspect passes victim from behind
Weapon: Gun
Detail: Removed victim's shorts
Actions: Rapes victim on ground
Verbiage used: "If you scream, I'll kill you." "Don't

look at me. "Shut up." "Put your coat over your head."
"Wait 10 minutes."

    Suspect Actions: Made victim lie on ground. Pulled
tube top over her face. Forced her to give oral sex. Re-
moved tube top and put shorts over her face.

There were many things in this spreadsheet that caught
Keats's eye.

First he noticed that five of the assaults took place near
the *David* statue in Delaware Park. He remembered that
that was the exact location where the Bike Path Killer's
1986 assault had taken place. That attack had long been
presumed to be the Bike Path Killer's first.

Then he saw how the things these victims said the rapist
said to them were similar to the verbiage the Bike Path
Killer had used. Like the way he told them to wait for a
specific amount of time. All of the Bike Path Killer's victims who survived—with the exception of the secretary
raped on the Ellicott Creek bike path who couldn't remember her assault—said they'd been given similar commands.

Also, four of the park victims described how their assailant made them put clothing, a ski mask, or their shirt
over their heads during the attack. Four of the Bike Path
Killer's victims reported the same thing.

But then, Keats noticed, the park rapes didn't involve
any kind of garrote device, or any strangulation for that
matter.

"Boss," Keats said to Nigrelli, "maybe I'm making
more of this than I should." He tossed the files to Nigrelli.

"What are you looking at?" Nigrelli said, curious as to
what Keats had found. He first noted Alessandro's name.
He'd known him. Nigrelli's father, a retired detective sergeant, had worked with Alessandro.

He then looked at the spreadsheet. "Holy shit,"
Nigrelli said.

They took turns reading each entry to each other.

The FBI profilers had told them that the 1986 case was probably not the first because the rapist seemed to know what he was doing. They had also said that the garrote was likely not the first weapon he used. Nigrelli and Keats were thinking that it was looking like the FBI profilers may have been right on track.

"This is kind of weird. We've got to write this down," Nigrelli said.

They ran out of Delano's office and dragged the filing cabinet into the headquarters conference room. On the wall was a big white dry erase board. On one side of the board the details of the Bike Path Killer's ten attacks, from the 1986 rape in Delaware Park to Joan Diver, had been written down. The task force members would see that list on the board each day as they got their assignments.

Keats grabbed a pen and started writing on the other side of the board. Nigrelli looked at the board and couldn't tell what Keats had just written. "Get out of here," he said, jumping up and grabbing the pen from Keats. "I'll write them down." Keats called out the details of each rape and Nigrelli organized them on one side of the board.

Standing back and looking at the two sets of cases, Nigrelli was astonished. "Josh, whoever did these, did these," he said.

"He didn't do ten attacks. He did sixteen."

Greg Savage, the sheriff's detective sergeant, walked into the room. He was famous for his cool-as-a-cucumber demeanor. Nothing ever seemed to faze him. He looked up at the board and, without even saying hello to Keats and Nigrelli, said: "Oh, that's the Delaware Park Rapist."

Keats asked: "What are you talking about?"

Nigrelli was stunned. "You know who this guy is?"

Savage explained that in 1985, he had just started out at the Erie County Sheriff's Office. His first assignment was working at the holding center in downtown Buffalo. A guy named Anthony Capozzi had been dubbed the "Delaware

Park Rapist," following his arrest after a series of rapes in Delaware Park.

Capozzi had been held in what had been considered the old side of the jail, Savage recalled. The old side was made up of jail cells with bars, rather than the more modern pods. The inmates kept on the old side were the ones the deputies had to keep a closer eye on.

Savage recalled how he'd see Capozzi sitting on his bunk, rocking back and forth, chain-smoking cigarettes while staring at the wall. He hardly ever spoke, except to ask for a light.

Savage remembered thinking back then that it was hard to believe that this man was capable of being a serial rapist. He'd seen inmates fake being crazy, but this man seemed to be the real deal.

Keats was confused. "Nah," he said, looking at the lists of rapes. "That's our guy."

Keats and Nigrelli explained to Savage what they had just found.

"That's not good," Savage said, "because I remember he was arrested for those," he said, pointing to the rapes in 1983 and 1984.

"Where is he?" Keats asked him.

Savage replied: "I think he's in state prison."

They all suddenly had the same gut-churning thought— was this Capozzi guy sitting in prison for something the Bike Path Killer had done?

26

Anthony Capozzi

Discovering the Delaware Park rapes file suddenly opened up an entirely new avenue for the task force members.

The rapes looked very much like the work of the Bike Path Killer.

They didn't know exactly what to make of this Anthony Capozzi guy, but they knew they had to dig further into his case. They were looking at the possibility of an innocent man in prison. And maybe there was something from his case that could yield clues about the man they were looking for.

Al Rozansky began combing through the rest of the files in the metal box to see if he could find more on the Capozzi case. The task force also requested the original case file on Capozzi from the district attorney.

From the files, they pieced together the case against Anthony Capozzi.

Throughout the 1980s, Delaware Park had been the scene of a string of rapes, and that had caused panic in the city of Buffalo. The park was a beloved landmark in the city, where many people had enjoyed taking strolls, walking their dogs, playing with their children, and going for pleasant jogs. Every summer, a troupe of actors put on Shakespeare productions, offering Buffalo a mini version of New York City's famed Central Park "Shakespeare in the Park" productions. People were particularly fond of the loop around the man-made lake in one portion of the sprawling park.

It had come as a shock that year after year, women were being raped in this park, often in the middle of the day, and that no one had been caught. Almost all of the attacks took place near the replica of *David,* which stood atop a hill that overlooked the lake on one side and the Scajaquada Expressway on the other.

There was plenty of speculation that one man was responsible for all the rapes. They were calling him the Delaware Park Rapist.

Every time a new attack took place, the police would increase patrols in the park and the park commissioner would order all the underbrush around the *David* statue removed. Warnings would go out to women about being alone in the park.

Then one day, William Buyers, a former police officer turned city official, noticed a suspicious-looking man near a Perkins restaurant on Delaware Avenue, not far from Delaware Park. He recognized the man, he told police. He said he had seen the same person in Delaware Park a day before the July 8, 1984, rape by the statue.

Buyer said that several months later, he saw the same man again by the Perkins restaurant. He tried to follow him but lost track of him. And then he saw him again on September 11, 1985. This time, he followed him and got his license plate number. He phoned it in to the police, who tracked the plate number to the home of Anthony Capozzi. They took his picture and showed it to the 1984 victim in a photo array. She identified him as her assailant. Capozzi was arrested on September 13.

Capozzi was from the west side of Buffalo. He was

twenty-nine. He came from a tight-knit Italian-American family. He was on the shorter side, about five-eight, had dark hair and a thick dark mustache. He also had a three-inch scar on his forehead.

About the time he was a teenager, he had been diagnosed with schizophrenia. His family did everything they could to help him, but his condition seemed to only grow worse as he grew older. His loved ones knew that he found comfort in taking long walks, particularly in Delaware Park.

But they were stunned when he was arrested. They refused to believe that their Anthony was capable of committing such an act.

The victims of the park rapes were brought in to view lineups that included Capozzi. Three of the women pointed to him as the man who had raped them. They were the 1983 victim, who was taking a shortcut from Buffalo State College when she was attacked, the April 1984 victim, who was walking through the park to get to a bus stop, and the July 1984 jogger, who was running around the park's Hoyt Lake. Sheila DiTullio, the DA office's first chief of its new Sex Crimes Bureau, presented the cases to a grand jury, and Capozzi was soon indicted on three charges of first-degree rape. But Capozzi steadfastly denied that he had hurt any of the women.

All the while, Capozzi remained behind bars. His family could not make the $50,000 bail the judge had ordered.

In the months that followed, Capozzi's lawyers, Thomas C. D'Agostino and Robert Schreck, filed many motions, including one to quash the lineup identifications. They argued that the decoys used in the lineup looked nothing like Capozzi, but the judge rebuffed their efforts.

At the time, DNA was only just beginning to be looked at for forensic purposes. So there was no real scientific evidence to link Capozzi to the rapes. All that scientists were able to determine from exams of the Delaware Park rape victims was the blood type of the assailant, type O.

Capozzi's attorney Thomas D'Agostino was desperate to find some way of exonerating his client. He believed he was innocent. He had Capozzi's blood tested, but it turned out to be O as well.

While Capozzi sat in jail, another rape took place in Delaware Park. It was on June 12, 1986. It happened at 9:30 A.M., near the *David* statue. The victim was a female jogger. The rape was a little different. He had a different weapon. This time, the attacker used a rope to wrap around his victim's neck.

Perhaps it was because of the new weapon, but only Capozzi's lawyers questioned how it could be that if the Delaware Park Rapist was behind bars, there had been another rape in the park.

A widely watched trial began in February 1987.

DiTullio, who had become an assistant attorney general (AAG), returned to criminal court on special assignment to handle the trial.

The three women Capozzi was accused of raping each took the stand, and all three pointed to Capozzi, identifying him as the man who had sexually assaulted them.

Buffalo News columnist Ray Hill described the July 8, 1984, victim's testimony. He wrote that she usually ran another part of Delaware Park, but she had decided that she wanted to run around the Hoyt Lake because it was a hot day.

She described her stunned reaction when the man grabbed her. *"There was a split second when I said to myself, 'What's going on here?'"*

"When he dragged me into the shrubs, it was dark and it looked like black death," she told the jury. *"It was almost like being in a little cave."* Hill wrote how she described being able to hear the traffic on the Scajaquada Parkway nearby, but she knew no one could hear what was happening to her. *"That's when I knew I was really in trouble. All the time he was doing it, I was thinking to myself, if I'm*

good and I behave myself, maybe I'm going to get out of this alive."

After the rapist was done and had run away, she said, she fell to her knees and prayed. She got up and started on her way out of the park when she ran into some joggers. Among them was a young girl. In a state of shock, the victim said all she could think of was the safety of this girl. *"I told them not to go that way because there was a man with a gun and she was only a kid,"* she said.

During cross-examinations, D'Agostino probed the witnesses about why none of them had mentioned a pronounced scar on Capozzi's forehead. None of the victims had ever mentioned a scar when they were questioned by police.

Capozzi's parents and sister took the stand and swore Anthony wasn't capable of violence.

D'Agostino also entered into evidence Capozzi's medical records that showed that Capozzi's weight had fluctuated between two hundred and 220 pounds during the years of the attacks. The victims had also described their assailant as being forty to fifty pounds lighter.

Capozzi never testified in his defense, D'Agostino making the hard decision that every defense lawyer has to make: would his testimony help or hurt him, especially when cross-examined by the prosecutor?

But in the end, the jury believed the victims' testimony, and Capozzi was convicted in the two 1984 rapes. He was acquitted of the December rape. His mother cried as the verdict was read, the *News* reported.

Capozzi was sentenced to 11 2/3 to thirty-five years in prison for the rapes of two of the women. He was sent to Attica Correctional Facility, a walled fortress that drew national attention in 1971 when inmates rioted and were later subdued in a bloody retaking by state police.

There were no more rapes in Delaware Park and the citizens of Buffalo believed they were safe again.

* * *

In the days after the task force members had found the information on Capozzi and the Delaware Park rapes, they found themselves walking into the conference room and staring at the white board. Detective Delano even made up his own version on a piece of cardboard that he kept with him to study on his own time. But it wasn't clear what they should do with this information.

In the meantime, they pressed on with their daily tasks. Patronik, Rozansky, and Monan had taken the assignment of getting Global Positioning System (GPS) coordinates for all the sites of the rapes and murders attributed to the Bike Path Killer. The FBI wanted to use those to map out the incidents to see if there was some sort of pattern. Their first stop was Amherst.

On Friday, December 22, 2006, Rozansky was sitting in the conference room with Patronik and Savage. He couldn't ignore the white board anymore.

Rozansky looked at his fellow investigators. "We gotta go," he said.

He meant to Attica.

The three men from the sheriff's department hopped in a car and made the roughly forty-five-minute drive to the prison. They asked to see Capozzi and he was brought out to see them.

He was a meek-looking man and he didn't seem terribly interested in the visit.

"Were you ever in Delaware Park?" Rozansky asked Capozzi.

"Yup, yup, yup. I know where Delaware Park is," Capozzi said.

The detectives were stunned. It was evident that this man was mentally disabled.

"Did you ever hurt anybody?" Rozansky said.

"I never hurt anybody. I play Frisbee. I play Frisbee," Capozzi said. "I have sisters. I wouldn't hurt any girl. I wouldn't hurt a girl."

Rozansky felt like he was talking to Rain Man, the autistic character portrayed by Dustin Hoffman.

Capozzi then asked the police officers if they were done.

"Can I go now?" he politely asked. "It's spaghetti night."

Rozansky, Patronik, and Savage left the prison in a state of shock. They were convinced Capozzi was mentally incapable of the cold, calculated rapes that he had been convicted of more than twenty years earlier.

Rozansky couldn't stop himself as tears started falling down his cheeks.

"Are you guys kidding?" he yelled. "Do you really think that this guy is capable of hurting anybody?"

The trio returned to Buffalo and shared what they found with the other task force members. They put in a call to Capozzi's attorney D'Agostino and left a message.

But it was the Friday night before Christmas Day and the city was grinding to a halt. The task force members knew nothing would get done Christmas week. They would have to wait until the new year for the files to come to find out more about Anthony Capozzi and to continue their hunt for the Bike Path Killer.

27

"Sanchez, Altemio C."

One of the first things the newly formed Bike Path
Rapist Task Force had done was bring in Dr. John Simich
and Paul Mazure, the DNA experts from the Erie County
Central Police Services Lab.

DNA had linked this serial rapist to three murders and
a half-dozen rapes. They wanted to know what more could
science tell the investigators about who their suspect was?
What clues did his DNA reveal?

"We had Dr. Simich come over and explain to us the
DNA," said Steven Nigrelli, the state police lieutenant and
one of the task force leaders. "Because we had heard
rumors, and it was in the *Buffalo News*, and it had gone
back and forth."

"They had been saying for four or five years now, there's
a high probability he's of Latino descent," Nigrelli said. But
they wanted to hear it from Simich himself.

He came out and broke down the DNA, and what the
percentages and odds were, Nigrelli said of Simich's presentation.

"He left it like this—there was a high probability that the
person we were looking at was of Latin descent."

Josh Keats, the state police homicide investigator, heard
Simich's presentation, then raised a question.

"Well, can I throw out every tip about a guy named Popolowski?" he asked.

Keats thought, *Why am I going to waste my time running down tips and leads on people with names like that?*

"Would it be a good investigative move to take all the Hispanics and go through them and eliminate them?" Keats asked.

Simich replied: "Yeah, that's probably not a bad idea."

So as other task force members started reviewing old rape cases, plotting the locations with GPS finders, interviewing people on the Clarence bike path who might have seen Joan Diver, and sorting through the 1,500 phone tips that had come in, Keats went through the case files that Amherst had accumulated since Linda Yalem's killing in 1990.

All the records from the hundreds of suspects Amherst had looked at were stored in about twenty large three-ring binders at Amherst police headquarters.

Keats went through the books' name directory and found everyone who had a Hispanic-sounding surname, calling on colleagues when he wasn't sure if someone's name sounded Mexican or Puerto Rican, or was a last name from other Hispanic countries.

When Keats had his list of Hispanic last names, he asked Betsy Schneider, a state police crime analyst assigned to the task force, for some help.

Schneider was not a cop. She had come to the state police three years before from a marketing company. She had since become an expert in researching the dozens of databases available to police agencies, and was working for the New York State Intelligence Committee, assigned to the Buffalo FBI office.

"Basically, the main thing I was offering the task force was to take some of the research workload off their plate, so they could be freed up and go out and do interviews," she said. "They get a tip of something on an individual and run it back to me, and I'd get a criminal history, DMV photos."

Nigrelli viewed Schneider as the task force's secret weapon. He had asked the state police brass for Schneider as a way to keep track of things.

"She was not only doing this research for us, but she was helping to connect the dots," he said. "We were actually going out and doing the interviews, but she was the funnel. She was the choke point. Betsy saw it all. You and your partner might be working on something, and you're myopic. Something that might come up that was minor in your interview? Well, it goes to Betsy and she sees it."

By this time, the task force had completed its move to its new headquarters downtown. But there was still much work to be done at the Amherst Police Department.

On December 22, the same day the sheriff's department detectives had gone to Attica to visit Anthony Capozzi, Keats and Schneider drove to Amherst with their list of Hispanic names. They headed to the second floor of the police department, where the detective bureau was located. On a long counter along one wall, all the binders related to the Yalem investigation were lined up.

Keats had already combed through the index to come up with eighty-one names of men with Hispanic-sounding surnames who had been questioned or been mentioned in some way in connection to the bike path investigation by Amherst police.

Now Keats and Schneider wanted to look at all the files connected to each of those eighty-one men, to see what kind of leads the Amherst police had on them, and why they'd been eliminated as suspects.

The names had been listed alphabetically, so Keats and Schneider decided they'd start on opposite ends. Keats began with the As and Schneider went to the end of the list; they started working their way through them.

The two stood at the counter for hours, carefully reading

through each file. They knew there was a chance that a good clue could lie somewhere in these meticulously kept files. They were determined not to miss anything.

All of a sudden, they heard a radio call go out over the PA system. There had just been a bank robbery in the town.

The Amherst detectives, who had been at their desks in their tidy cubicles, took off running for their cars. A short while later, they returned. The detectives had managed to catch the robber and were congratulating each other as they returned to the bureau.

In the meantime, Schneider had gotten to the last names starting with S.

She came across a binder that included the name "Sanchez, Altemio, C."

According to the name index, there were twenty-four entries associated with this name.

She was transfixed. She spent forty-five minutes going back and forth over the material.

"Josh, read this," she said, sliding one entry after another about this Altemio Sanchez character to Keats.

She was particularly interested in a file of interviews with Bob Bandish, Sanchez's fellow worker at American Brass. Two weeks after Linda Yalem was killed, Bandish had called Amherst police.

28

Bob Bandish

It had taken Bob Bandish those two weeks to summon up the courage to call the police, Bandish later said, because the Al Sanchez he knew, a guy he golfed with, who was a jitney driver on the overnight shift, was one of the nicest guys at the plant.

"I'll tell you, I was screwed up, my stomach, what are you going to do," said Bandish, a tall, lanky man who worked as a grinder at the plant.

But he finally felt the Amherst police should know what he knew.

Bandish worked the third shift at American Brass. He knew Sanchez not only from working the same shift at the plant, but also because they had both joined Bally's Total Fitness Center under a company plan that gave them reduced membership fees. He also golfed with Sanchez, and after work usually saw Sanchez at Bally's on the treadmill or lifting weights.

Sanchez worked in the factory's copper mill, driving a jitney and delivering metal to various parts of the plant. Bandish usually saw him before or after work because they worked in different departments.

"I'd see him there, shoot the shit with him," Bandish said. "We used to work a lot of overtime."

The police reports that Keats and Schneider looked at

showed that Bandish told the Amherst cops that as he was driving home from work on August 24, 1989, he looked up to see Sanchez driving by him on the Lockport Expressway, or the I-990, one of the interstate highways that ringed the Buffalo area. It connects with Millersport Highway, the route that Bandish took to drive home to Amherst from the plant.

"So I'm thinking to myself, maybe he's going to turn off at Sweet Home Road and go to the club," Bandish said. "Anyway, he didn't turn off at Sweet Home."

Bandish knew that Sanchez lived in Cheektowaga and thought it odd that he was going in the opposite direction, but he didn't give it much more thought.

Later that day, a fourteen-year-old girl was raped on the Willow Ridge bike path. Bandish mentioned it to a friend the next day at work, and also said he had seen Sanchez driving on the I-990 in the same area.

A year later, in September 1990, Bandish was riding his bicycle after work on the Ellicott Creek Trailway, a five-mile-long bike path that runs from Ellicott Creek Park, past the University at Buffalo, and finishes at Forest Road in Amherst. It's part of a flood control project, with huge ditches that carry runoff during heavy rains, and activists had gotten funding for a bicycle path to run alongside it.

"I remember it was a beautiful day. I think it was in the early afternoon," Bandish recalled. "Hey, here comes Al. So I stopped the bike, and we were shooting the shit."

Sanchez was wearing a jogging suit with an American Brass baseball cap from the plant.

"Al, what are you doing out here?" Bandish asked him.

"Ah, my wife," Sanchez told him. "She's taking a class at Buffalo State."

Bandish thought it odd, that if Sanchez's wife was taking a class at Buffalo State College, half an hour away, why would he be at UB?

"All right, I'm thinking to myself, what are you doing out here? You'd be over at the Buffalo State track, or

Joan Diver, a nurse, wife of a chemistry professor, and mother of four young children, was strangled on a bike path near her home in Clarence, New York, a wealthy suburb of Buffalo, on September 29, 2006. *(Photo courtesy of The Buffalo News)*

Diver was killed on the sixteenth anniversary of the Bike Path Killer's first victim, but she was not sexually assaulted, and no DNA was found on her body. *(Photo courtesy of The Buffalo News)*

A New York State Trooper walks on the bike path. Joan Diver's body had been found by volunteer searchers after the Erie County Sheriff's Department had suspended the official search.
(Photo courtesy of The Buffalo News*)*

Linda Yalem, a student at the University at Buffalo, was the Bike Path Killer's first victim. She was found raped and strangled on September 29, 1990, on the Ellicott Creek path that runs past the university. *(Photo courtesy of* The Buffalo News*)*

Majane Mazur, who turned to prostitution to support her crack cocaine habit, was found raped and strangled in a field near the downtown Buffalo baseball stadium before Thanksgiving Day in 1992. A DNA test twelve years later tied her murder to the Bike Path Killer. *(Photo courtesy of* The Buffalo News*)*

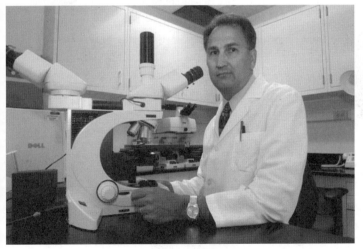

Dr. John Simich, director of the Erie County forensic lab, performed the DNA tests that showed the Bike Path Killer was likely Hispanic. *(Photo courtesy of* The Buffalo News*)*

Erie County Sheriff Timothy B. Howard, along with the police chiefs of Amherst and Buffalo, and the State Police, announces in November, 2006 that DNA tests show the Bike Path Killer had returned after a twelve-year absence. *(Photo courtesy of* The Buffalo News*)*

Members of the Bike Path task force came from the Erie County Sheriff's Department, Amherst and Buffalo Police, and New York State Police. *(Photo courtesy of* The Buffalo News*)*

Steven Nigrelli, then a State Police lieutenant and one of the task force leaders, comes from a police family. He is now a captain. One of his brothers is also a State Police captain and another brother is a Buffalo police officer. *(Photo courtesy of* The Buffalo News*)*

Scott Patronik, the sheriff's chief of technology, ran the task force's day-to-day operations with Nigrelli. He's a former State Trooper. *(Photo courtesy of* The Buffalo News*)*

Lt. Joseph LaCorte of the Amherst Police Department, a task force member who worked on the original Linda Yalem case.
(Photo courtesy of The Buffalo News*)*

State Police Investigator Josh Keats, left, and Sheriff's Senior Detective Alan Rozansky played key roles in the task force investigation. Rozansky wept after interviewing Anthony Capozzi and realizing he could not have committed the rapes he was in prison for.
(Photo courtesy of The Buffalo News*)*

Buffalo Police cold case detective Dennis Delano became the public face of the task force's battle to free Anthony Capozzi from prison. They were convinced the rapes had been committed by Altemio Sanchez instead. *(Photo courtesy of* The Buffalo News*)*

Betsy Schneider, a crime analyst for the State Police, helped identify Altemio Sanchez as the Bike Path Killer by searching databases for crime tips developed by the task force. *(Photo courtesy of* The Buffalo News*)*

Erie County Sheriff's Sgt. Greg Savage remembered Anthony Capozzi's first days in jail following his arrest as the Delaware Park Rapist. *(Photo courtesy of* The Buffalo News*)*

Lissa Redmond, a sex crimes investigator for the Buffalo Police Department, had an unsettling effect on Altemio Sanchez during his interrogation by the task force. *(Photo courtesy of* The Buffalo News*)*

Anthony Capozzi, who suffered from schizophrenia, took long walks to clear the voices in his head and was seen by a former sheriff's deputy in the park near where the Delaware Park Rapist had struck. *(Photo courtesy of The Buffalo News)*

Thomas D'Agostino, who represented Capozzi during his rape trials, remained convinced of his client's innocence twenty years after his conviction. *(Photo courtesy of The Buffalo News)*

Anthony Capozzi and Altemio Sanchez looked enough alike to be brothers. Capozzi was identified by two victims of the Delaware Park rapist, leading to over two decades in prison.
(Photos courtesy of The Buffalo News)

Wilifredo Carabello, Altemio Sanchez's uncle, had stalled the investigation into the Bike Path murders when he lied to the police about his nephew.
(Photo courtesy of The Buffalo News)

Altemio Sanchez is led away to jail after task force investigators matched his DNA to the victims using a dinner glass they had recovered.
(Photo courtesy of The Buffalo News)

Sanchez insisted during eight hours of questioning by the task force that he had no idea how his DNA was found on the women he was accused of raping and murdering. *(Photo courtesy of the Associated Press)*

After he killed Joan Diver on the Clarence Bike Path, Altemio Sanchez enjoyed himself with his wife Kathleen at a reunion of her former employer. Meanwhile, Joan Diver's husband, the police, and hundreds of volunteers searched the woods for her.

Christopher J. Burns, a New York Supreme Court justice, sentenced Altemio Sanchez to prison for seventy-five years to life for the three murders he was convicted of. *(Photo courtesy of* The Buffalo News*)*

Kathy Sanchez, a marketing manager for a company that produces oxygen for medical companies, was shocked by her husband's arrest but continued to support him in court. After the verdict, she filed for divorce. *(Photo courtesy of* The Buffalo News*)*

Josh Keats, Dennis Delano, Lissa Redmond, Anthony Capozzi, and Alan Rozansky. Members of the task force were on hand to greet Capozzi after they freed him from prison. He had served twenty-two years for the rapes Altemio Sanchez committed. *(Photo courtesy of Lissa Redmond)*

Anthony Capozzi in a quiet moment after all the excitement died down, once he had returned home following his release from the Attica Correctional Facility. *(Photo courtesy of The Buffalo News)*

Erie County District Attorney Frank J. Clark with Capozzi lawyer Thomas
D'Agostino after Capozzi's release. *(Photo courtesy of* The Buffalo News*)*

Altemio Sanchez with his attorney, Andrew LoTempio, as Sanchez was sentenced to spend the rest of his life in prison. *(Photo courtesy of The Buffalo News)*

Runners taking part in the annual Linda Yalem Safety Run on the campus of the University at Buffalo in 2005, near where Yalem was killed. The race drew more than 1,200 runners in 2008. After Sanchez's arrest, he confessed to having run the race six years after he killed her.
(Photo courtesy of The Buffalo News)

Delaware Park," Bandish thought. "Why would he be all the way here in Amherst?"

Bandish returned to the bike path on September 30 for a short ride before driving with his son to watch his other boy play football at Mercyhurst College in Erie, Pennsylvania, a ninety-minute drive from Buffalo.

"So we came back from the game," Bandish said. "Right at Sweet Home and the bike path, man, there was a ton of Amherst cops all over the place. Holy shit, I told my son, 'Hey, something big went down.'"

The next day's newspaper and television and radio news were filled with stories about the rape and murder of Linda Yalem, a twenty-two-year-old UB student who had just transferred from Long Island. She had been raped and strangled with a garrote.

Included with the stories was a composite drawing of a man who had raped two other women on paths in the area, including the fourteen-year-old girl on the day Bandish had seen Sanchez driving on the I-990.

The next day at work, Bandish talked it over with his friend at the plant.

They both agreed the composite looked like Al Sanchez, the friendly guy they golfed with and who belonged to Bally's with them.

Bandish's friend, who still works at the plant, and didn't want to be identified, had a hard time believing that Al Sanchez could have raped and killed someone.

"Do you think I should tell somebody about it?" he said Bandish asked him. "You hate to ruin a guy's life and put him under suspicion, if you're wrong. But on the other hand, if this is the guy who's doing it, you gotta do what you gotta do, you know?" That's when Bob decided to go talk to the police and tell them what he knew.

Even then, Bandish had qualms.

"Oh Christ, they're going to talk to him and I'm going to have to face him, you know."

After nine days, Bandish finally made the call.

Schneider and Keats were now both reading about Bandish's call on October 9, when he talked to Officer David Sperrazzo on the tip line that Amherst police had set up for the Yalem killing. He told Sperrazzo that he worked with Sanchez at American Brass, told him about seeing him the day the fourteen-year-old was raped, and seeing him on the Ellicott Creek bike path the day before Linda Yalem was killed.

The file showed that Amherst Captain Thomas Gould turned the tip over to two detectives, Joseph Ciliberto and Robert Fuller, to follow up. They drove to Bandish's house in Amherst, but he wasn't home. They called later, and were told by Bandish's wife to call back because he worked the night shift and had gone to bed.

The two detectives found Sanchez's address in Cheektowaga and drove out to Allendale Road to check out his house. One of the cars in the driveway was a light to medium blue Pontiac Grand Am. They made a note of the car and mentioned in the file that an Orchard Park woman had called in a tip that she had seen a car of the same color, though she thought it was a Dodge, parked near the bike path the day of Yalem's murder. She told police she thought she saw a couple fooling around, but after reading of the murder, she realized it could have been a man dragging Yalem into the woods.

The two detectives decided to sit on the Sanchez house. At 11:10 P.M., they watched a man leave the house, get into the Grand Am, and drive away. They followed him a short distance before losing him in traffic.

The next day, they checked with Buffalo State College on the parking permit they found when they were looking over Sanchez's car. College security told them it was assigned to Kathy Sanchez, Al's wife, who was a student at the college. They also finally found Bandish at home, and they heard firsthand what he had told Sperrazzo about seeing Sanchez.

29

Keats and Schneider
at Amherst

Keats and Schneider continued reading the Sanchez file. They learned that hundreds of tips continued to pour into Amherst police on the Yalem killing, and it wasn't until January 31 that two other detectives, Raymond Nitsche and Thomas Kenny, called Sanchez and asked him to come to Amherst police headquarters for an interview.

He agreed. Sanchez denied to the police that he had ever been on the Amherst path. He told them he had no objection when they asked about their checking his work schedule at American Brass. And he willingly allowed Amherst to take his fingerprints.

A month later, the records showed, Detective Kenny went to American Brass and looked at Sanchez's payroll records. On the day Yalem was killed, Sanchez was scheduled to work four hours of overtime, meaning he would not get out of work until 11:30 A.M. But the records showed he left work at 7:30 A.M., without explanation. The same records showed that on May 31, 1990, the day a thiry-two-year-old woman was raped on the same path, choked with a garrote and left unconscious, Sanchez had come to work an hour late and his pay was docked.

Detectives Nitsche and Kenny set up an interview with the human resources manager at the plant, Thomas Cervola, and gave him a list of the dates for the seven attacks attributed to the Bike Path Rapist.

Cervola reported back to them on March 4. Altemio Sanchez was not working at the time of any of the seven attacks.

Keats and Schneider were astounded. Why had they never heard about any of this before?

The next entry they found was on May 23. Sanchez's fingerprints had been compared to an unidentified print on a water bottle found near the scene of the rape of the fourteen-year-old. They did not match.

That puzzled Keats and Schneider because there had never been any mention of a suspect leaving a fingerprint at any of the rapes.

The most puzzling entry in the file came on January 24, 1992.

As a result of meetings all week with Capt. Gould, Lts. Keiffer, LaCorte, Melton, Dets. Meyer, Nitsche, Kenny, Klimczak and Dailey, the memo read, *the following suspects have been eliminated and removed from the IDMO (identity, method of operation) file.*

A list of the names of 131 people followed. Among the entries: Sanchez, Altemio C.

There was no explanation. Despite the report of Bandish, his coworker who had placed him near the scene of the fourteen-year-old's rape, plus the Yalem homicide, the similarity between Sanchez and the composite sketch, the similar-looking car he drove compared to the car the Orchard Park woman had seen near the bike path when she saw what she later realized could have been a struggle, the Amherst police had cleared Sanchez. They had let him go.

Bandish was never again contacted by the Amherst police. He never knew what became of his tip.

But he knew Sanchez had figured out that Bandish had talked to the cops.

"I'd see him at the plant," Bandish said. "I mentioned it to my friend, 'Man, he's not responding to me.' He was acting different."

Bandish said he eventually retired from American Brass early, because of health problems. He said the stress from having accused Sanchez was part of it.

Keats and Schneider left the Amherst Police Department that day with a lot of unanswered questions. The biggest one: why had Amherst let Sanchez go?

30

The Man at the Mall

The holidays had come and gone and now it was Monday, January 1, 2007. It was time for the task force to regroup and get back to work.

They had a new member now. Lissa Redmond was part of the team.

She walked into her Oak Street workplace and ran into Scott Patronik, her old friend. He led her to the back, where a cubicle had been set up for her. All of the offices had been snatched up by the other task force members.

Although a veteran cop, Redmond felt a little uneasy. She knew Patronik, had met Nigrelli before, and had started to get to know Delano. But she didn't know any of the other detectives at all and she couldn't help but notice that she was the only woman among them. Betsy Schneider would come by, from time to time, but she usually worked at the Buffalo FBI office, where she had better access to databases. Besides, Schneider was a crime analyst and not a cop. It was different.

But Redmond wasn't about to let any of that get in the way of her work. She was excited to be healthy enough again to be back at work, especially as part of this important task force.

During her first week on the task force, she was amazed

at how busy everyone was. Every member seemed to be working furiously on a tip or an angle, but all their efforts were directed at one thing: catching the Bike Path Killer.

It was so refreshing to Redmond, whose husband, Dan, was a Buffalo cop and the son of a retired Buffalo police inspector. During the eight previous years she had been assigned to the case, she'd rarely been able to devote any long stretch of time to it. The bosses had always said the case was a priority, but very few, except Redmond's direct supervisor, Lieutenant David Mann, ever gave her the time or resources.

Looking around at all these people working feverishly to catch the killer, Redmond thought: *This is it. If it is ever going to be solved, it's now.*

Among the items she brought with her to her new office was a photograph taken of the third Riverside High School student who was raped by the Bike Path Killer. The girl had been brought into the police department and was made to stand against a wall for the picture. The duct tape that the killer had used to bind her was still attached to her neck. Redmond had often looked at the girl in the photo and wondered, *How could someone do that to another person?* She tacked it up on her cubicle wall.

During the first week in January, Rozansky, Savage, and Delano were concentrating on the Capozzi angle. They put in a call to the district attorney's office to ask for Capozzi's file. They also tracked down Capozzi's defense attorney Thomas D'Agostino, who said he was out of town but would meet with the task force as soon as he returned.

During Christmas week, Schneider had done a workup on Altemio Sanchez at Keats's request. She ran his DMV records, which included his license history that showed various addresses where he had lived, as well as vehicles listed in his name. She did a criminal record check as well as an Accurint report, a research tool popular with law enforcement and journalists alike. It tracks all known addresses and phone numbers, relatives, neighbors, any kind of property owned by the person, bankruptcies, and liens. She also talked to a lieutenant at the Upstate New York Regional Intelligence Center and asked to get a hard copy of a DMV photo of Sanchez.

Keats was working on a second list, in addition to the list of Hispanic names. This one was for men who had been arrested in Erie County for patronizing prostitutes. Redmond concentrated on going through old rape cases in Buffalo.

On January 3, Rozansky and Patronik hooked up with Nigrelli and Delano to head over to Delaware Park, where they collected the GPS coordinates of the rapes in the 1980s that they had just learned about. They wanted to give that information to the FBI.

The next day, the DA's office called the task force office to say they had found the Capozzi files in what they called "the tombs" of the courthouse. Rozansky would pick them up the next day.

On January 5, the task force members contacted the FBI to let the profilers know about the old Delaware Park cases they had found. That evening, Patronik stayed late at work, even though it was a Friday night. He needed some time to read through the Capozzi file they had just received from the DA's office.

In the file, Patronik found a report that immediately caught his attention. It was from the 1981 rape that occurred in Delaware Park. The victim was a Buffalo State College student who had been raped near the *David* statue. Investigators back then had looked into the possibility that it could be connected to Capozzi, but it had apparently been excluded after she did not identify him during a lineup.

The police report was written by Sergeant Ronald Coyle, a respected detective at the Colvin Station in North Buffalo. Coyle had talked to the rape victim, who had filed a warrant for her unknown assailant, and told her to call him if she saw the rapist again.

She called Coyle after seeing the man at the Boulevard Mall with a blond woman and a young child, and jotting down his license plate, *427 TWJ.* Coyle traced the car to Wilfredo Caraballo, who lived on Buffalo's west side.

He says his car insurance is expired and the car is in his garage and has not been driven in months, Coyle wrote. *He shows me his car and that checks out.*

Coyle read him his rights, took three pictures of him, and then made up a photo array of Puerto Rican males with Caraballo's picture among them, but the rape victim said that was not the rapist.

I am closing this case for now, Coyle wrote in the report, *but I will check Delaware Park for suspect in blue jogging suit daily as I have been doing. I will re-open if she sees him or any new info comes in.*

Patronik called Rozansky. "I've been reading the files," Patronik said. "There's this lady. She was raped, and two days later, she saw the guy."

The investigators both knew what that meant. Who would have a better shot at identifying the rapist than this woman?

Rozansky teamed up with Savage to pursue this lead.

The next morning, Saturday, January 6, the investigators got Schneider started on a data workup on Caraballo and on the victim. They needed to talk to both of these people.

The DMV quickly provided an old photo of Caraballo from about twenty years ago, as well as what looked like his current address: a house on Potomac Avenue. Rozansky and Savage drove over to the address. No dice. Caraballo had moved away long ago.

Schneider came up with a list of other addresses associated with Caraballo, and Rozansky and Savage spent the next several days checking out those locations.

31

The Last Week

As Rozansky and Savage chased down the Caraballo
lead, Keats was pursuing Sanchez.

On Monday, January 8, and the following day, Keats sat
down with the human resources director at Luvata, the new
owners of the American Brass plant.

Keats had seen the Amherst report that Sanchez had not
been at work during the times the rapes and murders attributed to the Bike Path Rapist had occurred. Keats wanted to
see if that held true past 1990. He learned that it did.

He also met with Schneider, who had been working on
cross-referencing the various lists of possible suspects. She
had exciting news. She had compared the list of Hispanic
last names with men who had been arrested for patronizing prostitutes in Erie County. Two names had popped up.
One was a man who was already in jail. The other, Altemio
Sanchez.

Keats asked Schneider to keep digging on Sanchez. The
next day, she spoke with a special agent at the Social Security Administration. She wanted information on two people:
Altemio Sanchez and Wilfredo Caraballo. She faxed over
requests for the information.

On the morning of Wednesday, January 10, Keats
decided to stop by Sanchez's home to talk to him, and

try to get a DNA sample. The house was in Cheektowaga, a working-class suburb east of Buffalo and south of Amherst and Clarence.

He drove to the neatly kept home on Allendale Road, a pleasant, tree-lined street. He knocked on the door, but no one was home and Keats left. He would return again on his way back home. Again, no one was there.

The more Rozansky learned about Caraballo, the more it sounded like he was their guy. Rozansky was determined to track him down. This Caraballo character fit the profile pretty well. He looked like the composite drawings of the Bike Path Killer, although he seemed a little bit older than what the victims had indicated. But as a seasoned investigator, he knew that sometimes what victims of traumatic attacks remembered wasn't always accurate.

One of the relatives associated with Caraballo that Schneider found for Rozansky was a woman named Margarita Torres. The records showed she may have been Caraballo's sister.

On Thursday, January 9, Rozansky and Savage knocked on the door at the house where Torres lived. It was a two-unit house, with a downstairs and an upstairs apartment, typical of Buffalo neighborhoods.

A woman living in the downstairs apartment told the detectives that Torres wasn't home, that she was at work. The woman went on to say Torres was a cleaning lady at D'Youville College. It was a small private school just a few blocks away.

The detectives followed up on the tip and tracked down Torres at the campus.

They showed her the DMV photo of Caraballo that Schneider had turned up. "I don't know if that's him," she told them.

Rozansky and Savage were highly suspicious. *This man is her brother, and she can't identify a photo of him.*

"What do you mean you don't know if it's him," Rozansky pressed. "Look, I need to talk to him."

She said she thought her brother had moved back to Puerto Rico, but she wasn't totally sure.

Rozansky figured Torres was covering for her brother. He handed her his card and asked her to call if she heard from Caraballo.

Then he and Savage went to find another relative. Their records showed there was another brother in town. His name was Heriberto Caraballo, and his address was on Fargo Avenue. Rozansky and Savage knocked on the door. He wasn't home, but they took notice of the name on the mailbox: *Heriberto Sanchez Caraballo.*

The next day, Wednesday, January 10, Rozansky teamed up with Patronik and they headed back to Heriberto Sanchez Caraballo's home.

This time, he and his girlfriend were home. Rozansky knew he had to play it cool or they'd shut them down, like Torres had the previous day. He figured the family members were hiding something. Maybe they knew that Wilfredo Caraballo had been up to something.

Rozansky and Savage explained to Sanchez Caraballo and his girlfriend that they were investigating a crime and that they were just trying to rule out his brother, Wilfredo Caraballo, as a suspect. To do that, they needed a sample of a family member's DNA.

Sanchez Caraballo, amazingly, agreed. They handed him a buccal swab, which he jammed down his throat. He handed it back to them. Rozansky noticed that there was a little spot of blood on it. Rozansky laughed to himself. All he needed to do was lightly swab the inside of his cheek; but Rozansky figured, the more body fluids, the better.

They also let Sanchez Caraballo know that they really needed to talk to his brother, Wilfredo. Rozansky handed him his card, with his cell phone number on it, and asked him to pass the number along.

Rozansky packed up the swab, put it in an evidence box, and then he and Patronik headed north to the Riverside neighborhood, where three of the rapes had taken place. Since there were already out and about, they figured they'd head north along the Niagara River up to that neighborhood. They wanted to get the GPS coordinates for the rapes that had happened there.

Back downtown at the task force, Keats got a call on his cell phone. It was Schneider calling from the FBI offices a few blocks away.

She explained that the information from the Social Security Administration showed that Sanchez's mother's name was Luz Caraballo. It also showed Altemio Sanchez had been born in Puerto Rico. That fit with the DNA profile Simich had put together.

She said she was 99 percent sure that the man Keats was looking at, and the one Rozansky had been chasing, were related.

"Did you know there was a connection?" she asked Keats.

"No!" he replied, excited and incredulous.

Keats then called Rozansky and told him what Schneider had come up with.

They came to an agreement if one of them was able to track down the person each was after.

"Ask your guy about my guy, and I'll ask my guy about your guy," Keats told Rozansky.

That afternoon, Rozansky was sitting in his police car as Patronik hiked out to the railroad tracks off Military Road, near Hertel Avenue, with the GPS device. He was just a couple of blocks away from the old American Brass plant. This was just the kind of police work Patronik, who had a master's degree in computer science, relished. He loved gadgets and high-tech investigator tools. Plus, he was also an avid outdoorsman. Rozansky liked to tease him about being such a gung ho outdoorsy type that he'd camp out in snowbanks in the Adirondack Mountains.

Rozansky was waiting for Patronik to come back to the car when Rozansky's cell phone rang.

It was Wilfredo Caraballo. He was calling from his new home in North Carolina.

Rozansky jumped out of the car and gestured wildly to Patronik to come back. He pointed to his cell phone. Patronik came running.

"You looking for me?" Caraballo asked Rozansky.

Rozansky told him he was.

"Is this about the thing a few years ago?"

Rozansky was intrigued. He wasn't about to stop Caraballo's train of thought.

"Yeah, go ahead. Talk to me," he said.

"I not drive the car," Caraballo said, in somewhat broken English. "My nephew, Altemio, drive the car."

Rozansky asked: "Did you ever tell the police that?"

Caraballo responded: "I don't remember."

Patronik and Rozansky were very excited. They jumped into the car to head back to the Oak Street headquarters. As they drove, Rozansky called Keats.

"You're not going to believe this shit," Rozansky said. "His nephew had the car. And guess who his nephew was?"

Keats had a pretty good idea. "Altemio?"

"Yup," Rozansky said.

They met up at the task force and looked at the cross-referenced lists.

There was Altemio's name.

Rozansky pointed at it. "That's the Bike Path Rapist."

Keats was hesitant to believe it. "Yeah, right." He didn't want to get his hopes up.

The task force members decided that it seemed pretty

clear that they needed to talk to Altemio Sanchez. They also realized they couldn't take the chance of messing up this arrest. If he really was the killer, going up to his door and asking for his DNA could only cause problems. He had already murdered three women. What would keep a man like that from killing again if he thought he was about to get caught?

While they tried to figure out their plan, they decided to get the DNA sample from Heriberto Sanchez Caraballo to the CPS lab for Simich to analyze. He'd be able to tell if he had any blood relation to the Bike Path Killer.

This would be a priority job for Simich and he would make sure it would be done as soon as possible. With so many advances in DNA technology and Simich's years of experience doing DNA analysis for local agencies, Simich would be able to come up with an answer in twenty-four hours. The same test, with an infinitely lesser degree of accuracy, had been taken six months back when Amherst police first had the analysis done with their cases a decade and a half earlier.

32

Out of the Past

The task force members needed to know everything they could about Altemio Sanchez. They knew they'd only have one shot at arresting him. They needed to make sure he was the one. They didn't have his DNA yet, which meant they were facing the possibility of having to get a court order to get it from him. They wanted to have an air-tight case against him.

They started with the files they knew they already had.

Sanchez's name had popped up twice on a list of johns who had been arrested over the years in Buffalo, once in 1991 and the second time in 1999.

The task force members decided to get the original arrest reports.

The 1999 arrest report was easy to track down. The report technicians at central booking found it.

The report said that on September 23, 1999, at 10:45 P.M., Altemio C. Sanchez, DOB 1/19/58, was arrested on Congress Street, in the neighborhood where he grew up.

The report said he pulled up in a 1996 Ford van to where an undercover officer was standing at the curb.

"Get in," he ordered her with the ease of a regular john. The FBI profilers had said they believed the killer probably sought out prostitutes often.

"Do you want to stay in the van? I'll give you a blow job for ten dollars," she offered.

"Yes, I want to stay in the van while you blow me," he said.

"For ten dollars, right?" she said.

"Yes, get in," Sanchez said, at which point the officer signaled for backup and Sanchez was arrested on charges of patronizing a prostitute in the fourth degree.

The other report provided more clues. It was from the first time he'd been arrested.

The report said Sanchez was charged on May 2, 1991, at 1:50 P.M., on Virginia Street, near Mariner Street in Buffalo.

It was just a few blocks from where Majane Mazur had last been seen before disappearing a year and a half later.

According to the arrest report, Sanchez pulled up in his car and called to a woman who turned out to be an undercover vice squad officer.

"Did you call me over?" she asked him.

Sanchez then said: "Are you looking for some action?"

"Sure," the police officer said. "What do you want to do?"

Sanchez crassly replied: "How about a fuck?"

The officer said: "Okay. How much do you pay?"

"How much do you want?" Sanchez shot back at her.

"Whatever you'll pay?" she said.

"Twenty-five dollars," Sanchez suggested.

"Okay," the officer said, "you'll pay me twenty-five dollars for a fuck?"

Sanchez said, "Yes," at which point the officer signaled for backup and Sanchez was arrested. He was charged with patronizing a prostitute in the fourth degree.

The arrest report also noted that Sanchez had been driving a white 1988 Pontiac.

Mazur's boyfriend told police that he had last seen her getting into a white four-door Pontiac with a white man.

The task force members looked back over the DMV records Schneider had pulled up. They indicated Sanchez's wife had a white four-door Pontiac Sunbird registered in her name at that time.

All the arrows seemed to be pointing right at Altemio Sanchez.

On the night of Wednesday, January 10, Rozansky went to the Amherst Police Department. He knew Schneider and Keats had found Altemio Sanchez in those files earlier and they now needed copies of them. He began pulling all of Amherst's reports from when they had investigated and questioned him back in 1990.

Knowing the Amherst police might be a little prickly about this, Rozansky decided not to take the originals. Instead, he faxed the documents, one by one, back to the task force. Nigrelli, Keats, Patronik, McCarthy, and Ken Case, the district attorney assigned to the task force, were eagerly awaiting each page's arrival.

The task force members hovered over their fax machine, snatching each page as it came in.

"Blue car," they spotted on one page. That matched a blue car Sanchez had once owned. There were other intriguing coincidences.

At one point, Rozansky had skipped a page they needed. They frantically called him on his cell phone. "We need that page," Nigrelli told him. Rozansky found the page and sent it over.

The task force members had heard what Keats and Schneider had told them about the Amherst files, but now, as they read it, it was plain as day. Sanchez looked awfully suspicious.

Nigrelli called Schneider on her cell phone. "Good call," he told her. He was amazed that a civilian with little law enforcement background had made this discovery.

The reports were highly detailed and showed that the Amherst Police Department had been quite methodical in investigating Sanchez. They had clearly been interested in him. It just didn't make sense that they had decided to rule him out based on the fingerprint on the water bottle.

The next day, Thursday, January 11, the DNA results from Heriberto Sanchez Caraballo's buccal swab came back.

Rozansky and Keats were present when Simich called. They listened in on speaker phone.

"Statistically speaking, the sample you submitted has a familial relationship to the Bike Path Killer usually found in a first cousin or uncle," Simich told the investigators.

That sounded good, but Rozansky wasn't sure. "Talk to me in layman's terms. Are we hot?"

Simich replied: "Hot."

The task force had their answer.

The man they were looking for was Altemio Sanchez.

33

Who Is Altemio Sanchez?

Altemio Sanchez came to this country in 1960, just after the largest migration from Puerto Rico in American history. The postwar boom in the United States was slowing when Sanchez left.

The Sanchez family came to the United States for other reasons. They left Puerto Rico in a hurry. As he told investigators later, Sanchez was only two when his mother caught his father in bed with a prostitute. Luz Sanchez left her husband, Teraion, packed up Altemio, his older brother, Angelo, and his two older sisters, Bianca and Ida, and moved to Miami.

From there, she moved to New York City, where the nation's largest population of Puerto Ricans had settled. She lived out of her boyfriend's van with her four kids for a year. Then it was on to the Rochester suburb of Henrietta for a short stay before she came to North Collins, south of Buffalo.

The farms of North Collins and Eden are especially productive because of their closeness to Lake Erie's moderating weather patterns. There was plenty for migrant workers to do, especially in the fall harvest season, and labor bosses in Puerto Rico had over the years sent hundreds of migrants north for the picking.

His mother, Altemio later told investigators, was a heavy drinker. He remembered one time when she drank herself into a stupor that lasted for three days. The boyfriend who lived with her and the family regularly beat her, Sanchez said. He also told investigators that his mother's boyfriend sexually abused him for years, but yet he could not remember the man's name.

Like many of the field-workers from North Collins, Luz Sanchez moved with her family to the lower west side of Buffalo, where about 1,400 Puerto Ricans made their home at the time.

Altemio Sanchez was nine when he moved to Buffalo, and he remembered his mother moving the family from one cramped apartment to the other. He said it was almost like they moved every year, living on Plymouth Avenue, Massachusetts Street, Hampshire Street, and Fifteenth Street.

Elizabeth Fildes remembered the family well. Her father, too, had migrated from Puerto Rico to New York City, and had also worked in the fields of North Collins. He moved to Buffalo, worked at a couple of factories, and saved enough to open a small grocery on the corner of Hudson and West, Martinez Delicatessan.

"They lived everywhere," Fildes said of the Sanchez family. "Landlords would keep them for a while. Then they would get rid of them. The mom was always on welfare. She didn't have a job. The sisters I remembered were very well behaved."

Altemio used to hang out near the front of her father's store with other local tough guys, remembered Fildes, now an Erie County sheriff's deputy who handles human-trafficking cases. Her father would run the youths off.

"Almost anyone who was friends with him was of a criminal nature," she said of Altemio.

One of Sanchez's uncles was a street character, she said, who used to pick up soda bottles for deposits. "People called him calabaza, or pumpkin head," she said. "He was a real weirdo."

Another uncle lived directly across from her father's store, she remembered, and he fell in love with a woman who didn't want him.

"He came into my father's store, said he was going to buy some groceries. He took them back to the apartment across from my father's store, had a big dinner, and shot himself."

After Sanchez's mother sobered up, Fildes recalled, she became a Pentecostal.

"She went to the other extreme. The Pentecostal religion is basically the kind that everyone has to go to church every single day. She was very heavy-handed with them too," she said of Sanchez's mother.

Altemio's mother had one boyfriend after another through the years, Sanchez later recalled, and most of them beat her.

"I guess she was the best mom I could imagine," Sanchez later said, "but I had a lot of difficulties when I was growing up. She got beat up a lot by all her different boyfriends and I witnessed it. It caused anger inside of me about what I saw. A couple of times, she took her anger out on me, hitting me when I was young."

When he was a junior in high school, he said his mother told him that she tried to end her pregnancy by having an abortion before he was born. By this time, Luz Sanchez had given up drinking for religion, had become a born-again Christian, and married a man named Gonzalez.

"I love my mother, but it was just the way she made me feel, like we never had a real mother-son relationship,"

THE BIKE PATH KILLER 175

Sanchez later told an investigator. "She took her church more seriously than watching her son play sports. Every day, I'd come home from school and she'd be praying at someone else's house."

Sanchez developed into a good athlete at Grover Cleveland High School. He played on the school baseball team and hung out at the Boys and Girls Club, playing more sports after school.

He was not a good student, was socially inept by his own description, and never had a girlfriend until after he graduated in 1977 and enrolled in an industrial-arts program at Buffalo State College.

There he met his future wife, Kathleen Whitley, who came to Buffalo from central New York. They fell in love, and after he got her pregnant, Sanchez dropped out of school, got a job in a factory, and they married.

Kathy Sanchez was truly the light of his life. She was bright, energetic, the life of the party, and she, too, loved Altemio. It should have been the start of a new life for him.

34

Surveillance

The task force members were pumped. The killer seemed to be in their sights.

Now they had to come up with a plan.

They knew they were dealing with a very dangerous man. They also realized he was probably waiting for the day the police would come for him. Did he have a plan for them?

They decided first and foremost that Sanchez needed to be under twenty-four-hour surveillance. They couldn't take the chance of him slipping away.

Nigrelli and Patronik called up several of their most trusted detectives for the job. Nigrelli picked members of the State Police Violent Crime Task Force, and Patronik went to the sheriff's narcotics unit. These investigators were well seasoned in spying on the sly, and they had worked together on previous operations as well. Amherst also provided a couple of their officers to help out. The task force members also took turns doing the detail.

Two officers, each in his or her own unmarked police car, were assigned to each shift of the surveillance detail. One officer was to always stay in sight of Sanchez's house on Allendale Road. That position was referred to as the "eyeball." The other would wait on one or the other end of the street. That was the "tail car."

When the eyeball would see Sanchez leaving the house, the officer would let the tail car know which direction he was headed, and then follow him to his destination. Both officers had cell phones and radios to keep in contact with each other and with the Oak Street task force headquarters.

To make double sure they knew where Sanchez was, Nigrelli also put in an order for a GPS unit, known as a "Q-ball," which they planned to hide on Sanchez's car. But Nigrelli learned it would take a few days for it to arrive from Albany to Buffalo.

With the surveillance in place, the task force members discussed the possibility of arresting Sanchez right then and there. They consulted with Ken Case, who said they had the legal grounds to do it.

But they would have an airtight, open-and-shut case if they could get a DNA sample from him to match up with those from the victims. They could just go and ask for it, but that would just blow their cover.

They could wait for Sanchez to spit or throw a tissue away or something, but that could take forever.

Monan suggested they try the toothbrush charity stunt that he and LaCorte had pulled back in North Carolina. The other members knocked that idea down. Too risky, they decided.

As they looked through all the paperwork they had gathered on Sanchez, they had noticed that Sanchez had an expired gun permit. And he was no longer allowed to keep a handgun after his two convictions for soliciting a prostitute. That could conceivably give them an excuse to knock on his door and ask for his gun. It was possible to sometimes get some trace DNA off a trigger, if the gunman cocked it hard enough.

But then again, it also meant that Sanchez had a gun, and that they were asking him to approach them with a gun. That could lead to some serious trouble. Sanchez was a known killer and he would have nothing to lose by taking out a cop or two trying to arrest him. And, of course, the shootings in December of the two Buffalo police officers were still heavy on all their minds.

They mulled it over and decided the gun plan was their best bet. They figured that if it worked, it would kill two birds with one stone: they'd get his DNA and get his gun away from him, but they were prepared for the worst-case scenario.

On Thursday, January 11, two sheriff's deputies were selected for the task. Their job was to get him to hand his gun over. They were told to try to get him to cock it a few times so that some skin cells might slough off. They were also given a pen that had been wiped clean of any fingerprints and body oils. They were hoping that could snag some DNA as well when Sanchez used it to sign the form.

That morning, the deputies arrived and knocked at Sanchez's door. Sanchez, who had just recently returned home from his overnight shift at Luvata, answered. They told him that they were doing a roundup of guns from people with expired permits and said he was on the list. Sanchez bought it. They told him he needed to surrender his weapon. He agreed. He went back into the house and came out with it.

The deputies were nervous. What would he do? Did he suspect anything?

As they had been instructed, they asked Sanchez to cock the gun to make sure there were no bullets inside. He did as he was told. They then asked him to sign a form. The deputy who had the pristine pen went for it in his pocket, but he was so nervous he pulled out the wrong one. Sanchez used it to sign the form and said good-bye.

The deputies rushed the gun to the CPS lab and Dr. Simich got right to work.

The task force members were on pins and needles as they waited for the results.

* * *

The next day, Friday, January 12, Simich called with the bad news. There was no DNA on the gun. They needed to try again.

They decided they'd stick with the surveillance and just wait for a chance to grab something he ate or drank from, if he went somewhere to eat. The surveillance team tailed Sanchez as he went to work that night and then returned home Saturday morning. Two new surveillance teams replaced them: Chris Weber and Josh Keats in one car, and Ed Monan and Alan Rozansky in the other. It was evening when the two state police investigators called up Monan and Rozansky on their cell phone. They had to leave about thirty minutes early, they said, which meant Monan and Rozansky would be doing surveillance solo.

They figured it wouldn't be a problem. Their replacements were coming in half an hour. The state investigators left and Monan decided he'd drive past Sanchez's house a few times to make sure they didn't miss him. He drove down to one end of the block and then turned around, when all of a sudden he saw Sanchez and his wife in their car headed straight for them.

Monan and Rozansky were caught off guard, but they weren't about to let Sanchez get away. They called up their bosses and let them know what was going on as they followed the Sanchezes.

They headed northeast for about 3.5 miles, from Cheektowaga over to Williamsville, a village within Amherst. They came to a stop near a popular gift shop on Main Street and parked their car. They didn't get out. Monan and Rozansky sat and watched them. About ten minutes later, the Sanchezes were on the move again. They kept heading east on Main Street until they got to Clarence. They stopped again, this time at the parking lot of a butcher shop. They didn't get out of the car again.

The light went on again in the car.

"It looks like they're reading something," Rozansky said. They figured it was a map. A few minutes later, Sanchez turned the car around and started heading west on Main Street. They went past the gift store and ended up in front of Sole, a popular, trendy restaurant that features Latin-influenced dishes.

Rozansky wasn't exactly primed for the surveillance detail. His family was mad at him. His sister had flown in from out of town. The Rozanskys were Jewish and Saturday night was supposed to be a night for the family to gather to break the Sabbath. Rozansky had a job to do, and he explained as much as he could to his sister that he'd have to be late to dinner.

Al and Kathy Sanchez were seated at a table along a wall at Sole. Rozansky and Monan made their way over to the bar. A football game was on the TV above. The detectives ordered sodas—they weren't about to risk anything by having a cocktail. They were quickly joined by Mike Rose, another Amherst detective. He and Greg Savage had been scheduled to relieve Monan and Rozansky. Monan asked to speak to the manager.

Rebecca Klauk came out to the bar, where she saw the three detectives standing and talking to her bartender.

Monan took Klauk away from the bar into a hallway and explained, without giving any details, why they were there.

"The two customers at the table are part of an investigation," he told her.

Klauk asked to see his badge and ID card, then asked what she could do to help.

"Don't move anything from the table," Monan said.

Klauk didn't think that was a good idea. "It might be a little strange," she said, explaining the diners would find it unusual.

"Well, all we need are the glasses," Monan told her. She told the server not to move them.

Sole attracted a hip, upscale crowd, and while Klauk had no idea who the couple was, she remembered Sanchez looking like he might have been a college professor out on a date with his wife.

He seems like the guy who taught my college English class, she thought.

The police were using the classic way of obtaining a DNA sample from an unsuspecting perpetrator. Rozansky couldn't count the times he'd offer a soda to a suspect in an interview room. "Want a pop?" he'd ask, and the perp would grab it, drink it, and not think anything as it was cleared away. Just a drop of saliva could yield the telltale DNA that the cops needed to make an arrest.

As the Sanchezes dined, the detectives took turns walking past them. They wanted to get a good look at Al Sanchez. It was so strange seeing him, having a pleasant dinner with his wife, knowing that he very likely was a serial rapist and killer. They watched and waited until the Sanchezes finished their meal. When they left, Savage was in place to follow them.

Rozansky, Monan, and Rose went over to the table and began trying to figure out which objects Sanchez would have touched or put his mouth on.

They carefully began bagging the items: silverware and a glass with a straw. Rose suggested getting his linen napkin. They bagged it too.

The other diners were shocked as they watched the cops scooping up the glasses. Among them was a woman who had grown up with Al Sanchez. She had recognized him there in the restaurant. She had remembered him and his brother as bad news. Later that night, she called her friend Elizabeth Fildes. "You'll never believe what I saw," she told Fildes. They had no idea what the police wanted with Sanchez. It seemed serious, but they had no idea of the magnitude.

Monan and Rose offered to take it to Dr. Simich's lab.

He would be there waiting for it to arrive. Rozansky had no problem with that. He didn't need to be the one to deliver the goods. He needed to get home to make amends with his family.

The Amherst detectives drove the bagged tableware downtown. Monan held the bags in his hands, refusing to take his eyes off them. He wanted to make sure there was no way anyone could challenge the evidence's chain of custody.

But the Sanchezes weren't done with their evening. Greg Savage and Greg McCarthy from the sheriff's department took over the surveillance. They followed the Sanchezes as they drove to a Borders bookstore. The Sanchezes split up in the bookstore. Al Sanchez wandered into the cookbook section, selected a stack of Spanish cookbooks, and sat down on the floor. He leisurely thumbed through the books as the cops watched him.

After an hour or so, he met up with his wife in the store and the two went to the bookstore café to order some coffee drinks. They sat down at a table and sipped their coffee. Savage snuck back into the kitchen and asked the staff not to touch the Sanchezes' cups. They agreed.

But then Al and Kathy Sanchez got up from their seats with their paper coffee cups and started walking out the door. Savage and McCarthy tailed them and watched as they chucked the cups into a trash can before getting into their car. Once it looked like the Sanchezes were in their car, the detectives carefully went into the trash can and picked up the cups. They needed to make sure they had every opportunity to find DNA. Those cups were rushed to Simich as well.

The cups were dropped off. Simich got to work first thing in the morning. He promised he would have an answer for them by 5:00 P.M. the next day. The task force members all prayed that their plan had worked. All they needed was one tiny drop of DNA and Sanchez could be arrested.

The next day, the task force members tried to go about their everyday lives. But they couldn't help but think about the DNA testing that was under way. It would be proof, beyond any doubt, that Al Sanchez, this man they'd watched have a pleasant meal with his wife, who liked cookbooks, who had a normal job and a tidy home, was the Bike Path Killer.

Several of the task force members couldn't help themselves and came to work. Patronik was there. So was Monan, as was Redmond. LaCorte, who had largely worked out of Amherst, even came down to hear the big announcement. Nigrelli had come by for several hours but had to leave to take his son to a swimming pool party for his hockey team at a Cheektowaga hotel.

Nigrelli picked up the golf club again and began swinging. The others paced and Redmond said to herself that it seemed like they were in a hospital waiting room, waiting for a baby to be born.

The investigators were all hopeful, but at the same time, they'd been in the same position before. The Amherst cops had been ready to bet their paychecks on the North Carolina man when the DNA came back saying he wasn't the rapist they were looking for.

Don't get too excited, LaCorte kept saying to himself. *We've been disappointed so many times.* He imagined the phone call coming in and Simich saying: "Sorry, it's not the same guy." He hated to think of the task force having to start all over again. But then again, LaCorte had done it before. And there was no giving up. Not on a case like this.

Nigrelli had to leave before the call came. He drove home, picked up his family, and drove to the hotel. The kids were clearly having a ball as they splashed around in the indoor pool, but Nigrelli couldn't enjoy himself. He couldn't stop thinking about the DNA test that was under way. His family members accused him of being detached.

As the 5:00 P.M. hour neared, the task force members in the office gathered in the conference room and waited. They were quiet. No one had much to say. There was only one thing on their minds: did they have the right guy? It was all coming down to the results of this one test.

At precisely five o'clock, the phone rang. It was Simich. He was a man of his word.

"You've got your man," he told the task force members.

The strongest DNA came from Sanchez's napkin, he told them. Then the cup at Borders, and finally the glassware from his table at Sole.

No one was surprised, but they were all elated.

Redmond couldn't believe it. She had spent so many years on the bike path case. And now, they finally had their guy. She was so happy, so amazed. She knew that she'd never have a moment like this again in her career as a police officer.

The hair on the back of LaCorte's neck stood up. He couldn't believe it. It was almost like he hadn't heard the words. But that's what Simich had just said: *"You've got your man."*

Patronik immediately called Nigrelli.

"It's him," he said.

Nigrelli was driving, but he threw his hands up in the air for a moment. He began cheering with delight. And then, in the next second, he found himself getting choked up. He was overwhelmed as he thought of all the victims and all the hard work that so many men and women in law enforcement had put into trying to find this man over so many years. He then called Keats, Weber, and Schneider.

Rozansky was at his home, playing with his dog, when his cell phone rang. Patronik let him know the good news.

Now all the task force had to do was arrest Sanchez.

But how?

35

The Arrest

They needed a plan.

Patronik and Nigrelli sat down with Ken Case, the assistant district attorney, to come up with one. Over the last couple of days, as they had grown more and more confident that Altemio Sanchez was the Bike Path Killer, they had thrown around ideas about how they should go about arresting him. They wanted to get him as soon as possible, but they also wanted to make sure they got it right. There was no way they were going to take the chance of this guy getting off on a technicality.

They knew that Sanchez would be headed to work Sunday night for his overnight shift and would head back sometime Monday morning. The simplest way to get him, they decided, would be to follow him home from work and grab him as he was going into his home.

It was decided that Ed Monan and Greg McCarthy would be the ones to interrogate Sanchez first. Monan, because he was from Amherst, where Linda Yalem was killed, and McCarthy, because he was one of the investigators in the Joan Diver murder.

So they were to be in one of at least three cars that would follow Sanchez back from the Luvata plant Monday morning. Whoever arrested him was to stick him in the back of their car so that questioning could begin right away. He was then to be driven down to the sheriff's department detective bureau downtown.

After Sanchez was in custody, the plan was for Redmond and Weber to pick up Kathy Sanchez and take her to the Amherst Police Department, where she'd be questioned.

They arranged for crime scene investigators from each law enforcement agency represented on the task force to be ready to search Sanchez's house for any evidence. They didn't know if he had kept a journal, mementos, newspaper clippings, or any other possible items that could help in his prosecution.

They also rounded up several state troopers, who were to fan out across the region to track down witnesses and victims. They were to show a photo of Sanchez to them to see if they recognized him.

The plan was set.

Everybody was told to be at the Oak Street headquarters by 7:00 A.M.

Nigrelli couldn't sleep that night. He tossed and turned as he went over every possible scenario. He thought about everything that could go wrong. He thought about questions to ask Sanchez. He ended up at the office by 5:45 A.M.

Even Patronik, a famous late sleeper, showed up early.

The others were ready to go by 6:30 A.M.

One surveillance car, with state investigators Andre Dunlop and Darryl O'Shei, had been waiting all night outside the Luvata plant in Riverside. They were soon joined by Rozansky and Savage in one car, and Monan and McCarthy in another.

They realized it was highly likely that with three cars tailing him, Sanchez would eventually figure out that he was being followed. But at this point, they figured, it didn't matter. The important thing was to not let him out of their sight for a single second.

Just after 8:00 A.M., Sanchez left work and got into his car. The three cars followed.

From the Luvata plant, Sanchez started heading east. But instead of going home, he seemed to be heading to Amherst. They later learned he had a doctor's appointment at an office on Sheridan Drive and Harlem Road. He had had shoulder surgery recently and was having it checked out. The task force members had wondered whether he had aggravated the injury when he attacked Joan Diver. The autopsy showed she had fought him hard.

Monan and McCarthy were told to switch gears and start heading toward his house, where they were to wait for Sanchez.

Sanchez came out and got back into his car. But instead of getting on Interstate-290, which was right near the doctor's office, and would have been the fastest way home, he got onto a side street. And then another and then another. He would stop his car and then keep going.

Sanchez clearly wasn't headed to Cheektowaga.

He slowly wound his way from Amherst, west into Buffalo. He drove past Delaware Park. The task force members started to wonder whether Sanchez was trolling for a new place to attack.

He eventually ended up in his old neighborhood on the west side.

O'Shei radioed back to Nigrelli: "He's onto us. He's got us made. He's driving to shake the cow."

He also added that the roads were getting icy. A light rain had started to fall and it was starting to freeze over on the ground. It was Martin Luther King Jr. Day, so the roads weren't terribly busy. But still, it was getting a little hairy as they were tailing this increasingly erratic driver.

Nigrelli asked: "Are Monon and McCarthy there?"

O'Shei said they were moments away from catching up to them.

Nigrelli and Patronik looked at each other. What were they waiting for?

"Take him off," Nigrelli said. "It's a wrap. Take him into custody."

O'Shei and Dunlop and Rozansky and Savage flashed their lights and pulled Sanchez over.

They walked up to his car. Rozansky took the lead.

Sanchez looked calm as he opened his car door.

Rozansky firmly, but not violently, pulled him out.

"Sir, we need to talk to you," Rozansky said coolly. It was a proud moment for Rozansky.

Rozansky made a concerted effort not to touch Sanchez's car. He didn't want to mess with any potential evidence. He cuffed Sanchez and put him into the back of Monan and McCarthy's car.

Sanchez did not ask why he was being arrested.

36

Kathy Sanchez

As Altemio Sanchez was being driven to the sheriff's office in downtown Buffalo, Lissa Redmond and Chris Weber waited in their car for Kathy Sanchez to leave the house. She was headed to her car when the two detectives approached her.

They told her they needed to ask her some questions.

Kathy Sanchez seemed extremely confused and scared. She had no idea what a Buffalo detective and a state police investigator were doing there in front of her home in Cheektowaga.

"Look, we can sit in the car, [or] we can go in the garage. Let's just get out of the rain," Redmond said.

Kathy Sanchez invited them into her house.

There was no easy way to break the news to this woman, so Redmond just came out and said it.

"We believe your husband is the Bike Path Rapist," she said.

"No, that can't be," Kathy Sanchez replied.

"Well, you need to tell us why that can't be."

They explained to her that they wanted to continue questioning her at the Amherst Police Department.

They also asked if they could search the house, even

though they had already obtained a search warrant. Kathy Sanchez agreed and signed a consent form.

Redmond thought about what a beautiful home it was. She then thought about the picture-perfect life that Kathy Sanchez thought she had had with her husband. From the research they had done on Altemio Sanchez, Redmond knew the couple had a nice life together. They had this house, their jobs, and their handsome sons.

Redmond wondered how she'd react if someone suddenly came up to her and told her that her husband had twelve bodies buried in the backyard. *You'd look at them and go, you're nuts,* she thought. And that's exactly what Kathy Sanchez was doing. She seemed to think this was all one very big, very surreal mistake.

Redmond got the feeling that Kathy Sanchez had absolutely no idea what her husband had been up to. She didn't get any sense that she was covering for him or hiding anything from the police. Redmond felt terrible, absolutely terrible, for this poor woman whose life was unraveling before her eyes.

37

Questioning
Kathy Sanchez

Redmond and Weber brought Kathy Sanchez back to the Amherst Police Department. They spent the next nine hours questioning her.

At first, they talked about all the milestones in the Sanchez lives. How they met. When they got married. The birth of their sons. Their jobs. The trips they had taken together.

And then the investigators began explaining what her husband was being charged with.

Kathy Sanchez seemed very frightened. She was getting worked up. She couldn't believe what she was hearing.

But she acknowledged that she'd heard some of this before. She said her husband had already been questioned about the Bike Path Killer case.

Redmond and Weber were fascinated.

Kathy Sanchez explained to them that the Amherst police had questioned her husband years ago in connection to the case, but there was nothing to it. It wasn't him, she insisted to them.

Despite being upset, she remained cooperative. She

answered every embarrassing question the investigators brought up.

They asked her about her and her husband's sex lives. She said there was nothing unusual about it. They asked if he ever got rough with her. She said no. They asked if he had ever choked her during sex. She said no.

They brought up the vasectomy they believed he'd had. Testing on the semen that had been found on Majane Mazur, who was killed in 1992, and the fourteen-year-old Riverside girl, who was raped in 1994, indicated that sometime during that period the assailant had lost his ability to produce sperm. They believed the most likely explanation was that he had had a vasectomy.

Kathy Sanchez confirmed it.

She also acknowledged that she was aware that her husband had been arrested for patronizing a prostitute. She knew only about one arrest, though.

"She's a nice lady," Weber said. "Not the sharpest knife in the drawer, not a whole lot of common sense. Very nice, articulate."

He believed she had no idea what her husband had been up to. "I just think she was a happy-go-lucky lady who lives this life," Weber said. "She worked days, her husband worked nights. She was happy as a clam."

During the interview, she began asking whether she should talk to a lawyer. Redmond and Weber didn't want her to, but they couldn't stop her. She didn't, though.

She also got several calls from her two sons. Michael was in Lancaster, New York, near Clarence, and Christopher was in San Diego.

Michael had seen the news and wanted to know what was going on. He agreed to come to Amherst with the detectives. They laid out the evidence against his father.

"Your father is being charged with homicide," Weber explained to Michael Sanchez.

He went through the list of girls and women who had

been raped and murdered by Sanchez. He explained that in seven of the cases, DNA had been found and that the evidence all matched his father's DNA.

"Wait a minute," Michael Sanchez said. "You're telling me that my father's DNA was found in those girls?"

Weber replied: "Yes."

Michael Sanchez looked at his mother. "He's fucked."

Kathy Sanchez didn't want to hear that. "Shut up, Michael."

But Michael Sanchez could see the writing on the wall. "He's screwed, Mom."

He spoke with his mother and they ended up calling a lawyer for Altemio Sanchez. They knew he would need one. Michael Sanchez's girlfriend worked for a local attorney, William Mattar. He specialized in handling car injury cases. "Hurt in a car? Call William Mattar" was his slogan.

Mattar was obviously not qualified to handle a homicide case, and referred Sanchez to local defense attorney Andrew C. LoTempio.

38

Sanchez in the Box

Altemio Sanchez sat quietly in the back of Greg McCarthy's truck. Ed Monan, in the front passenger seat, had the feeling that Sanchez was going through what he was going to say and do as he was questioned.

The detectives were dying to start asking him questions, but they didn't want to be too hasty. If Sanchez lawyered up, that would end all chances of a confession. And they needed a confession to keep the case from having to go all the way to trial.

They were just a couple of miles away from the sheriff's office in downtown Buffalo, where Sanchez was to be interviewed, and there was no use in starting the interrogation right then and there in McCarthy's truck. Monan decided he'd spend the few minutes it would take to get downtown trying to build a rapport with Sanchez. He didn't have a tremendous amount of experience with drawing confessions out of homicide suspects. But having been a detective for much of the last decade, he'd learned that going all out on a perp right from the get-go rarely ever worked.

Monan had learned from the sheriff's deputies who obtained Sanchez's gun four days earlier that he was unloading a set of golf clubs when they approached him. Monan was an avid golfer himself, so he started talking to Sanchez about golf. He asked him about which courses he had gone to, which ones he preferred, things like that. Anything at all to get him talking. That was the key.

Sanchez spoke up a couple of times and Monan was glad. Maybe his approach would work.

Very soon, they arrived at the Erie County sheriff's detective bureau in a five-story brick building on West Eagle Street, where cops share the same elevator with county election workers whose office is on the floors below. The building was adjacent to the Erie County Holding Center, which the sheriff's office oversees.

A handcuffed Al Sanchez was led out of the police car and into the detective bureau. He was escorted straight to an interview room. Unlike most interrogation boxes portrayed in many TV cop shows, there was no one-way mirror. The room did come equipped with a CCTV camera that beamed images to a monitor in another room nearby.

There had been some debate about who should be the first to interview Sanchez.

This was a homicide investigation, and the most experienced homicide interrogators were the state police investigators: Keats, Weber, and Nigrelli.

But the state police didn't have a single bike path case of their own, so the decision was made to start off the questioning with McCarthy and Monan.

Both men were narcotics detectives and didn't have much experience at drawing a confession in a homicide case, but they knew the two homicide cases—Yalem and Diver—inside out. It made sense to give them the first crack at Sanchez.

As they settled in their chairs in the interview room, Monan made sure to read Sanchez his rights. He wanted to do things by the book. He didn't want to take any chances with the legalities. While he didn't want Sanchez to ask for a lawyer, he certainly didn't want to extract a confession and then have it thrown out because he had failed to Mirandize Sanchez.

Sanchez looked somewhat nervous, but not terribly so. He had his hands between his thighs. He wasn't acting crazy. He wasn't protesting his innocence or even demanding to know why he had been brought in to the interview. Mostly, he seemed cold and detached.

Monan and McCarthy talked to Sanchez as the rest of the task force members gathered around the CCTV to watch. They suddenly realized that no one was transcribing the interview. Buffalo police report technicians were supposed to take shorthand of the session, but in the rush to arrest Sanchez, it was one of the items overlooked. Betsy Schneider, the state police crime analyst who helped wrap up the loose ends that led to his arrest, grabbed a pen.

We wait twenty-five years to do this interview, and suddenly we don't have anyone in place, Nigrelli remembered thinking.

The district attorney's office had advised against videotaping the session, so there was no recorded version of what was said, only a transcript that Schneider began and the report technicians finished once they were rushed over.

Sanchez sat quietly, almost calmly at the table, dressed in a black pullover zip-up jersey with silver stripes running down the sleeves and a pair of blue jeans. He had a slight paunch he hadn't worked off since his shoulder surgery, which hung over a black belt.

Before he led cops around town for more than half an hour before they finally pulled him over, he had worked an eight-hour shift at the brass factory. He hadn't had anything to eat, but he didn't act tired and he didn't ask for any food.

Monan and McCarthy were soon joined in the box by

sheriff's detective Rozansky, the lead detective in the Diver homicide.

Every interviewer has his own style. Some like to build a rapport with the suspect, acting as a friend trying to draw out information, trying to get him to tell his life story, and seeing if they can get him to confess. That's what Monan had been trying to do in the car.

Others try a more confrontational approach: "Look, we arrested you because we know you're guilty. We've got all the evidence we need, why not make it easy on yourself and we'll try to get the district attorney to give you a break."

In the interview room, Rozansky, Monan, and McCarthy decided to take that road, boring in on him right off the bat. They wanted him to understand that he was in deep trouble and they had all the evidence they needed to book him. He needed to know that there was absolutely no wiggle room.

"We have the DNA," they told him. "We're not trying to gang up on you. . . . It's over. You don't have anywhere to go."

"We want your side of this," Monan told him. "We want you to give us a chance."

"Who are you looking for?" Sanchez asked them. "I'm telling you, I'm not the one. I'm sitting here trying to be as nice as possible to you. I can just bring my lawyer, but I'm not gonna do it. I'm not responsible for any of this stuff you're talking about. You keep drilling me, saying we know you're the one."

Monan laid his cards on the table to the man who had walked out of Amherst a free man more than fifteen years before. Cutting Sanchez loose still stung.

"We don't need to get anything out of you," Monan told him. "We don't need to do that. We have the DNA evidence. That's all we really need. We want to give you a chance to tell us what happened."

"What happened where?"Sanchez asked him.

"On the bike path in Amherst."

"I don't know anything about Amherst or the girls you're saying that I met or had bad sex with them," Sanchez said. "I am lost."

McCarthy told Sanchez they had trailed him to Sole, got his DNA from his glassware, trailed him to Borders, where they picked up his coffee cup. McCarthy fibbed and told him they also got DNA from the handgun they recovered from him the week before, even though there was no DNA recovered from the gun.

"You're saying you want me to commit to something I didn't do," Sanchez told the three detectives.

Outside the interview room, the crowd of task force investigators watched and listened to the interview through a monitor, rapt and stunned that Sanchez continued to deny any connection to the rapes and murders.

Detective Dennis Delano had just arrived with Ken Case, the district attorney assigned to the case.

"We heard Ed saying, 'We got your DNA, we know you did it,'" Case said. "You're not going to get Al Sanchez to confess like that. He's a very controlling, manipulative person. He was trying to take control."

Delano was irritated. That's no way to get a confession, he told Case, and angrily went back to his office at Buffalo police headquarters.

Case had to agree with Delano.

"You're not going to convince Altemio Sanchez that he's not driving the bus," the prosecutor said. "Ed was screaming at the guy. He's calm. He's taking back control."

And so the interview went, hour by hour, as the detectives laid out the evidence, showed him pictures of the victims, telling Sanchez that they had his DNA, that after nearly thirty years of his rapes and murders, it was over.

"That's what you say," Sanchez responded, over and over again.

The only time he opened up was when someone asked about his family, or his golfing.

"My irons are Excalibur and my woods are Cobra," he told them. "They've got the highest titanium. That's what I started out with. Right now, they're coming out with these big drivers."

It became clear to the detectives in the box with him, and the investigators watching him outside, that Sanchez thought he was going to walk away from this, just like he had done after the Buffalo police had questioned his uncle about the car Sanchez had used when he was seen at the mall by one of his victims. And when the Amherst police questioned him about Yalem's murder.

"How long do I have to stay here?" he asked two hours into the questioning. "I told you, I can't answer any more questions."

Rozansky told him they found his DNA in Joan Diver's car.

"I have never drove anybody or whoever's car you're talking about," he replied. "I was not in her vehicle."

He had only been in Clarence to golf, was never on the bike path, and he was never on the Ellicott Creek Trailway, where Yalem was murdered, he told them.

"But what do you want me to say?" Sanchez asked them. "I never knew the girl. I never was out on the bike path. I've never been to any of those places. I never did anything to those girls."

He told them that Amherst detectives had asked him the same questions about Yalem years ago.

"I mean, the same thing happened to me in Amherst," he said. "They drilled me. I was in there, I don't know, for a couple hours. Two detectives were drilling me the same way you are."

Shortly before noon, four hours into the interview, Sanchez lost his cool.

"These crimes you're saying I committed, I didn't do," he told Monan. "If you're gonna arrest me, do it now. Call my wife and explain it to her. Go ahead and I will slap the biggest lawsuit against the sheriff's department. I'm telling you the truth."

At one point, during a pause in the questioning, Rozansky looked at Sanchez and said, "I'm trying to figure out why you did it."

"I'm trying to figure out the same thing myself," Sanchez replied.

Was it a slip in his façade? Did he actually mean it?

A short time later, Rozansky asked him about the absence of sperm in his semen. When the Bike Path Killer raped his last victim in 1994, the fourteen-year-old girl near the railroad tracks in Riverside, there had been no sperm in his semen.

"Ever had a vasectomy?" Rozansky asked.

"No," Sanchez replied.

Rozansky gave him another chance.

"Never had a vasectomy?"

"No, never," Sanchez said again.

While the detectives continued to question him, other investigators called Lissa Redmond and Chris Weber, who were interviewing Kathy Sanchez in Amherst.

She confirmed the operation, and the information was passed back to the interviewers.

"They just talked to your wife," McCarthy told him. "She told them you had a vasectomy in '93."

"I'm telling you right now," Sanchez told him. "I never had a vasectomy."

"Your wife just said you did," McCarthy said.

"Then bring my wife in then," Sanchez replied.

But Sanchez realized it was no use holding out any

longer, if his wife had told them. He finally admitted he had had the vasectomy.

"I never tell people that," he said. "It's an embarrassing thing."

As the interview dragged on, someone brought a radio into the interview room so Sanchez could hear news of his being in custody as the Bike Path Killer.

But he still wouldn't give up anything, other than to say that his wife and sons would be devastated by what was being said about him.

"I would never have hurt, never hurt another woman," he said. "I would never lay a finger on my wife, so why would I lay a hand on someone else? I'm not a violent person whatsoever."

"I'm not the kind of person who could do something like this," he added. "Take somebody else's life? Why would I rape somebody? I have a good life. Good job. Good kids and a good job and a good wife."

Monan tried another tack.

"Do you think there's a chance that at some point in your life," he asked, "you're gonna regret not talking to us?"

"I'm being honest with you on my momma's grave," Sanchez said. "I didn't have anything to do with any of those girls, any of those rapes, any of those murders. If you can't believe me . . ."

The afternoon dragged on. Someone brought in McDonald's Happy Meals. The detectives ate. Sanchez watched them, refusing food or anything to drink.

They kept playing the news broadcasts on the radio. Sanchez told them that though he was innocent, the news would destroy him.

"My life is ruined," he told them.

Rozansky tried another route. He asked Sanchez to

let them swab his mouth for a DNA sample that would clear him.

"I don't believe in swabs," Sanchez said. "I don't want to do it."

Finally, at 5:00 P.M., the task force switched interrogators. Josh Keats, the state police investigator, entered the room. Lissa Redmond had been called in from Amherst, where she and Weber had spent the day with Kathy Sanchez.

Monan was disappointed that he hadn't been able to get a confession out of Sanchez. He knew that would have made things a lot easier for everyone: the police, the court system, but mostly the victims. But he also realized that Sanchez had been waiting for this moment for more than twenty years. He'd probably been rehearsing this scene in his mind over and over.

39

The Box, Part II

By the afternoon, Redmond was absolutely exhausted. She had been grilling Kathy Sanchez all day. And now they wanted her to come talk to Altemio too. She was to team up with Josh Keats for the job.

When she walked out of Amherst, she saw that the light rain from the morning had turned to a miserable, wet, slushy snow. A patrol officer from Amherst was assigned the task of driving Redmond down to West Eagle Street. As they made their way to Buffalo, they passed an accident on the road, and the patrolman had to stop and call it in.

Redmond walked in and saw her fellow task force members crowded around the monitor.

Keats was already in the room but hadn't really started interviewing Sanchez just yet. Redmond joined him. Everyone else had already given a shot at interviewing Sanchez, or had been listening in. Redmond had no idea what ground they'd already covered, so she just sort of went in there and winged it.

A change seemed to come over Sanchez as Keats and Redmond introduced themselves.

"Those are two very experienced interviewers," Nigrelli said. "Lissa does sex abuse interviews all day long. Josh does homicide interviews. He pitches themes at people. That's what we're taught. Give them an out. If they're going to go for it, you've built an out for them."

"Josh Keats is one of our best interviewers," Nigrelli said. "He knows [Sanchez] is involved at St. Aloysius Church. People of Latino descent are very involved in the Catholic faith, so Josh went in with that belief. It's a great pitch. That's just knowing your guy. So Josh went in with that pitch and it worked. All of a sudden, he likes Josh."

Sanchez was suspicious of Redmond at first. He thought she might be a psychologist.

"At one point," Redmond says, Sanchez pointed at Keats. "He says, 'He's a detective, those other guys are detectives. You're something else. You're more than a detective.'

"No, here's my little badge," Redmond said. She told him she was usually assigned to the sex offense squad.

She brought a different style after years of interviewing those charged with sex crimes.

"I was used to dealing with sex offenders and pedophiles," Redmond said. "I wasn't a homicide detective. I was used to dealing with the mind-set of a sex offender. They don't view themselves as bad people. I call it the demon. You've got a demon in you that you can't control and it comes out—where, like, with homicides, sometimes people kill people in the heat of the moment. They've really pissed them off, it's an act of passion, revenge. There's a motive. Whereas with sex crimes . . . it's their pent-up motive, their need to control, to hurt. But they can seem perfectly normal the rest of the time."

Redmond didn't find it as strange as others did that Sanchez could pass himself off as completely normal while committing these horrendous crimes.

"A lot of times with pedophiles, you find they're the nicest [people], because how else could they get a child to trust them? If they were a big, scary, nasty person, no child would come within ten feet of them. They have to have a

kind and gentle persona to gain that trust. Sex offenders
also do.

"You don't picture a guy jogging down a pathway," she
said. "Someone who looks perfectly normal, who can walk
out of the crime scene and the police wouldn't grab him. It's
a detachment from the victims. He can love his wife. He can
love his kids. He can be good to his sister. He can do everything for everyone, he can detach himself from the victims,
do all these horrendous things, but they don't view themselves as a bad guy. So I tried to play on that. I think that's
where I was striking a chord. 'I'm not a bad guy. I may do
bad things, but I'm not a bad guy.' And give him that out."

Redmond had spent the whole day without eating. She
was starved, but all that was left in the Happy Meal boxes
were some cold French fries and the toy that came with the
meals. Redmond picked up the toy and started playing
with it. She couldn't figure out what it was. From the box,
it looked like a hairless mole rat.

She looked at Sanchez.

"Did you eat?" she asked him. He said no.

A big bell went off in both her head and Josh's.

"You don't really believe that we have your DNA, do
you?" she asked him.

"Well, that's what you say," Sanchez replied. "You say
you do."

"He really didn't think we had anything on him," Redmond recalled, "so I'm sitting there with my hairless mole
rat. I'm starving, I didn't eat anything all day. I would have
eaten anything. I didn't know who touched the fries, so I
didn't eat them. This guy had worked all night. And you're
telling me he's not going to eat or drink?"

Sanchez seemed friendlier, he opened up more, but he
still would not admit to a single rape or murder over the
next hour as the questions continued.

Sanchez kept bringing up calling a lawyer. He didn't quite ask for his lawyer, but he kept mentioning it. Nigrelli, Patronik, Case, and Frank Sedita III, the district attorney's homicide chief, were starting to get a little nervous. The last thing they wanted to do was to create grounds for any statement Sanchez made to be thrown out of court.

Plus, it had been eight hours since they'd arrested him, and Sanchez wasn't giving up anything. He wasn't budging. He wasn't even drinking any water.

Nigrelli decided it was time to pull the plug on the interrogation. He walked into the interview room and looked at Keats.

"It's a wrap," Nigrelli said, running his forefinger across his neck.

Then Sanchez stood up.

No one knew what was going on.

Then it occurred to Nigrelli; Sanchez thought he had beaten the cops again. He thought it was just like it was back in 1990 in Amherst. He believed he had outlasted the detectives and that everything was going to go back to the way it was. He still hadn't understood, after all of this interrogation, that the police really did have solid, irrefutable DNA evidence against him.

Nigrelli lost his temper.

"You're not going anywhere," he told Sanchez. "You're never going home. You're going to jail for the rest of your life."

Sanchez looked startled.

"We weren't lying," Nigrelli said. He walked out of the room and found a deputy. He asked for his handcuffs and handed them to Keats.

"Cuff him," he told Keats.

Sanchez put his wrists together in front of him.

"Oh no," Keats said. "We're doing this Troop F–style."

"Troop F–style" was something Keats had learned in the academy. It was the textbook way to handcuff a suspect. It was often used for the arrests of the worst of the worst on the streets of New York City.

Keats ordered Sanchez to put his hands behind his head. He slapped one cuff on one wrist, then pulled that arm down to the small of his back. He then yanked the other arm down and cuffed that wrist too.

Sanchez turned ashen. He had an "Oh shit" look on his face. It seemed that Sanchez was finally beginning to understand that his thirty-year charade was over.

Redmond grabbed her coat and walked into the interview room. She stared Sanchez in the face. "Hey, Al. Good luck," she said.

Sanchez was silent. He seemed to be thinking: *You really weren't kidding.*

After staring down Sanchez, Redmond headed outside. The icy rain from the morning had turned to snow. There was a thick blanket of snow on the unmarked police car she'd borrowed that morning.

She was absolutely exhausted. She felt like she'd just done twenty rounds with Mike Tyson. She mustered up enough energy to clear off a small spot on the windshield and she began driving. Her car was over at the sex offense squad, just a couple of blocks away.

She was slowly trying to make her way over there when a traffic cop pulled up behind her and flashed his lights. She rolled down her window.

"Lissa?" the surprised traffic cop said. He'd been set to give her a ticket for unsafe driving because of her snow-covered windshield.

"I'm just exhausted," she said.

"Are you okay?" he asked. She realized she must have looked really pitiful.

"I just need to go back to my car and go home," Redmond said.

The cop knew that Redmond was part of the bike path task force. He had an idea of what kind of a day she had had. He didn't write her up. "Just be careful," he scolded her.

Redmond made her way to her car, drove home, and collapsed from exhaustion. Within a month, she would be hospitalized with pneumonia.

In the meantime, a discussion was under way as to where Sanchez was headed next.

The Amherst police desperately wanted to bring him back to their town and have him arraigned in the town court. He was being charged with the Yalem murder, along with the Mazur murder. Sanchez wasn't being charged with any of the rapes, because the statute of limitations on rape had long since expired. That law had changed that summer, but it didn't apply retroactively. But there certainly was no statute of limitations on murder. Charges had already been drawn up against Sanchez in the Yalem and Mazur murders. A grand jury was to be convened soon on the Joan Diver murder.

The other task force members balked at the thought of moving Sanchez to Amherst. They thought it made much more sense to keep him in Buffalo. He was going to be locked up at the Erie County Holding Center, which was next door to the sheriff's office. It didn't make sense to drive him out to Amherst and then bring him back.

Ken Case made the call. He said Sanchez stayed in Buffalo.

Then came another logistical matter: getting Sanchez to the jailhouse.

It was decided that Sanchez would have to make the walk of shame. The press was more than eager for photos and video of a handcuffed Sanchez being walked to jail.

A deputy had suggested that they put Sanchez in the back of a patrol car and drive him through the garage into the jail sally port. It would be the most hassle-free way to transport him.

The task force members had other plans. They wanted Sanchez to have to do a perp walk.

Nigrelli, who liked to call the perp walk the "walk of shame," knew this could turn very political. He first checked with Ken Case to make sure there was no legal reason to not do the perp walk. Sanchez's photo had been released hours ago to the media, and it had been splashed across screens across the region all day. Case said there was no problem.

Nigrelli and Patronik then began making calls. They wanted to make sure every agency that had been involved in the arrest that day was represented on the perp walk. They arranged for some troopers and deputies to line the path that Sanchez would be forced to walk. They called up Dennis Richards, the chief of detectives for the Buffalo Police Department, and had him send over a couple of uniformed officers. They did the same with LaCorte, asking for Amherst cops to be sent over.

Once all the jurisdictions were represented, Sanchez was slowly walked through the honor guard of officers. Still and video cameras were trained on Sanchez. Flashes went off in rapid succession. Sanchez looked numb.

He was walked over to the jail. He was taken to the high-risk unit, the same one where Anthony Capozzi had been locked up more than twenty years earlier. Except this time, the right man was behind bars.

40

Reaction

As Al Sanchez was being questioned by the task force, the rest of Western New York learned for the first time that the man who had been raping and murdering women for decades was finally in custody.

Erie County sheriff Timothy Howard, who led the call for the task force after the Bike Path Rapist's DNA was found in Joan Diver's car, led his fellow lawmen in a self-congratulatory press conference to announce the arrest.

"Ladies and gentlemen, all of Erie County can rest a little easier today, because the monster known as the Bike Path Rapist has been taken into custody," Howard told a packed press conference.

"This serial rapist and murderer who eluded law enforcement for more than twenty years was arrested earlier this morning. He is being interviewed as we speak. Finally, finally, after intense investigations, which have spanned more than twenty years, the murder victims will get their justice. . . . And because of this arrest, the rape victims can also get some type of closure."

Buffalo police commissioner H. McCarthy Gipson was the next to step up to the podium. He attributed the arrest to "good old-fashioned police work" and a "three-pronged" investigation. But he did not give any details. DNA analysis and FBI profiling played important roles, he said, but once again offered no explanation.

Next, Amherst police chief John Moslow told the reporters that the DNA match was 100 percent. "This predator is off the streets," he said.

Sanchez had not yet been charged, his lawyer not yet hired, prosecutors hadn't begun work on the indictment, and here was Erie County's chief law officer calling him a monster and the Amherst police chief saying it was 100 percent certain that Sanchez was the Bike Path Killer.

DA Frank Clark provided the reporters with a little more information. He said the case came to a head based on information provided by a 1981 victim and was bolstered by a tip from FBI profilers that the killer more than likely patronized prostitutes, and that the DNA profile had shown he was Hispanic.

But it would take a couple of weeks before all the incredible details about how the task force had worked together to find the killer would be known.

The police officials' comments came back to haunt them immediately, as Andrew C. LoTempio, a former city judge who returned to defense work midway in his term, became Sanchez's lawyer. LoTempio filed motions asking that charges either be dismissed, or a change of venue granted because of the inflammatory remarks.

"We were so certain," Sheriff Howard later said of the evidence against Sanchez. "I still think that's exactly what he was. I think to stand near him—and there were times when I went to the jail to get a feel—I really felt I was in the presence of evil. And I really felt this was a person with so much evil to betray everyone, his wife, his kids, his neighbors, that's evil to the core. And he is a monster."

No one would dispute that what the Bike Path Killer had done over the years was monstrous. But once word got out that Al Sanchez was accused of being the Bike Path Killer, anyone who knew Sanchez was shocked.

Newspaper, television, and radio reporters fanned out into his neighborhood, his church, his workplace, and asked those who knew Sanchez what they thought.

Neighbor Ed Van Volkenburg teared up as he talked to a reporter for the *Buffalo News.* He had known the Sanchez family since they moved to Allendale Road in 1986, when the Sanchez sons were just boys: *"He's got a beautiful, wonderful wife and two sons," Van Volkenburg said. "I personally watched those boys grow up. . . . He's a great neighbor and a wonderful, wonderful family man."*

Jerry Donohue rushed home from work after his wife, Nadine, called to tell him of all the police cars in the neighborhood the morning Sanchez was arrested, and she then spent the morning in tears.

"Our kids grew up with their kids," she said. Sanchez had helped coach the Cleveland Hill Little League team.

Dave Heffron, of North Tonawanda, worked at Luvata with Sanchez for eighteen years and found his arrest unbelievable.

"We were really close," Heffron said of a man he described as one of his best friends. "I just couldn't imagine even him possibly doing the things he did. The guy was just the opposite of what you'd expect this person to be. I think pretty near everybody at the plant felt that way. To us, he was just such an outgoing person. He helped everybody, he got involved in charities. I think a lot of us are still in shock."

Heffron, like others, felt sympathy toward Sanchez's wife, Kathy.

"I'll tell you," he said. "I believe his wife knew absolutely nothing about it or even sensed anything. He got caught, he was in trouble a few years ago, when he had some contact with prostitutes. I think she almost left him because of things like that.

"But this other part," Heffron said of Sanchez as the Bike Path Killer, "it's still kind of unbelievable. It's hard for me to accept it, because I was one of his closest friends. I mean, we went to parties together."

Wayne Bordonaro, a landscape contractor who worked at Luvata with Sanchez, often golfed with Sanchez, and, in fact, had golfed with him at Ivy Ridge in Clarence, the same week that Sanchez was now accused of killing Joan Diver on the nearby bike path.

"We were good friends," Bordonaro said. "We went out to dinner with him, he's been at parties at my house. I golfed with him, worked with him. His locker was right next to mine at work. It's pretty shocking. I just can't believe it. Everybody can't say he was the nicest guy in the world and not mean it."

At the time of the interview Bordonaro has a picture of Sanchez on his desk, one that his wife is bugging him to get rid of.

"Me and the boys golfing at Glen Abbey in Canada," Bordonaro said.

Bob Bandish, who had gone to the Amherst police about Sanchez sixteen years ago, could not believe that Al had finally been arrested.

Bandish had retired early from American Brass, partly because of the stress caused by going to the police about Sanchez, the friendliest guy at the factory.

"I figured I'd die never knowing whether it was him or not," Bandish said. "He had everything. He had his family, he had golf. He loved golf."

41

A Dream Come True

The night before the arrest, Elizabeth Phillips said a prayer.

She was weak from her chemotherapy, but she did not pray for her own health. Instead, she prayed that the Bike Path Killer, who had taken her daughter away from her, would be caught.

"I hope they catch him tomorrow," she said. She had no idea that the Bike Path Rapist Task Force was on the verge of snaring the man who had murdered Majane Mazur.

When she drifted off to sleep that night, groggy from her meds and the agony of battling cancer, she dreamed about her daughter.

She often saw Majane in her dreams. But this dream was different from those she had had in the past. Her dead daughter came to her, she said, and told her that her long wait was coming to an end. She said that the police had found the man who had killed her.

Phillips remembered feeling moved by the dream. She felt touched. She didn't know what to make of it. She thought maybe her daughter was just trying to send a kind message to try to ease her discomfort from the chemo.

The next day, Phillips and Christine Mazur were out at a Burlington Coat Factory store in Greenville. They were out looking for housewares for Christine's new apartment. She was moving in with her boyfriend. They were expecting a baby.

Phillips and Mazur were thumbing through some colorful prints in the poster section when Mazur's cell phone rang. It was a 716 number.

Mazur figured it was another reporter wanting to do yet another interview. She didn't pick up the call but checked the message. It was *Buffalo News* reporter Maki Becker. It sounded like something big had happened.

She called back the number.

"What do you think?" the reporter asked.

Mazur had no idea what she was talking about.

"They just caught him," the reporter said.

Mazur was in shock. She turned to her grandmother and told her the news. They threw their arms around each other and began bawling their eyes out. They didn't care that they were in the middle of a store. This was the moment that they'd been waiting for fifteen years.

Elizabeth Phillips's prayers had been answered.

Christine Mazur got the closure she had sought for most of her life.

For so many years, the investigators in Buffalo had told her that she just needed to have hope—that someday the case would be cracked.

And now, finally it had happened.

"I'm just so glad," Mazur told the reporter. "It hasn't sunk in yet."

Christine told the reporter that she believed her mother was at peace now and was looking over her family. She said she believed her mother had a message for her: "All of us can stop worrying now."

When they got back home, Christine immediately got on the computer and started looking for any information on the man who had been arrested in her mother's murder. Altemio Sanchez's mug shot popped up on her screen.

She was disgusted. She studied his upturned chin and downturned nose. She thought he looked a little like a troll. She hated to think that this was the last face her mother had seen before she died.

Christine Mazur began thinking about the other women that Sanchez had murdered and raped. She shuddered at how he had used the garrote on them: how terrifying that must have been, and how horribly painful.

The arrest had initially felt like a big breath of fresh air to Christine. But now, all of a sudden, she began to worry.

What if the police have the wrong guy? What if he is the right guy, but then a lawyer somehow gets him off on a technicality or something? Could this man walk away a free man?

42

Steven Diver
Learns of the Arrest

Lost in the excitement over Altemio Sanchez's arrest was the reaction of Steven Diver, whose wife's killing and the drop of sweat from the Bike Path Killer found in her car had led to the formation of the task force and Sanchez's eventual capture.

Diver himself had come under suspicion after sheriff's investigators looking into his wife's disappearance had questioned the detail he gave about where his wife's body could be. He suggested places where she might be found, even drew a map that investigators seized as if it were evidence.

They also had had an outside consultant run a SCAN test on Diver's written statement, a report that had labeled Diver a suspect.

When a sheriff's lieutenant told Diver they would be giving him a lie detector test on Saturday morning, with his wife still missing, he hired a lawyer. He wasn't going to trust the detectives with his liberty.

And now, he was told that Altemio Sanchez had been arrested and charged with his wife's killing.

Diver was thrilled that Sanchez had been arrested, but appalled that he had been able to elude police for decades.

"There was evidence and there were many eyewitness

accounts," Diver said. "These were not perfect crimes. There were attempted rapes that produced eyewitness accounts and the composite sketches. Why weren't these crimes linked together? Sanchez could have been caught in connection with Linda Yalem's murder, where there was a lot of evidence and prior crimes. Had he been caught, years of misery and Joan's death could have been avoided."

A man who felt wronged by the initial investigation saw the rightness of bringing together investigators from multiple departments.

"The task force had the will and resources to solve Joan's murder," Diver said. "They had to ask questions again, revisit sources, and reanalyze assumptions that were made previously."

But why wasn't this done before? Diver asked. Why did it take his wife's killing for police to get their act together?

Diver didn't buy the theory that the killer had to strike again before he was caught.

"The only forensic evidence they found was Sanchez's DNA, which they already had from several other cases," he said. "The only thing that Joan's murder contributed was yet another wave of outrage, and this resulted in the formation of the joint task force. The task force showed the kind of creativity, [cooperation], and determination that represents the best of law enforcement."

He contrasted that with the man they arrested, Altemio Sanchez.

"Sanchez is the worst possible excuse for a human being," Diver said. "He victimized women all through his life. He lived a life of deception to those around him. It is hard to imagine a worse or more evil thing. It is hard to imagine how his crimes have affected women's choices and their sense of personal safety. Having this monster out there has affected our quality of life for years."

43

Sanchez in the Dock

Altemio Sanchez awoke early in the Erie County Holding Center the day after his arrest. He was going to court that morning for arraignment on charges that he killed Majane Mazur, the prostitute who was found strangled in a field off Exchange Street in 1992.

District Attorney Frank J. Clark eventually intended to charge Sanchez with the murders of Joan Diver, last September 29, and Linda Yalem on the same day in 1990, but this single charge was enough to hold Sanchez for now.

The courtroom of Erie County judge Michael L. D'Amico was crowded with reporters, task force members, and others who were curious to see in person the man who was accused of being the Bike Path Killer.

Heavily guarded by court deputies, Sanchez shuffled into the courtroom, his arms and legs shackled. He looked in the audience and saw his wife, Kathleen, and their son Michael. His other son, Christopher, had not been able to get there from San Diego.

"She can't believe it," Sanchez's attorney Andrew C. LoTempio told reporters. "Nothing in his life fits [with what he is charged with]."

LoTempio entered an innocent plea on behalf of

Sanchez, and outside the courtroom, he reminded reporters that his client, under the law, was presumed innocent.

"Just because police say there's been a DNA match doesn't mean he's guilty and will be convicted," LoTempio said.

The defense lawyer asked D'Amico that the defense be given its own DNA and blood samples.

"I want our experts [to test them]," he told the judge. "I've never heard of a one hundred percent DNA match," he added. "I'd like to see that."

Clark, a prosecutor for the last nearly thirty-five years, admitted afterward that LoTempio was right.

"When I say it's one in one hundred billion," Clark said of the possibility the DNA could belong to someone else, "that's not a certainty. But it's one in one hundred billion."

Clark also expressed confidence that the snatching up of Sanchez's glassware at Sole restaurant, allowing task force investigators to get his DNA, would be upheld.

"In our opinion, he has no expectation of privacy on those items, so we were free to take them without any court order," he said.

And with that, Sanchez was held without bail and returned to the holding center, while the prosecution and defense settled in for what could be one of the most visible and highly watched trials in Erie County since Leon Czolgosz was convicted, in the same courtroom, for the 1901 assassination of President William McKinley at Buffalo's Pan-American Exposition.

Kenneth F. Case and his boss, Frank A. Sedita III, would try the case for the people.

LoTempio, a former city judge, was hired by Kathleen Sanchez to defend her husband.

LoTempio, forty-three at the time, was a former Golden Gloves boxer who handled nearly forty homicide trials in his career as a defense lawyer.

In 2003, halfway into a ten-year term as a Buffalo City

Court judge, LoTempio walked away from the bench and returned to defense work.

"Criminal defense is what I was meant to do," LoTempio told reporter Dan Herbeck of the *Buffalo News. "I'm good at it. I love trying cases. . . . I missed that every day while I was on the bench."*

He would need all of those skills to defend Sanchez.

The task force, one of its members, Dennis Delano, later said, had presented to the prosecutors Altemio Sanchez on a silver platter, all neatly tied up and ready to go.

In reality, the prosecution still had a lot of work to do. Case and Sedita sent the investigators in search of the past rape victims, to get new statements from them and DNA samples.

The hardest thing for the task force investigators was to realize that they could never charge Wilfredo Caraballo, "Uncle Freddy," who lent Sanchez his car after the 1981 rape, and then lied to police about it.

Frank Clark sympathized with those who thought he should be charged with something, but said the statute of limitations had long expired. And he said Caraballo did what other members of a family might do when the police come knocking at the door.

"It was predictable, understandable that he wouldn't provide evidence," the district attorney said.

Clark was also quick not to judge Buffalo police for not pursuing the case further in 1981, once Caraballo said his car had not been used.

"It's a single case," he said of the 1981 rape. "We're not looking for a serial rapist here. It's one of dozens of dozens of dozens of cases (assigned tó police). They get to the blind alley and they stop. It's too bad they stopped, but it's understandable. And where do you go from there? Do you assume the uncle is lying? They took it at face value, and they stopped."

Prosecutors had an FBI agent visit Wilfredo Caraballo

222 Maki Becker and Michael Beebe

in North Carolina and get a statement from him on what he told Patronik and Rozansky on the telephone before his nephew's arrest.

Caraballo confirmed that he did indeed lend his car to Sanchez, and that he denied that anyone had used the car when Buffalo detectives came to his house.

I lied because I was so scared for him to get arrested, because there were so many innocent people in jail for something that they did not do, Caraballo said in the signed statement. *But still do not believe he did all this.*

The prosecutors also had to begin preparing for LoTempio's expected change of venue motion, with the defense lawyer claiming that Sanchez could not get a fair trial in Buffalo because of all the pretrial publicity.

And they took LoTempio at his word that he would challenge their DNA evidence, how the samples were obtained, how they were kept all those years, and how they survived the chain of custody. Anyone who watched the O.J. Simpson trial knew that scientific DNA explanations could easily confuse a jury.

And they also had to take the Yalem and Diver cases to a grand jury, so there would be murder indictments in all three cases. They hoped to win D'Amico's ruling that they could use the past rapes, even if they were barred from prosecution by the five-year limit, to show Sanchez's methods were consistent.

D'Amico, however, would not be making any more rulings in the case. After he discovered that Sanchez belonged to the same church as he did in Cheektowaga, St. Aloysius, he recused himself. State supreme court justice Christopher J. Burns would be the new trial judge.

44

The Nightmares Return

For the first few days after Altemio Sanchez's arrest, Suzi Coggins felt totally numb.

She couldn't believe that the man who had raped her twenty years earlier had finally been caught. When she saw him on the news, her first thoughts were of how much he had aged. Sanchez had had a full head of hair when he attacked her. Now he was bald. He seemed almost humble, she thought.

But his eyes. She recognized those right away. Those were the same eyes that had bore into her so angrily as he yanked the cord around her neck and pulled her up into the air. She could never forget those eyes.

Coggins was stunned to learn that this monster had been living such a normal life all these years. She felt bad for Sanchez's wife and kids, but then it began to make sense to her that was why he hadn't been caught all this time. He seemed perfectly normal. Nice even. If Sanchez had seemed evil or demented, the police would have figured it out much sooner.

Seeing him again brought back a flood of terrible memories. She found herself on edge, even though she knew that she should feel safe. She went into a convenience store and had a moment of panic when she saw a man with a mustache and a similar face to Sanchez's. But then she shook herself out of her state.

Silly, he's in jail, she said to herself. And she was able to breathe a sigh of relief. That felt good.

But soon the nightmares started. Coggins began having terrible dreams of being chased and of someone or something suddenly grabbing her out of nowhere.

She would scream, kick, and claw in her sleep until her boyfriend, Barnesy, would rouse her from the terrible nightmare.

"It's okay. It's okay. You're having a nightmare," he'd tell her, then hold her until she calmed down enough to go back to sleep.

One day, she was at the supermarket when she saw a karate studio flyer posted on a community bulletin board. She was momentarily intrigued, but she kept going without writing down the number. That night, she had another nightmare. In the morning, she'd decided she'd had enough of bad dreams.

She asked Barnesy what he thought. He thought it was a great idea. She found the number for the Dragon Defense Academy in Orchard Park and set up an appointment for a private lesson.

The instructor, who specialized in street fighting, showed Coggins an array of self-defense tricks. He showed her how hitting different spots on the neck would affect an attacker and how to poke someone in the eyes.

Coggins was shocked by one move he taught her. If an attacker was reaching for her, she was taught to grab one of his fingers with one hand, grab the next finger with her other hand, and then pull the two fingers apart until she heard a cracking sound. He called it "wishboning." She was simultaneously supposed to kick the attacker in the knees and then twist his arm around. She couldn't believe someone could actually do that to another person.

But the lessons quickly began building up Coggins's self-confidence. Karate made for great exercise and she was feeling in control of her life again. She wished she had done it years earlier.

She soon began sleeping through the night again. The nightmares stopped.

Four months later, Coggins was sitting on the couch talking to her daughter when Barnesy came home after working some overtime. He asked Coggins's daughter to leave the room for five minutes so he could have a private conversation with Coggins.

The daughter wouldn't leave. So Barnesy began nibbling on Coggins's neck and she began to giggle.

"What are you saying?" Coggins's daughter asked.

"Nothing," Coggins replied, still giggling.

Then Barnesy leaned in close to her ear. "How about after you get everything straightened out, we get married?"

Coggins wasn't sure she heard him right. "What did you say?"

Coggins's daughter was angry. Her mom wasn't paying any attention to her. "What did he say?" she demanded to know.

"Are you serious?" Coggins asked Barnesy. Her daughter stomped away in a huff. She didn't pay her any mind.

Coggins looked at Barnesy, stunned by his proposal. "Okay," she said.

Coggins had always had doubts about marriage, even when she had gotten married before. But being married to this man sounded like the best thing she could possibly imagine.

45

In Hindsight

The police officials who announced Altemio Sanchez's arrest had been coy about giving out details. The suspect was still being interviewed and hadn't even been charged at that point.

But within hours, the real story began to emerge.

Reporters at the *Buffalo News* learned about the 1981 victim spotting Sanchez in the Boulevard Mall, just days after she'd been raped. They were told about how the Buffalo police had tracked the license plate to Sanchez's uncle.

Word then got out about how Amherst police had interviewed Sanchez shortly after the Linda Yalem murder, but they had let him go because his fingerprints didn't match those found on a water bottle near the scene of the 1989 Willow Ridge bike path rape.

It proved to be an embarrassment to the Amherst police. The department had prided itself on its meticulous and methodical investigations. The police had spent countless hours and all the manpower they could muster on the case, and it had turned out that they had had the killer right in their grasp.

Lieutenant LaCorte remembered thinking when the task force found the documents in the Amherst binders about Sanchez's interview: *I hope it wasn't me.*

It wasn't LaCorte, but he, Ray Klimczak, and Tom Gould had all been part of a meeting in which Sanchez, along with more than one hundred other men who had been investigated for the Yalem murder, were formally eliminated as suspects.

The discovery of the information sent the Amherst police trying to figure out what had gone wrong.

They all knew Sanchez's name from the binders. They had all read his file several times and knew that he had been very thoroughly investigated, before being eliminated as a suspect. So, how could they have passed him over?

First they realized their mistake had been in not getting a DNA test on Sanchez. They realized that around the time Sanchez was interviewed, the FBI had asked them to limit the number of blood samples they were sending in.

"We probably should have taken his DNA," acknowledged Tom Gould, who was retired in Florida now.

He remembered Sanchez from the file and he remembered how his investigators had told him about Sanchez. "He was one of about one thousand people interviewed," Gould said.

At the time, the tip from Bob Bandish was interesting, but it didn't seem all that compelling. Bandish had said he saw Sanchez on the bike path and on I-990. "You gotta go with your gut, and they didn't think it was the guy," Gould said.

The Amherst police certainly hadn't ignored Bandish's tip. There were pages and pages of notes about how the police had done surveillance on Sanchez's home and gone to his workplace. They had even brought him in for questioning.

The Amherst police found the mug shot they had taken of Sanchez in 1990. It showed him nearly bald, like he was now. The 1989 victim, and his previous victims, had described the assailant as having a full head of hair. The 1989 victim was also shown the mug shot book with Sanchez's photo in it, and the police said she never recognized him.

Gould recalled all the other efforts his officers had put into trying to catch the killer. He remembered all the officers who had waited on the bike path in camouflage. He had put out female officers as decoys on the path as well. He had also ordered new safety measures, from putting in clear Plexiglas shelters along the path, so that anyone sitting in them could see all around them, to emergency phones. He worked with *Unsolved Mysteries* to do a show on the investigation.

"We could have saved a couple of lives," Gould said.

But he was glad to know that the detailed investigation into Sanchez in 1990 had eventually helped catch him.

"This was the biggest case I ever had in my career," he said. "It was a very empty feeling when I retired and I hadn't solved it. I was so happy when they got this guy. It just boggled my mind that he was living right near us."

But Amherst police weren't the only ones who had come close to catching Sanchez.

The Buffalo police had had the potential of catching him all the way back in 1981. The officers had done their job in tracking down Wilfredo Caraballo. He lied to them when he said no one had used his car. They had gone to the trouble of taking his photo and showing it to the rape victim. It was hard to say if they could have done more.

Then four years later, the Buffalo police arrested the wrong man for the Delaware Park rapes. But here, too, they had done the investigation by the book. They got a tip from a well-respected city official and the victims had identified Anthony Capozzi as the man who had raped them.

The sheriff's office had also slipped up. They had called off the search for Joan Diver after a day of searching. Boy Scouts ended up finding her body the following day. It was possible, as her husband had pointed out, that DNA could have connected her case to the Bike Path Killer sooner.

There were many "what-ifs" and the media was in a frenzy over who had messed up this and who had failed to do that.

But in the end, all of these missed opportunities had led the task force to Altemio Sanchez. It had taken over a quarter of a century and cost three women their lives, but they had finally done it. Western New York was proud and grateful for that.

46

No More Murders

Klimczak was elated when he heard that the Bike Path Killer had been caught. Lieutenant LaCorte had given him a call right after the arrest, just before the word had leaked out to the media.

Got the bastard, Klimczak said to himself.

When he heard about Altemio Sanchez, and the picture-perfect life he had been living, he realized that the FBI profilers he had met with at Quantico after the Yalem murder had been dead-on.

They'd said that the killer would not come back to Amherst, and that he'd go back to the area where he felt most comfortable. After the Yalem murder, Amherst police had saturated the town's bike paths with patrol officers. They installed emergency phones on the paths as well. They were constantly giving tips to the local press to keep the story alive. Klimczak believed that Amherst had successfully scared Sanchez away.

Indeed, after Yalem, he went back to the places that he felt most comfortable: downtown Buffalo, where he killed Mazur—it was just a couple of miles from where he grew up, and where he was used to picking up prostitutes.

And his next attack was in Riverside. The areas where he attacked all three of the Riverside High School students were within walking distance of the old American Brass plant, where he'd been working this whole time. You could actually see the plant from the open field where he raped those three girls.

The profilers had also said that the killer led a normal life. How true that had turned out to be. Sanchez had a wife and kids, a good job, and a nice home in the suburbs.

But then Klimczak learned that the Amherst police had had Sanchez in their grasp and had let him go. That ate at him.

He didn't know how that could have happened. He wasn't the one who had interviewed Sanchez back in 1990. He wished he had been, not that felt he could second-guess his colleagues' work.

Klimczak had been so obsessed with the case back then that he regularly double- and triple-checked alibis of anyone he interviewed. He wondered if he had been the one to interrogate Sanchez, if he would have picked up on some suspicious behavior.

He remembered how Lieutenant Gould would sit all the detectives down and have them go over lists of suspects that hadn't been 100 percent ruled out. They had combed through all of those files and did everything they could to make sure they hadn't missed anything. But, of course, they had, and there was nothing that could be done about it now.

At least the killer had finally been arrested. After all these years, they had gotten him. No one else was going to die at his hands. It was over.

It meant Klimczak would no longer feel compelled to take a detour on the I-990 when getting back to his home so that he could peer over the edge onto the Ellicott Creek bike path to see if someone was lurking there.

It meant he could finally stop patrolling the bike path in his neighborhood in Clarence and start now to enjoy walking it, like everyone else did and should.

47

Still More Work

The Bike Path Killer was in jail. The task force had accomplished what so many other police officers over so many years had never managed to do.

But their work was not done.

First they had to make sure their case against Altemio Sanchez was solid. There were many people who needed to be reinterviewed and much evidence to be sorted through. The district attorney's office needed it all in order to present the three murder cases before a grand jury.

The task force also began receiving calls from women who said they believed they'd been raped by Sanchez. The investigators weren't surprised. They had a feeling that there were other unsolved rapes out there that had yet to be connected to Sanchez.

Then, of course, there was Anthony Capozzi. He was still in prison.

On the white board at Oak Street, the next assignments for the task force members had been written down next to their names.

Redmond had a victim to interview. Keats had a witness to talk to. Weber was supposed to do some research. Delano's assignment: free Capozzi.

It became something of a catchphrase. People would leave notes on Delano's desk that read: *Free Capozzi*.

Sanchez's arrest had given Capozzi's family the miracle that they had been waiting for.

Every day, since Anthony Capozzi had been arrested on September 13, 1985, his mother, Mary, went to Holy Angels Catholic Church, where she would say a novena to the Virgin Mary.

"Please, God, make my son free, if it's your will," she told the *Buffalo News* that she would also pray. *"Give us peace, all of us, but most of all, my son Anthony."*

Twice a week, the family would drive out to Attica to meet with Capozzi. They observed how prison had worn him down. They worried about how his already-precarious state of mental health was affected by his harsh life.

John Justice knew Capozzi both from serving time with him at Attica, and because he, like Capozzi, received psychiatric treatment in the state prison system.

Justice was a teenager in the suburban village of Kenmore, just north of Buffalo, when he went berserk one day and killed his parents and brother, and then killed a neighbor with a car as he sped from his house. He was locked up with Capozzi in the Erie County Holding Center in 1985 while they both awaited trial.

"Anthony did hard time," Justice said of Capozzi, who had the dual problem in prison of being convicted of sex crimes and having psychiatric problems. "He used to put out cigarettes on his nose so people would think he was a tough guy and leave him alone. He had a permanent mark on his nose."

Justice's relatives sometimes came with the Capozzis at visiting time, and Justice said those in the prison or the psychiatric center, where they both were treated, were always happy for the Capozzi family's visits.

"Anthony's sisters were gorgeous," Justice remembered.

"Everyone tried to be in the visitor's rooms when they came."

Each time they'd visit, Capozzi would ask his parents why he had been locked up. He didn't understand how he could be in prison for something he didn't do. "When can I come home?" he'd ask them. They never knew how to respond.

Despite his mental illness, Capozzi had never waivered from his insistence that he did not rape the women in Delaware Park, even though it could have helped him get out of prison earlier. He appeared before the parole board five times over the years and, without fail, he always refused to admit that he had raped the women. New York State law requires inmates to acknowledge their crimes before they can be released on parole.

Anthony Capozzi was up for parole again in a couple of months.

This time, with Sanchez under arrest, Mary and Albert Capozzi were hoping that Anthony would finally have a real chance at freedom.

But it wouldn't be as easy as that.

Dennis Delano and Lissa Redmond sat down with the deputy district attorney, Frank A. Sedita III, to talk about Capozzi. Sedita explained that while there seemed to be reason to suspect that Sanchez had committed the rapes that had sent Capozzi to prison, there was no proof.

The DA's office would need solid evidence that irrefutably exonerated Capozzi if it was going to ask a judge to release him from prison. They needed DNA evidence, or something just as compelling.

As far as they knew, there was no physical evidence left from those two decades-old rape cases.

This requirement wasn't about to stop the bike path task force. They had found a killer who had eluded police for a quarter of a century. They could find the proof to spring this innocent man from prison.

Delano and Redmond went back to the task force office and racked their brains for ideas on where they might find old evidence. It occurred to them that many of the victims from the 1980s had been treated at Erie County Medical Center (ECMC), so perhaps their rape kits might be in storage there somewhere.

Redmond called the hospital and asked to speak to someone at the lab. She was given another extension, where she explained to a woman that she was looking for anything that may have been stored from rape kits done in the 1980s. The woman said they didn't have anything like that, but she said she'd have Redmond talk to someone in quality assurance to verify that. Redmond talked to another woman at quality assurance, who said there were no old rape kits stored at ECMC.

It seemed like a dead end.

In the meantime, Capozzi's new parole hearing date was coming up.

The media, which within a couple of weeks of Sanchez's arrest had run out of stories on the killer, began turning their attention to the Capozzi case.

Donn Esmonde, a columnist for the *News,* interviewed Delano about the Capozzi situation. The column, which appeared on January 28, 2007, was titled "A Mission to Uncover the Truth."

Delano, who knew that pressure from the media was Capozzi's best hope, talked to Esmonde about the case. He said that he was convinced he was innocent. "I would bet my career on it," he told Esmonde.

"It breaks my heart," Delano was quoted as saying, *"that he has been in jail these 20-odd years."*

Delano explained that most of the evidence that could have been used to exonerate Capozzi was lost or had been destroyed long ago.

"If I can find one Q-tip [of evidence]," he said, *"that would seal it."*

The *News* editorial board soon took up the cause as well. "Time Already Is Nearly Served, But Justice Demands Expedited Review," read the title of an opinion piece that ran on February 4.

Delano was determined to convince the district attorney's office to do something to help Capozzi. But there was little DA Frank Clark could do without new evidence. Clark suggested that he would write a letter to the parole board explaining the new circumstances. Delano decided he'd testify at Capozzi's hearing to try to help him out, but these were no guarantees for Capozzi's release. They needed proof.

48

Uncle Freddy

Wilfredo Caraballo, Altemio Sanchez's uncle Freddy, had so far been spared public exposure since he told the task force the week before that he had lent his car to Sanchez on the day in April 1981 that one of his rape victims saw him at the Boulevard Mall.

Caraballo admitted that he had lied to the Buffalo police officers who knocked on his door after they traced the ownership of the 1970s model Oldsmobile 88 to Caraballo.

That changed the day of Sanchez's arrest. Lou Michel, a reporter with the *Buffalo News,* got a tip that Caraballo had been one of the keys to breaking the case.

Michel found Caraballo living in North Carolina, where he had moved after leaving Buffalo, and surprised him with a phone call.

Michel, with fellow *News* reporter Dan Herbeck, is the author of *American Terrorist,* the story of Oklahoma City bomber Timothy McVeigh. He had struck up a friendship with McVeigh's father, and had become the only reporter Timothy McVeigh would talk to at first.

Michel's reputation of getting anyone to talk worked again, and Uncle Freddy was soon confessing to him over the phone.

"If I knew he did something like this, I would have

238   *Maki Becker and Michael Beebe*

reported it," Caraballo said of his nephew Altemio. "If I knew he was doing all this raping, I would have reported it. That's bad. I've got three daughters myself and grand-kids, and I don't want anything to happen to them."

Caraballo insisted he had not lied to the police officers when he told them that no one had been driving his car for the past month.

Members of the Bike Path Task Force thought that strange, because he had told them the previous week that he had lied to the police.

Caraballo told Michel that after the detectives came to his house to ask him about his car, he went to his nephew and asked what he had been doing with the car.

"I was mad at him because the detectives came to my house," Caraballo told Michel. "I said to my nephew, 'Have you done anything wrong? Because they were here looking for me.' He said, 'No, Freddy, I didn't do anything wrong.'"

"I didn't really believe him because of his eyes," Caraballo said. "You know, when people lie, you can see it. I suspected something happened, because the cops would never come to the house without a reason."

Instead of admitting that he had lied to police, Caraballo told Michel at first that it was an oversight that he hadn't told detectives about lending his nephew the car.

Then he said he might have been motivated not to tell the police "because many innocent people end up in jail." Or, he said, he might have wanted to protect a family member until he found out more.

The public reaction in Western New York was immediate.

If there was anyone who was as unpopular at the moment as Altemio Sanchez, accused of being the Bike Path Killer, it was his uncle.

Had Caraballo not lied to police—if he had said Sanchez had used his car, and detectives had shown the picture of Sanchez and not Caraballo to the rape victim—twenty-five years of rapes and murders could have been prevented.

But law enforcement could do nothing but bad-mouth Caraballo for not coming clean.

Even if they could have once charged Caraballo with a crime—and nothing they could charge him with matched the seriousness of his lie—the statute of limitations would have expired long ago.

DA Frank Clark said that even at the time that Caraballo first lied, the only charge would probably be obstructing justice, a misdemeanor.

"Would we have? If we got the guy?" Clark asked. "We rarely prosecute in situations like that. It's difficult, it's very difficult."

Clark gave an example.

"Mother takes the stand and provides an alibi for the son," he said. "Are you going to prosecute the mother for perjury? Nobody does, nobody does."

Clark didn't condone it, but he said he understood why Caraballo lied to police.

"I think that he reacted in a manner that other family members react in situations like that every day," the district attorney said. "It was predictable, understandable that he wouldn't provide evidence. That's just a fact of life.

"We see cases all the time where guilty people are acquitted because witnesses are either afraid to come forward or refuse to come forward," he said. "That happens all the time. So to think that a family member wouldn't provide police with information that might have led to the nephew's arrest and charges in this is unfortunate, but it happens every day."

49

A Legal Problem

Sanchez was behind bars, held without bail. The arrest had gone by the book. He'd been charged with the Majane Mazur murder.

But there was a problem. A potentially huge problem.

Frank Sedita met with several task force members to discuss the situation.

He explained that DNA test results from the bodily fluids found on Linda Yalem didn't technically match the DNA results from the tests done on the tableware from Sole or from the coffee cup at Borders.

DNA, or deoxyribonucleic acid, is the material in cells that contains genetic information, and its use had transformed the field of forensic science.

It wasn't that they had the wrong guy. The problem was that DNA technology had evolved so much that the test results showed different things.

Ken Case, Sedita's fellow prosecutor, explained it this way. Say you have an eight-track tape player, the state of the art for personal recording back in the 1970s. You want to take the eight-track recording made back then and play it on an iPod. And, of course, you can't.

The DNA machines they used in 1990 did not even

exist in 2007, so there was no way to even test the Sole and Borders samples using the old machines.

This had the prosecutors very worried.

Sedita, Case, and members of the task force sat down once again with John Simich at the lab.

Simich explained that the FBI test at the time of Yalem's murder in 1990 used the DNA testing method known as restriction fragment length polymorphism (RFLP). It required a sample as large as a quarter, and had not been used in years as DNA technology improved.

There was no good way to compare DNA using the RFLP method with the more modern polymerase chain reaction (PCR) analysis, or the newest short tandem repeat (STR) analysis.

"So, what you have are apples, oranges, and grapes," Sedita said. "You can't compare one to another."

"We said to Simich, 'What can we do?'" Sedita said. "Simich said he had no way of doing RFLP. You'd have to get more specimens."

Sedita said they checked with Dr. Woytash at the morgue and found they indeed did keep slides from autopsies. They got slides from the Yalem and Mazur autopsies, redid the DNA testing, and the problem was solved.

But a bigger battle loomed in the courtroom.

LoTempio, who had left the city court bench halfway through his term because he missed defense work, had filed a slew of motions.

He had asked for a change of venue, saying the sheriff's comments about Sanchez being a monster tainted the jury pool, and he was filing what is known as a Molineaux motion, named for a 1901 case argued before the New York Court of Appeals, trying to keep out evidence of Sanchez's alleged rapes.

Molineaux laid out the guidelines on whether the uncharged crimes—Sanchez's other rapes—would aid the jury's decision to get at the truth, or would be so prejudicial to him that they would destroy his chance of getting a fair trial.

Law school students study for Molineaux by using a memory device, "MIMIC," or motive, intent, modus operandi, identification, and common scheme.

Sedita felt comfortable he could win the motion before the court. And as he put it, the appellate division in Rochester rarely, if ever, grants motions for change of venue.

LoTempio wasn't so certain.

"You make the change of venue motion to the Fourth Department Appellate Division in Rochester," LoTempio said. "I gathered all the newspaper articles and made a tape of all the television stations' reports. You have to begin to pick a jury, once you establish that it's impossible, then the appellate division judges decide on the change of venue."

LoTempio also hoped he could persuade Burns to try the three cases separately, and keep out the evidence from the rapes in the Molineaux motion.

The worst-case scenario for the prosecution was if LoTempio would win both motions.

While Sanchez had been booked on the Mazur murder, it wasn't necessarily the strongest case on which to prosecute him. The victim had been a prostitute, and Sanchez had admitted to patronizing prostitutes. He'd even been arrested for doing so twice. LoTempio could easily argue that Sanchez had indeed had sex with Mazur, but he didn't kill her. If a jury didn't know about the other murders or rapes, there was a chance he could be acquitted.

Then there was the Joan Diver case. It was far from airtight. The prosecutors had DNA evidence—but it was a trace amount on the ignition switch of her car. There was no DNA found on Diver's body. There was none found at the crime scene. In fact, there was no physical evidence anywhere except in the car. Sanchez could say that he helped Joan Diver with her car one day when it broke down or had put her groceries in her car. Or since he was unlikely to testify, his attorney could make those suggestions. It would be a stretch, but there was a chance that it could provide just enough reasonable doubt that a jury wouldn't convict.

The Linda Yalem case had been considered the strongest case against Sanchez. She was a student and he had no relationship to the university. He had raped her, before killing her. His fluids had been found in her body, but now the test didn't match because of the difference in technology. LoTempio could easily make a point about the retesting. And with the DNA in question, a jury might be tempted to acquit.

Ed Monan, who was among those at the meeting with Simich, was surprised and upset. All along he had thought that the Linda Yalem case was a lock. For more than sixteen years, he'd been hearing about all the DNA evidence the police had on the Bike Path Killer. And that all they needed was to match it to a person. Here, they had done just that, but it wasn't enough.

50

"Might Be
Worth a Call"

On January 25, Lieutenant LaCorte received a phone call at his office. It was from a woman who said she had been raped as a teenager in 1977, in Angola, a tiny town on the southern outskirts of Erie County. She had seen the photographs of Altemio Sanchez in the newspapers and believed that he was the one who had attacked her thirty years earlier.

The woman said that when she was thirteen years old, she had been riding her bike on Lakeshore Road when she noticed a man drive his car by her slowly, four or five times. She kept riding. When she passed a blind curve, she saw the car stopped with its hood up.

The man stepped out from behind the hood of the car and asked the girl how far it was to Point Breeze, a beach. She said it was a few more miles down the road. She kept riding when she noticed the sound of footsteps behind her. Suddenly the man tackled her, pulling her off the bike and into the grass. He began choking her with his hands until she passed out; then he raped her.

LaCorte recognized the MO. It sounded strikingly sim-ilar to another unsolved attack that had happened in

July 1984 in Evans, a town just a few miles from Angola. Lieutenant Sam DeJohn, of the Evans Police Department (EPD), had been investigating that case and had contacted LaCorte several times about whether it could have been the work of Altemio Sanchez. He hadn't been able to connect the cases because the victim's rape kit had been lost.

LaCorte called DeJohn to let him know about the case. DeJohn called the woman the next day to hear her story.

Amherst police, along with investigators from Hamburg, which is near Angola, began looking into the 1977 case. DeJohn helped out too. He tracked down a couple of old detectives sheets on the case, but they needed more information.

LaCorte arranged for DeJohn to team up with Ed Monan to meet with the woman. They set up the meeting for February 8. Monan drove down to Evans, and then the two took one car out to the woman's home in Gowanda. After interviewing her for a couple of hours, they began heading back to Evans. By that time, a miserable snowstorm had begun. Western New York is famous across the country for its snow, and nowhere in the region does it snow more than what is known as the Southtowns of Erie County, such as Evans, Angola, and Hamburg, where lake-effect snow from Lake Erie piled up.

DeJohn began bemoaning the fact that so much of the evidence that they needed to see if their cases were linked was lost or had been thrown out.

"Do you suppose ECMC keeps stuff like that?" Monan asked.

"I don't know, Ed," DeJohn said. "Every time I go to ECMC for an autopsy, I see things like body parts in formaldehyde they save."

The men then stopped for lunch in Evans.

Monan was still fixated on ECMC. "It might be worth a call," he said, suggesting he would do so.

"No, you don't," DeJohn said. "When I get back, I'll

give them a call, talk to somebody, and see if there's any possibility."

DeJohn considered it a total shot in the dark. He didn't believe ECMC would have kept rape kits for three decades. He figured by calling he'd just be assuring himself that he had covered all the bases, and then would cross that off his list of things to do.

The next day, DeJohn called the medical examiner's office at ECMC. He was then told to talk to Ann Victor-Lazarus, head of quality assurance. He told her what he was looking for and Victor-Lazarus asked him to send her a request in writing on his police department letterhead.

He complied and faxed the document over. Almost a month later, on the morning of March 1, Victor-Lazarus called DeJohn.

She said she couldn't find anything from the 1977 case, but she had located slides containing a vaginal swab taken as part of the rape kit of the 1984 Evans victim.

DeJohn was totally surprised. He thought all such evidence was long gone.

He asked Victor-Lazarus if there were other slides at the hospital.

"Yes," she said. "We have other slides here."

It turned out that the hospital's pathology department had kept slides from rape kits dating from 1973 to 2002, the year the CPS began handling all the county's rape kit lab work.

Victor-Lazarus told DeJohn that the hospital policy mandated that he now get a court order for her to hand the slides over to him.

DeJohn shot off an e-mail to Frank Sedita at 11:10 A.M.: *I have an open rape case from 1984. Victim resides in North Carolina. She stated from looking at photos it was indeed Sanchez. ECMC has located forensic slides containing suspect's semen from rape kit. I am very certain the*

*DNA will match that of Sanchez. ECMC requires a court
order for me to obtain the evidence.*

A little later, at 2:36 P.M., DeJohn sent a follow-up
e-mail to Sedita: *Frank, I'm getting the files together for
my '84 case for you. Question: is there any possibility that
there is forensic evidence, on file, at ECMC regarding
Delaware Park rape cases that can be tested for DNA?
Just a thought. I'm sure it's been done.*

But, of course, it hadn't. Redmond had asked several
hospital staff members about the possibility of such slides,
but she had been told they didn't exist. Over the years,
other officers and attorneys had asked ECMC about the
slides. They were always told there was nothing left from
the rape kits.

Frank Sedita then sent out an e-mail to everyone connected with the Bike Path Task Force. He explained what
DeJohn had found: *The following should be done. We
should check ECMC to determine whether there are any
vaginal slides from (suspected) Sanchez victim rape files,* he
wrote, then listed their names. The old slides could help bolster his case against Sanchez. New technology in DNA
might even be able to come up with positive matches on the
ones that hadn't been matched before.

He then continued: *As you are aware, members of law
enforcement and the media have an opinion that Altemio
Sanchez committed two rapes for which Anthony Capozzi
was convicted. In fairness to Mr. Capozzi, I think ECMC
should also be asked to locate any vaginal slides from the
following women.* The names of Capozzi's alleged victims
were listed.

Dr. James Woytash, the chief medical examiner who
also happened to be the head of ECMC's pathology department, got the e-mail and immediately confirmed existence of the rape slides collection. He knew about it
because he was the one who had overseen it, until 2002.

Up until that moment, no one in law enforcement had ever asked him about the slides.

When Delano got the e-mail on his task force computer, he yelled over to Redmond. She was sitting in her cubicle, which was two offices away. In between them was Keats's office.

"Lissa, did you call ECMC about those slides?" he bellowed.

"Yes, Dennis, I called them and they told me they don't have them," she replied.

"Goddamn it," grumbled Dennis, still yelling. "Do I have to do everything myself? I'm going to call about those slides."

Redmond yelled back: "Dennis, you know what? You gotta do what you gotta do. I already told you they didn't have them."

Redmond was exasperated with Delano, but she had tremendous respect and affection for him too. He had become something of a father figure to her lately. In fact, many people mistook him for her father.

She jokingly blamed him for her recent bout with pneumonia, which had sent her to the hospital in February. Delano always kept the windows open in his office and in the car, even in the dead of winter, and Redmond teased him that that was the reason she had gotten sick.

"Well," Delano said. "I'm going to call."

Delano called the hospital and provided a list of all the names of the victims whose slides the task force was looking for.

Two weeks later, Woytash called Sedita and let him know that almost all the slides had been located. The hospital needed a search warrant to release them. Four days later, a judge signed off on the warrants. Rozansky and Monan went over to the hospital where they were met by Victor-Lazarus. They handed over their paperwork and they got the slides, which they promptly delivered to CPS, where DNA testing was set to begin.

But this time, they learned, it would take six to seven weeks.

Redmond was upset. "We don't have six to seven weeks," she said. "Anthony Capozzi comes up for parole on April fourth."

They needed the results from the slides before that hearing. Sedita agreed, and had Dr. John Simich, the lab's DNA expert, expedite the results from the slides of the two 1984 victims that Capozzi had been convicted of raping.

"I go to see Simich at the lab. 'You're going to get a shitload of stuff to test, but I need priority on the two cases tied to Capozzi,'" Sedita said.

"'I want to know if Capozzi is the Delaware Park Rapist,'" Sedita explained. "'If he is, fine. If not, we have to get his ass out of jail.'"

But even then, the DNA tests took time because the slides were preserved with a polymer coating that had to be taken off just so. You do it too fast or use the wrong solution, you destroy the slide. So while everyone waited for the results, the slides sat in a bucket of solution that slowly ate away the protective coating.

On March 28, the results were back.

As expected, Capozzi had not raped either woman. The real rapist was Altemio Sanchez.

Frank Clark held a blockbuster press conference on the shocking matter with Thomas D'Agostino, Capozzi's attorney, at his side.

"At last, he's been vindicated," D'Agostino said. "He's always said he didn't do it."

D'Agostino announced that he was filing a motion to have Capozzi's conviction vacated, and Clark said he would not retry him.

As Clark and D'Agostino were announcing the stunning news to the media, the Capozzi family gathered around a speakerphone to call Anthony. They shared with him the wonderful news that he was going to be released from prison.

Anthony Capozzi seemed confused, the family members told the *News*. He asked how he'd be able to get home and who would pick him up.

His sister Sharyn Miller laid it out for him. *"No, Ant. You're free. You're a free man."*

Capozzi replied: "Really?"

51

Out of Attica

The excitement over Capozzi's vindication came with great soul-searching and angry finger-pointing.

Clearly, the justice system had failed Capozzi.

Investigators with the DA's office had contacted the two victims of the 1984 rapes ahead of the press conference to let them know of the new developments. They were both aghast. One of the women fell to the floor and broke down crying, realizing her testimony had helped put an innocent man in prison for more than two decades.

Sheila DiTullio, the prosecutor who had put Capozzi behind bars, was now a state supreme court justice. She declined to speak to the press but released a short, contrite statement: *I deeply regret the outcome of this case. I realize it brings little comfort or consolation to Mr. Capozzi or his family. I handled this case fairly and honestly based on all the evidence and information that was available at the time. This is the most troubling and upsetting circumstance in my 25 years as a lawyer and judge and I am truly sorry for what happened in this case.*

Angry accusations flew back and forth between the district attorney's office and ECMC about why it had taken until then to find the slides. Both sides blamed each other for lack of communication.

But in the meantime, there was still the matter of getting Capozzi out of prison.

It was not going to be a simple or fast matter.

First there was a series of hearings that were to take place. And then, there was the fact that Capozzi had just recently been transferred to a mental-health facility by the prison.

But Justice Richard C. Kloch Sr., who supervises state judges for criminal cases, agreed to expedite Capozzi's case, allowing him to bypass hearings. Arrangements were also made for him to be transferred to the Buffalo Psychiatric Center, which happened to be located just about a mile from his family's home.

On April 3, the Capozzi family, along with attorney Thomas D'Agostino, gathered at the psychiatric hospital to welcome Anthony back.

Word got to the task force members that Capozzi was being freed. Delano, Redmond, Rozansky, and Keats happened to be at the task force that day when the call came. They all jumped into a car and headed over to the pysch center.

They were all waiting together in a conference room when Anthony Capozzi walked through the door a free man. His parents, sisters, and brother all wrapped their arms around him, thrilled that he was not only out of prison, but vindicated too.

For the first time in nearly twenty-two years, they all sat down together and posed for a family portrait. Mary Capozzi had always resisted taking a family picture, because Anthony was not there to be in it. It was a truly happy moment for the Capozzi family.

Anthony Capozzi then went to greet his attorney and the members of the task force.

He recognized Rozansky right away from when he'd come to visit him at Attica.

"I remember you," Capozzi said. "You came to visit me."

He handed Rozansky a piece of hard candy. Capozzi told Rozansky that the candy was a good-luck charm. Rozansky was touched by the gesture.

Capozzi then met the other task force members who had helped free him. He seemed a bit taken with Redmond. "They didn't build police officers like this when I was there," he joked.

Looking at Delano, he said, "We look alike." Delano thought that was pretty funny.

Watching the happy scene before her, Redmond was struck by the thought of how far-reaching the Bike Path Killer case had been. Here was this poor innocent man who had spent more than two decades in prison because of Sanchez. And then there were all of those women who had endured unimaginable horror, and then had to live with that the rest of their lives. These women were scattered all around the country now. She had met the ones who were now in the Carolinas, when she flew down to interview them. There was one who had moved to Chicago. There was another in Tennessee. She felt proud to have been part of this extraordinary investigation.

Although Capozzi was out of prison, he still couldn't go home, and that was confusing to him.

Because of the state of his schizophrenia, it was decided that he needed to stay at the psychiatric center for at least a few weeks to help him make the transition from prison to life outside.

But that Sunday, which happened to be Easter, he was allowed to go home to enjoy a nice ham and lasagna dinner with his family.

He returned to his old neighborhood to find all the trees decorated with blue ribbons, to welcome him home and to honor the Virgin Mary, to whom Mary Capozzi had prayed every day for nearly twenty-two years. Capozzi got a hero's welcome from the neighbors. As he walked around the old neighborhood, everyone stopped to shake his hand and congratulate him.

He returned to the psych center, but over the next few months, he would come home to his parents' house every weekend. When they'd go out, strangers would ask to shake his hand and buy him a drink. On one weekend, he and his family, along with the task force members, were treated to a big celebration party at Sole, the restaurant where Sanchez and his wife dined under surveillance.

Capozzi was eventually transferred out of the hospital and into an assisted-care facility.

In the meantime, state legislators passed a law streamlining the process for wrongly accused inmates to sue the state. They named it Anthony's Law.

A year and a day after his release from prison, Anthony Capozzi filed a $41 million lawsuit against New York State.

52

The List
Keeps Growing

Within a couple of days after the arrest of Sanchez, half of the task force members had gone back to their respective departments.

So, for the most part, the only ones left were Delano and Redmond from the Buffalo Police Department, Keats from the state police, and Rozansky, Savage, and McCarthy from the sheriff's office. They had plenty to do.

The phones were ringing off the hook.

The DA's office was calling every few hours, asking for this or that. They were determined to build as strong a case as possible against Sanchez. He was still maintaining his innocence and seemed determined to let his case go all the way to trial. They needed to piece together his entire crime history.

It seemed like everyone on the planet wanted to congratulate the members of the task force. And the media were phoning in every two seconds. The reporters were hungry for details of how they finally cracked the case.

But the task force also began hearing from past victims of unsolved rapes.

At least a dozen women called the task force in the days

after Sanchez's arrest saying they believed they'd been raped by Sanchez.

It was a daunting task to sort through all of these potentially connected cases. Redmond, who was used to dealing with rape victims from her time with the SOS, handled a lot of it.

In most of the cases, the women couldn't remember key details that would have helped Redmond find their files. Some hadn't reported the rapes to the police when it happened. Others didn't know which precinct they'd gone to. At least one woman said it had happened in another state. Almost all of them failed to pan out.

Except for one.

A woman called and said that on July 14, 1985, she had been raped by a man who looked just like Sanchez.

The date alone made Redmond take notice. That was exactly one year to the day before Suzi Coggins's rape. They knew Sanchez had a thing for anniversaries. He killed Joan Diver on the sixteen-year anniversary of the murder of Linda Yalem. Then there was a creepy discovery that *Buffalo News* reporter Michael Beebe, the coauthor of this book, had made. As the paper's former running columnist, he had sources who kept lists of people who participated in old races. He discovered that Sanchez had taken part in a memorial race for Linda Yalem in 1996. It was the first year the run had fallen on the actual anniversary of the student's murder.

The victim explained to Redmond what had happened to her. At the time, she was a street prostitute. This man she believed to be Sanchez had picked her up in downtown Buffalo. He drove her to a secluded spot on Exchange Street, but it apparently wasn't secluded enough. So he insisted on driving her elsewhere. She wasn't happy with the plan.

That's when he wrapped a rope around her neck and

began to pull it in an effort to keep her under control. He drove her south to Hamburg, where he found an isolated field. There he took off her clothes, raped her, and left her naked.

A neighbor saw the woman emerge from the woods naked, went to help her, and called the police. At first, Hamburg police handled the case, but then it was taken over by the Buffalo police. It had never been connected to the Bike Path Killer case.

But there were so many elements that fit. He had used a rope to choke her. It would have been the first time he had done that. She was a prostitute. The detectives had figured Majane Mazur couldn't have been the only prostitute that he had abused. And then there were the locations. He went to Exchange Street, which was where he murdered Mazur, and then he drove her to Hamburg, near the spot where he raped Suzi Coggins a year to the day later.

The woman's rape was put at the top of the task force's list of likely cases that were connected to Sanchez.

The task force also learned about two other rapes back in 1977 that fit Sanchez's MO.

Al Sanchez was still in high school at the time of the first rape.

It was 1:30 A.M. on May 26, 1977. It was at Delaware Park. If the rapist were Al Sanchez, he was a month away from graduating from Grover Cleveland High School. The rapist approached a young woman in her car. He showed her a knife.

"Do not resist," he told her. He ordered the woman out of the car and forced her into a patch of bushes. There, in the dark, he made her take off her clothes and then lie down on the ground.

He tied the woman's hands and put a gag over her mouth.

He then raped her, there on the ground. When she would try to move, he tightened the gag further.

When he was done, he took the woman's purse and went through it. "How much money do you have?" he asked. Then he fled.

He clearly liked what had just happened.

Less than two months later, on July 18, he struck again. This time, he chose Shoshone Park, located in North Buffalo, near a set of railroad tracks.

This time, the urge struck him at 9:30 A.M. Broad daylight. Daytime would soon become his preferred time to prey on his victims.

The rapist walked up to a young woman, nineteen years old, the same age as Sanchez.

Instead of a knife, the rapist used a gun. "'My name is Dave,'" the victim would later recall he told her.

He forced the teenager to take her clothes off and get down on the ground.

He began to rape her and then stopped. "Do me by mouth," he commanded as he held the gun to the young woman while making her perform oral sex on him.

"Did I hurt you?" he asked when he was done. He then riffled through her purse and slipped away.

With the prostitute and the two cases from 1977, the total number of women police believed Sanchez had raped was up to fifteen. He was unsuccessful in raping another. And he had murdered three women.

The DA's office wanted to know definitively whether these cases were connected. They also wanted fresh DNA swabs from all the known victims. They weren't taking the chance of Sanchez's attorney questioning the accuracy of their DNA tests.

Prosecutors hoped to win a judge's ruling allowing the use of past rapes, even though they could not be prosecuted because the statute of limitations had expired, to show a pattern of rapes that Sanchez had committed through the years.

That was going to be tough getting the DNA samples. Many of the victims had moved out of the area. Others had married, and police and prosecutors had lost touch with them over the years.

It was decided that the task force members would fly out to meet some of them to reinterview them and get new oral DNA swabs.

Lissa Redmond, Scott Patronik, Josh Keats, Dennis Delano, and Greg Savage took the state police plane to the Carolinas. There they met with the 1981 victim, the woman who had seen Sanchez in the mall after her rape and had given police the license plate number of the car registered to Sanchez's uncle, Wilfredo Caraballo. And they also saw the 1986 victim. The Carolinas were a popular destination for Western New Yorkers who had tired of Buffalo's winters and lack of job opportunities.

The 1981 victim was gracious with the officers, but she was angry too. She couldn't believe that the man whom she had identified had gotten away with raping her and hurting so many other women. Had the police tied Sanchez to the use of his uncle's car then and arrested him, there might never have been any other attacks or three murders.

The 1986 rape victim bore the scars of her attack. She was now in her late sixties, her fingers were still bent. She had managed to get her fingers underneath the garrote that Sanchez had pulled around her neck. She believed that by doing so, she saved herself from being killed.

Rozansky went to Tennessee, where he met the 1994 Riverside High School student whose picture was still up at Redmond's cubicle, the last rape attributed to Sanchez before he was accused of killing Diver twelve years later. She hadn't heard anything about his arrest.

Meanwhile, in the Town of Tonawanda, Brian Moline wanted to talk to the task force about a cold case he was working on, the July 1, 1985, murder of fifteen-year-old Katherine Herold.

Moline, a detective whose father was the former town supervisor, was struck by the similarities in Herold's attack and some of the Bike Path Killer's victims.

Herold's body was found lying across the CSX tracks, just inside the Village of Kenmore border with Buffalo, by a train crew. It was half a mile from where Al Sanchez worked at American Brass.

Herold appeared almost doll-like, her head resting on the tracks. She was dressed in a T-shirt, blue jeans, and cowboy boots.

There was a deep gash over one eye, an angry red line from a garrote surrounded her neck. There was a similar gouge in the back of her hand, as if she had gotten it inside the noose that killed her.

Moline got autopsy and crime scene photos of the Bike Path Killer's other victims.

He compared the abrasion from the garrote that was left on Joan Diver's chin, apparently where it had slipped until the killer could get it wrapped around her neck.

A nearly identical pattern was on Kathy Herold's chin.

Herold had not been raped, but then neither had Joan Diver, who had fought her attacker.

Herold's older sister, Jennifer, said Kathy was a dancer who performed in a recital with her friend Ani DiFranco, before DiFranco became a national recording artist. Her sister was very athletic, and would likely have fought her attacker.

Jennifer said her sister had become rebellious since the

death the year before of their father, the director of the Buffalo Museum of Science.

Tonawanda police had dropped their investigation years before, figuring that it was someone in the rough crowd that Herold had been hanging around with.

Moline thought it was worth taking a look at Sanchez.

"The way I see it, looking at the other crimes he committed," Moline said, "there are similarities that cannot be ignored and have to be investigated."

The task force agreed and shared information with him.

But district attorney Frank Clark said until Moline could come up with some forensic evidence that Sanchez was involved, it was an interesting coincidence only.

"I mean coincidence isn't evidence," Clark told the *Buffalo News. "The fact that she was found near American Brass is interesting, in terms of looking to see if it was Sanchez. But from an evidentiary standpoint, it's kind of a minor circumstance."*

Jennifer Herold spoke of the pain that whoever had killed her sister had caused Jennifer since her sister's death.

"I've sat across a table for over twenty years now, looking at a chair where my sister should be sitting," she said. "My sister should be here with me, helping me with Mom. My sister should have a hundred kids, she was so great with kids. My sister should be here arguing about stuff. She was a funny, funny girl. She was smart and she had this potential to be an amazing person.

"She wasn't a throwaway kid," she added. "She wasn't a bad kid. She was going through a high-school rebellion, everybody does."

53

Amassing
the Evidence

Case and Sedita still had not indicted Sanchez in the Diver homicide. All they had was the DNA found on her car's ignition switch. There was no other physical evidence. They and the task force had no doubts that Sanchez had killed her, but could they prove it before a jury?

All that showed, they knew, was that he had been in the car at some time. It didn't prove that he killed her. It didn't even prove that he had moved the car the day of the murder.

But Alan Rozansky, the task force member from the sheriff's department, was told to talk to a witness who had told a sheriff's deputy that she sold a length of cable to Altemio Sanchez at a Clarence hardware store.

Rozansky tracked down Jane Peterson, who worked at Hector's Hardware in Clarence. She told him she sold four feet of cable to Altemio Sanchez for 60¢ the last week of September 2006, just days before Joan Diver was murdered. She identified Sanchez from an array of pictures she was shown.

"There were two reasons she remembered the sale," Sedita said. "One, it was noninsulated wire. Everyone always buys insulated wire. And he wanted it cut to exactly four feet."

They took the wire to James Woytash, who did the autopsy on Joan Diver.

"Woytash looks at the wire, looks at photos of Joan Diver's neck," Sedita said. "He's nodding. He said, 'I said the diameter was an eighth of an inch. The diameter of this wire is an eighth of an inch.'"

Then he compared the abrasions on Joan Diver's upper neck, where the garrote had left almost a tread mark. Then he looked at the photos of underneath her chin, where the cord had cut so deeply, the skin had come off.

"It had to be a noninsulated wire," Woytash said. He said he would testify that was the murder weapon.

Sedita then had the Buffalo police photographer take photos of the noninsulated wire and the mark on Joan Diver's neck and blew them up.

"The pattern is a lock and key with the ligature marks on Joan Diver's neck," Sedita said. "We go to Clark. He said go for it, indict him for Joan Diver."

Sedita also did some computer work on his own. He got the photo of the ligature marks on Linda Yalem's neck, and put them side by side with the photo of Joan Diver's neck.

He marked both photos with triangles, where the cord cut in. They were indistinguishable.

When this case went to trial, it would be part of Sedita's summation to the jury, shown on a PowerPoint presentation on a big screen. Sedita knew from past trials how much attention jurors paid to visual presentations.

"They're killed sixteen years apart on the same day —just looking at them, and you're telling me that's a coincidence?" Sedita asked. "Are you kidding me?"

Ken Case was adamant about putting Kathy Sanchez before the grand jury.

"There was only one person who could possibly be his alibi," Case said. "That was her. She was still standing by her guy."

Frank Sedita disagreed. He said Clark and John De-Franks, the number two prosecutor in the office, wouldn't go for it. Case went to them both and won their approval.

"I sat down with her for half an hour before she went into the grand jury," Case said. "I said, 'I'm sorry. I'm sorry that you went through this. I can't even imagine what you've been through with this.'"

Kathy Sanchez testified, the prosecutors put in their other evidence in the Yalem murder, and new evidence in the Diver case, and Sanchez was indicted. He was arraigned on March 12, in the murders of Majane Mazur, Linda Yalem, and Joan Diver.

At the same time, LoTempio started laying out the case to Sanchez in his visits to the holding center.

He told Sanchez that he would try to get the case moved from Erie County; he told him he would try to get separate trials for each murder; he said he would try to keep out evidence of other rapes.

"I told him the sort of things they would present, a map of where you worked and lived and where the crimes took place," LoTempio said.

"As we got more and more into it, he asked, 'Is my family going to hear the details about all this stuff?'"

LoTempio said they would, if he lost the Molineaux motion.

54

The Serial Killer's Wife

In the days following Al Sanchez's arrest, the media, local and national, began looking for any scrap of detail they could find on him.

And that meant going after his family.

Kathy Sanchez's home phone was deluged with calls from reporters, begging to interview the wife of the serial killer. Her son Michael roared at TV cameras as news crews tried to interview him in front of the family house on Allendale Road.

On one occasion, Kathy Sanchez returned to her home to find a newspaper reporter and a TV crew staking out the house. They were careful to stay just outside her property line so that she couldn't call the cops on them.

Her son wasn't there to ward them off so she sat in her car, parked in the driveway. She made a series of phone calls on her cell phone and refused to look back at the reporters who waved at her, trying to get her attention. After several exasperating minutes, she started her car and drove away. The media did not follow.

Kathy Sanchez didn't know what to think about her husband's arrest. She thought for sure it was a terrible, terrible

mistake. She visited Al and called him as often as the jail
would let her. She met with his lawyer and emptied out her
husband's 401k plan to pay for his legal fees.

All the while, the local radio shows were filled with
speculation about whether Kathy Sanchez knew what her
husband had been up to all these years. Some callers said
there was no way she couldn't have known. People were
saying horrible things about her complicity.

None of the task force members believed Kathy
Sanchez had any clue about her husband's sick proclivi-
ties. Mostly, they felt sorry for her, although they couldn't
understand why she was continuing to stand by her husband knowing that there was a mountain of DNA evidence
proving Al Sanchez's guilt.

But accepting that her husband was a serial rapist and
murderer meant realizing that the last three decades of her
life was a lie. The happy milestones she had shared with
her husband over all those years would be shattered by the
knowledge that, while he had been so loving to his family,
he was also committing terrible, unspeakable acts.

Kathy had met Al while they were attending Buffalo
State College. She got pregnant and they decided to get
married. The wedding was on July 5, 1980. Their first son,
Christopher, was born in October. A couple of months
later, she was pregnant again.

From what Al Sanchez would later tell investigators, he
was thrilled about being a dad. "I always wanted kids at an
early age," he said. "I wanted a family."

If the task force was right, Al Sanchez had been involved
in a rape of a twenty-one-year-old Buffalo State student on
April 14, 1981. Kathy would have been about four months
pregnant with their second son, Michael.

It was this victim who, two days after the attack, spotted Al Sanchez at the mall. Next to him was Kathy, who
was pregnant, and holding their six-month-old son.

The task force had linked Sanchez to three attacks—

two rapes and an attempted sexual assault—around Thanksgiving and Christmas, 1983.

Earlier that very year, Al Sanchez had taken his job at American Brass and chose to work the night shift so that he could watch his two little sons while Kathy went to work during the day.

The next year, Sanchez was accused of committing two more rapes. One was on July 8, 1984. That would have been just three days after his and Kathy's four-year wedding anniversary.

Almost exactly a year later, on July 14, 1985, he raped a Buffalo prostitute, leaving her in Hamburg. And then exactly a year after that, he raped Suzi Coggins in Hamburg.

In May of 1986, after years of living in rental apartments, the Sanchezes bought their house on Allendale Road. The next month, Al Sanchez was accused of returning to Delaware Park for one final rape there.

Over the years, Al Sanchez had been a model dad. He had doted after his sons. He put them through private school and coached youth baseball and the church basketball team. Once the boys were older, the Sanchezes had enjoyed traveling. They went to Paris and London, Las Vegas and Florida. They took Mediterranean cruises.

But in the meantime, Al Sanchez had been raping and killing women, as well as patronizing prostitutes. He got caught twice, and Kathy Sanchez had known about one of those arrests. There had been another time when she suspected he was having an affair with one of her friends. She forced him to move out of the house for a few months. She was deeply upset by the two incidents, but she had no clue that her husband had been holding much darker secrets.

On September 29, 2006, the day Al Sanchez murdered Joan Diver, he met up with his wife at a downtown Buffalo bar. Her former employer, Barrister, a legal publishing company, was hosting a reunion party. A friend of Kathy's snapped a picture of the happy couple at the party.

That photo had been widely circulated in the media, ending up on TV and in the newspaper, as proof of Al Sanchez's Jekyll and Hyde personality. Here he was with his wife, both wearing name tags, smiling with drinks in their hands. You'd never know from looking at Sanchez that he had just killed a woman, whose husband and police were still searching for her body.

The task force members saw that despite his horrible crimes, Al Sanchez seemed extremely devoted to his wife. During their interviews, he had often grown emotional when they mentioned Kathy. He kept telling them he was worried about how his arrest would affect her. "She's got a heart murmur," he told them.

Several of Al Sanchez's victims and the families of his murder victims said they felt for Kathy and her children and didn't blame them at all.

"I really feel bad for his wife and kids," Suzi Coggins said.

"It's just sad how many lives he can destroy," said Christine Mazur. "To think how disgusted you'd be. He's out there raping and then coming home and lying in her bed. And his kids. I can't imagine. . . . They're going to have to move out of New York."

About two weeks after Sanchez's arrest, Lieutenant Nigrelli was at a Wegmans supermarket in Cheektowaga when he saw Kathy Sanchez. She looked at him and then dropped her head quickly. She had recognized him. He also thought she had finally accepted the terrible truth that her husband was indeed the rapist-killer that the police said he was.

In July, she had a conversation with her husband's probation officer.

"My heart is broken," she had said. "I can't believe anybody I'm connected with could hurt people he didn't even know in such a horrendous way. He is probably the last person on earth I would believe could do this or be capable of it. My sons can't believe it either. They love their father so much. Never once did he ever strike me as someone being even a little bit crazy or a little bit odd."

55

Guilty

Altemio Sanchez was to appear in court before State Supreme Court Justice Christopher J. Burns on May 16 for routine pretrial motions.

But something was up. Burns scheduled the session in a newly built ceremonial courtroom in the old Erie County Courthouse. There were court security officers everywhere.

The press had also gotten wind of something. Television stations sent their top correspondents. This was not an ordinary motion.

In the courtroom were members of the task force who had arrested Sanchez. His wife, Kathleen, sat in the second row, holding her brother's hand. Steven Diver made his first courtroom appearance, sitting in the front row.

When Sanchez shuffled in, again locked in handcuffs, leg cuffs, and chains, he looked like a beaten man. He was dressed in a dark suit, white shirt, and red tie, but he did not make eye contact with anyone as he sat next to his attorney, Andrew C. LoTempio.

When the proceedings began, it became clear immediately that this was anything but routine.

Sanchez stood as his attorney announced that his client was pleading guilty to all counts of the indictment.

Before he accepted the guilty pleas, the judge asked

Sanchez what he did to Linda Yalem, the first count of the indictment.

"I strangled her," Sanchez said, his head down.

Kathleen Sanchez burst into tears, squeezing the life out of her brother's hand.

He said the same thing about Majane Mazur, about Joan Diver.

Steven Diver could barely control himself.

"When I heard him say that he strangled Joan," Diver later said, "I wanted to bash his brains out. He succinctly said in a muffled, feeble voice, 'I strangled her.' I am not sure how I restrained myself. Intellectually, I realized that I could not achieve much in an outburst and it would simply harm my credibility in the sentencing later on."

Diver said a Higher Power kept him from acting on his urge.

LoTempio told the judge that Sanchez had decided to plead guilty after they discussed the evidence against him, ten days to two weeks before.

"Once I spoke to Mr. Sanchez," LoTempio told the judge, "he decided it would be best for his family and the family of his victims to save them from hearing the details of the case. He is saving his wife and children from hearing those dirty details."

Gregg McCrary, a former FBI profiler now in private practice, had worked on the Bike Path Rapist cases when he was an agent in Buffalo. He scoffed at Sanchez's reasons for pleading guilty.

"I think there's reason to question that," McCrary told Michael Beebe, who covered the court proceedings for the *Buffalo News*. "Because someone like this, who's done what he's done, has no compassion for the victims. He's shown that repeatedly. No one with any compassion or empathy could possibly act like he acted against these victims. So, is he doing that to protect them? I'm skeptical of that."

What Sanchez really feared, according to McCrary, was admitting his failure in court.

"What we know about narcissists is that they're hypersensitive to criticism," he said. "So, what he would be forced to face in court are his own failures, the fact that they have this airtight evidence. They got him. There's no running room here."

Kathy Sanchez continued her refusal to say anything to reporters. But in the first signs of a break with her husband, she issued a statement through her attorney.

The family of Kathleen Sanchez expresses its deep sorrow and heartfelt prayers for the family and friends of so many victims, the statement read. *It is unimaginable to us that someone we have truly loved and respected for so many years could be capable of such violent acts, and we are sincerely sorry and filled with grief for your tragic losses.*

LoTempio told reporters outside the courtroom that once Sanchez had decided he would plead guilty, he asked the lawyer to tell his wife of his decision.

"No, you have to tell your wife," LoTempio said he told Sanchez. He brought Kathleen Sanchez to the jail, and her husband told her that what the police said about him was true, he indeed was the Bike Path Killer.

LoTempio explained to reporters that he had considered using an insanity defense for Sanchez.

He said his client had a deep-rooted animosity toward women stemming from his childhood, and that he was unable to control his impulses.

"Much like an alcoholic or drug addict, that's when someone can't control their impulses," LoTempio said. "Please don't make it as me making excuses for him. There is no excuse."

He said Sanchez acted on these dark impulses, then returned to a normal life as husband and father, and a friendly guy to his coworkers and neighbors.

"He raised two children and they were leading normal lives," LoTempio said. "Obviously, there was this Dr. Jekyll and Mr. Hyde."

LoTempio told reporters not to blame Kathleen Sanchez, or even suspect that she knew anything about her husband's crimes.

"Law enforcement in this community went almost thirty years without putting two and two together," he said. "So it's not out of this world that she wouldn't put two and two together."

Burns, the judge, did not require Sanchez to detail his crimes, nor admit to any of the rapes the task force said he committed.

LoTempio told reporters that Sanchez had discussed the rapes with him, and that he had passed on the information to prosecutors. He said his client might sit down with prosecutors if they gave him some reason to do so.

Clark, the district attorney, nipped that in the bud.

"I won't consent to one day off his time, not one day," Clark said. "If he's so remorseful, let his conscience be the motivating factor."

Clark said when Sanchez returned for sentencing in August, he'd instruct his prosecutors to seek the maximum term, seventy-five years to life. With Sanchez nearing his fiftieth birthday, it would ensure he would never again be a free man.

Clark sympathized with the rape victims, whose rapes would not be punished, but said he would agree to nothing for Sanchez if he admitted to them.

"Would you want to be the person who was responsible for giving him a sentence that he could get out while he could still walk, talk, and chew gum?" Clark asked. "Not me."

What happened? Why did he plead guilty?

LoTempio said he honestly did not want his family to have to listen to the crimes he committed.

Before the overtures on pleading guilty began, Frank Clark and the prosecution team continued to speculate whether Sanchez would actually go to trial, or plead.

"We were doing what-if scenarios," Clark said. "What if he does this, what if he does that. There were two camps. One camp was, he's going to plea. And they were positive. The other camp? He's not going to admit anything, he's going to make us go the whole nine yards."

What camp was Clark in?

"I didn't think he was going to plea," the district attorney said.

He was surprised when the overture came to the prosecution from LoTempio.

"He might want to plead," Clark said of Sanchez. "Then it was, he might want to plead to one. Then he'll plead to two, but he's not going to plead to Diver."

Why not Diver?

"The reason he wasn't going to plead to Diver," Clark said, "was for some reason, he didn't want to admit publicly to his wife that he had done Diver. And it came to us, would we take a plea on two and not the third? And then have to go to trial on the third."

Clark ruled it out.

"If I'm going to try this lawsuit," he said, "I'm going to try the whole thing. And if he's going to plead, he's going to plead to three homicides."

Frank Sedita, who handled the plea negotiations with LoTempio, had his own suspicions on Sanchez's reluctance to admit killing Joan Diver.

"From discussions I had with his lawyer," Sedita said, "I got the impression that after his prostitution arrest, and after his wife caught him cheating, he made some kind of promise to her that this was going to stop. If he pleaded guilty to Yalem and Mazur, that would be before this promise. If he admitted Diver, then that meant he had lied to his wife.

"It sounds weird," Sedita said of the logic involved, "but this is a pretty twisted individual."

There was also another piece of evidence that the prosecution would try to present at trial.

During the search of the Sanchez home following his arrest, investigators found two computers. One was upstairs and was obviously the family computer. The second was downstairs in the basement, obviously Sanchez's private space.

There, hidden in files that took a forensic computer specialist to find, was Sanchez's porn collection.

"It was very vicious rape stuff," Sedita said. "It was gross, very disgusting, disturbing."

Presenting that at trial would have been one more layer of the real life that Altemio Sanchez had led all those years.

56

Relief

Suzi Coggins learned about Altemio Sanchez's decision to plead guilty from a *Buffalo News* reporter.

"Oh, my God," she exclaimed. "That's awesome."

She was ecstatic and overwhelmed with a sense of relief. It was the best thing she could have imagined from this decades-long ordeal.

Coggins had been dreading the thought of testifying in court. She knew her case couldn't be tried because of the statute of limitations on rape, but she had faced the possibility of being called to the stand to help bolster the murder cases against Sanchez.

She also knew that a trial would have meant daily media coverage. She didn't want to have to hear about this awful man day after day after day, like she did when he was arrested.

She had worried about how such a trial would affect not only her, but all the other victims, and the families of the women who were killed. She thought of Joan Diver's children who would have been exposed to all the horrible details of Sanchez's other attacks.

"He's earned an ounce of respect," Coggins told the *News* reporter.

She was happy to learn that somewhere in the twisted

soul of Altemio Sanchez there was a conscience. She figured he did it to save his own family from further embarrassment. Whatever the reason, she believed it was the right thing for him to do.

She asked Captain Shea if there was any chance that she could talk to Sanchez one on one. She had a lot of things she wanted to say to him. Mostly, she wanted to be able to look him in the eye and tell him: "You didn't destroy me. I'm fine and I always will be. Now you have to deal with all your sins."

Shea told Coggins such a meeting wasn't possible. Sanchez wasn't talking to anyone. Sanchez did, however, admit that he had raped Coggins. That made her feel a little better, knowing that he acknowledged it.

Now she felt like she could put that horrible chapter of her life behind her for good and get on with her life.

She and Barnesy had decided they were going to move to Arizona. They were going to start a new life together. It would be a wonderful opportunity for her and her children.

She was also going to pursue her dream of going into business as a psychic reader. She had the gift; now she wanted to put it to use. She was going to start the business with a friend and call it Mystic Journeyz.

Coggins knew she'd miss Western New York terribly. It was the only place she had ever lived, but it was time for her to move on.

57

A Meeting with the Prosecutor

Sanchez had come to Sedita's office on August 3 to talk about what rapes he had committed. With Sedita were John Cleary, the district attorney's chief investigator, and James Murphy, who was Sedita's top investigator in homicide. Sanchez came to the session with his attorney, Andrew LoTempio.

There was no recording of the session, but Sedita shared his notes with the authors of this book.

"I've never interviewed a serial killer before," Sedita said. "And I don't want to ever do it again."

As he had earlier told Moira Roberts, the probation officer who issued her findings in a sealed report to the court, Sanchez told of the physical abuse of his mother by her boyfriend, but he denied to Sedita ever being sexually abused himself.

Notwithstanding homicides, Sedita's notes show, *defendant estimated he raped between 10 and 12 women. Defendant said he raped women because of what he "saw in my mother."*

He said he had never struck his wife, and could not

explain why he raped and murdered in light of his seemingly stable life.

Sanchez said he chose his victims at random but planned the locations where he attacked.

For example, Sedita wrote, *defendant would mentally take note when observing a relatively isolated but regularly frequented area, like a shortcut or bike path. Defendant said he would often reconnoiter the area and select a spot where he could grab a victim from behind, drag her into cover, assault her with reduced risk of detention, and make a quick escape to his car, which he usually parked nearby.*

Why did he rape?

Defendant said he liked to be aroused, but added it was not the sex, but control of his victims that aroused him.

How did he feel during a rape?

Defendant said he felt like he had control. When asked how he felt after a rape, particularly in light of mundane day-to-day living, defendant said he knew what he had done was wrong, but "it was like I went from husband and dad to animal."

Sanchez said he got the urge to rape when he was alone, and that the urge became particularly strong when he spotted an area well suited for an attack.

After a rape, he said, he felt nervous and would calm himself by stopping at a store or eating something before returning home. He said he didn't want to encounter his wife immediately after a rape.

Sanchez also denied that he had ever used a wire during the rapes, always rope, and denied that he had bought the noninsulated wire at a Clarence hardware store the week before the Diver murder.

He explained his twelve-year absence—from 1994, when he raped the fourteen-year-old Riverside High School student, to his 2006 murder of Joan Diver—as a fear of being caught.

Sanchez told Sedita that he never meant to kill Joan Diver or Linda Yalem, but did so because each of them had fought him during the attacks. He said he did not rape Diver because she had fought so hard, and that he was scared after she died.

He denied raping Yalem after her death, but Sedita noted in his report that Sanchez had told the probation officer that he had raped Yalem after he killed her.

He denied any significance in the fact that he killed Diver and Yalem on the same day, sixteen years apart.

He said the day he killed Joan Diver, he drove to the Galleria Mall, where he threw away the garrote in a garbage Dumpster, and bought a new shirt, the one he was pictured wearing that night at his wife's reunion party.

Sedita and the investigators then asked him about twenty-two rapes that task force investigators believed he had committed.

He was told that he was suspected of raping seven women in Delaware Park, and that DNA evidence tied him to five of those attacks. He claimed he only committed two rapes in the park.

He admitted raping the woman who later identified him at the Boulevard Mall after Sedita told him his DNA matched, and the woman had recently identified him in photo arrays.

He denied a December 19, 1983, rape in Delaware Park, despite the fact that his DNA was found.

At that point, LoTempio told him that some of his denials did not make sense and that it was no time for manipulation. Sanchez then admitted raping the woman, but he continued to deny he used a gun.

He again denied an April 3, 1984, evening rape near Hertel and Elmwood Avenues, one of two rapes that Anthony Capozzi was falsely imprisoned for. Confronted with the DNA evidence, he claimed he could not remember if he raped her.

He also denied the second rape attributed to Capozzi, even when confronted with the DNA evidence.

But then he admitted he did rape the women that Capozzi was imprisoned for. He said he never told the police, even anonymously, that an innocent man was in prison because he was scared.

Defendant also admitted Capozzi's conviction made it easier for him to continue raping women.

He also denied raping the woman in Evans on August 15, 1984, the case that led Evans Lieutenant Sam DeJohn to discover the DNA evidence stored at ECMC from old rape cases.

He said he could not remember raping a prostitute on July 14, 1985, after first driving her to Exchange Street, the place where he killed Majane Mazur, and then driving her to Hamburg, where he raped her and choked her unconscious with a garrote.

He admitted a June 12, 1986, rape in Delaware Park, after being told his DNA was found, and being shown the double ligature marks on her neck.

He denied a May 26, 1977, manual choking and knife-point rape in the Elmwood-Bidwell area.

He admitted raping Suzi Coggins near Frontier High School on July 14, 1986, even though there was no DNA evidence.

He admitted raping a Riverside High School student in a junkyard without the need for Sedita to tell him his DNA was found.

He admitted a May 1, 1989, rape in the Riverside area after he was shown the double ligature marks on her neck. He admitted the rape, again without Sedita having to tell him his DNA was found.

He admitted raping and choking the fourteen-year-old cheerleader in Willow Ridge on August 29, 1989, in Amherst.

He also admitted the May 31, 1990, rape of the business-woman on the Amherst bike path.

He admitted the October 19, 1994, rape of the fourteen-year-old girl from Riverside High School, his last rape before killing Joan Diver twelve years later.

He denied raping three women at gunpoint in Shoshone Park in 1977.

He also said he told his Uncle Freddy, or Wilfredo Cara-ballo, that he had raped the Buffalo State student in 1981 when he borrowed his car and the police questioned his uncle.

Defendant said that admission soured their previously close relationship, Sedita wrote.

In response to Investigator Murphy's questions, defendant also admitted his Uncle Wilfredo looked disapprovingly at him because he knew defendant continued to rape. Defendant nodded when Investigator Cleary asked whether this was their "dirty little secret."

The final tally after the three-hour interview was that Sanchez admitted murdering three women and raping twelve others between 1981 and 2006.

58

Sanchez Is Sentenced

Altemio Sanchez's sentencing was supposed to take place on August 2, 2007, before state supreme court justice Christopher J. Burns. However, it was pushed back to August 14 with no explanation.

Steven Diver had asked for the delay months before because he had to attend a chemistry conference out of town, and he did not want to miss testifying at the sentencing. Few people knew that, though.

Some members of the Bike Path Task Force who arrested Sanchez had their own theories for the delay. They figured it was because of Frank Sedita's interview with Sanchez, which had not yet been made public.

Neither Sedita nor Clark would confirm the interview, but in an August 10 story in the *Buffalo News* by court reporter Matt Gryta, Andrew C. LoTempio confirmed the session.

"There is apparently another side to Sanchez that prompted him to come forward to give those other women sense of closure," LoTempio said.

Members of the task force were furious. Sedita did not know the case the way they did. He may have prepared to try Sanchez, but he wasn't as familiar with the rapes he committed over the years as they were. Kenneth F. Case, who had left the district attorney's office to work for the State Judicial Conduct Commission, was the attorney assigned to the task force.

The bottom line, task force member Dennis Delano complained in an e-mail to a reporter, one of this book's authors, *is that the task force spent many long hours investigating this case, and brought it to a successful resolution, and Frank Clark, through Sedita, cut us out of our own investigation, knowing that they did absolutely nothing except read our reports and documentation on it.*

Clark had an easy answer. Sanchez, through his attorney, asked to speak to Sedita. He was under no obligation to talk to anyone.

It was also learned before the sentencing that Sanchez had filed charges against a fellow inmate in the holding center, who had attacked Sanchez after he learned his last name and what he was in jail for.

As soon as I said my name, Sanchez, he immediately started assaulting me, striking me about my head, Sanchez said in a complaint filed in June about the fellow inmate William Harris. He said the man also aggravated his surgically repaired shoulder.

The charges went nowhere, but they served as a reminder, if any were needed, that Sanchez would need protection in prison because of his sex crimes.

Sheriff's deputies who staff the holding center also said that they had caught Sanchez hoarding blood pressure pills, and worried that he was planning to take them all at once in a suicide attempt.

Sanchez fit the image of a downtrodden man as he shuffled into court under heavy guard, his handcuffs and leg cuffs again shackled to a chain around his waist. A dark gray suit and white shirt hung on him like he had lost a lot of weight.

The first rows of the courtroom were filled with relatives of his murder victims. Steven Diver was there, as was Ann

Brown, the only sister of Linda Yalem. Members of the task force who arrested Sanchez were there, as were members of the press. One of his rape victims, a former prostitute who had been choked and left for dead by Sanchez, sat in the back of the courtroom with a counselor.

For Steven Diver and Ann Brown, this was the first time they were able to confront the killer of their loved ones, allowed to address the court. They did not shy away from the opportunity. Christine Mazur was eight months pregnant and thought it best not to travel from North Carolina to see the man who had killed her mother, Majane.

Brown told the judge how she and Linda Yalem, just two years apart, grew up in Southern California. Ann was eight and Linda was six when their father died, and the bond between the sisters grew even stronger as their mother raised the two girls by herself.

When Brown was in New York City getting her doctorate, Linda decided to transfer to the University at Buffalo to be nearer her sister. They had talked that summer about Linda's plans to run the New York City Marathon. Brown and her husband would be there to cheer her on.

Brown said she received a call from the university's public safety office on September 30, 1990, telling her that Linda had failed to return from a training run the day before. They asked if she had heard anything from her sister. She had not. Brown called her mother in California and was on the next plane to Buffalo.

A young woman had been found strangled on the bike path, Brown learned when she arrived, but she told Linda's roommates that maybe it wasn't Linda. But, of course, it was.

"I learned of what happened to her and it is worse than your worst nightmare," Brown told the court. "My little sister was raped and strangled. Her nose and mouth were left taped shut. The killer left her lying in the dirt with her T-shirt over her head, and her pants pulled down.

"How do I live with that?" Brown asked. "It still tortures

me. Linda was robbed of her life. She can't graduate from college, get her first professional job, or have children. All this and more were taken away from her. My mom and I were left to live with that."

Brown talked about how close she and her sister were growing up, how they rode Big Wheels together, played with Barbies, hung out together in high school. Linda was the maid of honor at her wedding.

"Every time I see sisters together, I feel pain," Brown said. "I miss all the day-to-day things that we would have done together."

The two times she really needed her sister, Brown said, she was not there. First, when she learned that her daughter was diagnosed as autistic. And last May 28, when their mother died.

"My mother felt some relief about the killer being caught," Brown said. "I am grateful that she knew this before she died. I take solace in knowing that no other women and their families will be harmed by this killer.

"People said to me that catching the killer will bring closure," she said. "But I live with this day in and day out, it is the story of my life, and closure will only come when I'm not here anymore. Even though the killer took the life of my only sister, he did not take my life. I have not given him the power to ruin me. I know that Linda would have wanted me to live my life with dignity, to raise my children, and to live despite what he did to our family.

"I respectfully ask that you give the most severe sentence," she told Judge Burns, "so this killer will not take another life, mutilate another family, or destroy another woman."

Sanchez kept his head down throughout Brown's statement, but his wife, Kathleen, sobbed throughout, rocking back and forth at times.

* * *

Steven Diver was next. He nearly brought tears to the eyes of those in the audience as he read the poem his eight-year-old daughter, Claudie, wrote about her mom being the best on Joan's last Mother's Day.

"The court should know that Joan's life, its importance to her, to me, and to my children cannot be fully described," Diver said. "The grief that we have suffered due to her loss is not easily expressed through the use of language. Joan did not just die, she was horribly and violently accosted and murdered. She suffered."

Diver urged the judge to study the autopsy photos of his wife, as he did.

"I have thought about what must have happened to Joan thousands of times now," Diver said, "how she was viciously attacked and killed. She was strangled with a metal cord that was wrapped so tightly it seemed to cut into her. It looks like her throat was sliced. Can you imagine the pain she suffered?

"She was running on a clear, beautiful day, full of life," Diver said. "She then presumably saw Sanchez and abruptly felt searing, burning pain as the cable cut into her neck. She couldn't breathe, and though she kicked and clutched, she could not break his hold. Her face shows swelling due to repeated blunt-force trauma. For some absolutely inhuman reason, he beat her in the face after he killed her. Compare her radiance in life with her puffy, swollen face in the autopsy photo, and imagine the violence of the strangulation and how hard he beat her. This act of brutality is so heinous, it raises this immoral, inexcusable crime to the highest level of punishment."

Diver told the court about what Joan did in life, how she helped the Boy Scouts and Girl Scouts, had become involved in a group working with new mothers, called Mommy and Me, how she planned to return to nursing now that their youngest child was going to school.

He said how his wife had grown up in the mountains of Utah, and had passed on her love of nature to their children.

"She respected all of God's creatures and their right to exist in our world," Diver said of his wife. "She liked to walk, run, and hike. Joan loved to listen to the birds, to smell the dampness in the deep woods, to feel the warmth of sunshine on her face. I was always amazed at her childlike fascination with the natural world, and her appreciation for beauty."

He talked of her devotion to their four children. "She imparted to them a respect for others, a love of education and reading and compassion.

"Now Joan is no longer able to take care of them, to listen to their observations, to help them solve their problems, to give them advice, to help them do their homework, to treat their wounds, to hold them when they need comfort.

"She was probably thinking about them when she was running on September twenty-ninth, before she was surprise-attacked and killed," Diver said. "She never stopped thinking about them and caring for them until she was made to stop thinking and made to stop breathing. Now four children are motherless, thanks to a senseless and incomprehensibly arbitrary act of brutal murder. And there is no doubt that Sanchez is guilty of this, by his own admission of guilt, 'I strangled her.'

"The day he murdered Joan," Diver said, "he went home and went out to a party with his wife and appeared normal and merry. This ability to brutally prey and kill without any regard for the victim, then turn it off and go back to a seemingly functional life shows deceit, sociopathy, and complete lack of concern for anyone except himself."

Sanchez should be locked up forever with no possible chance of ever being a free man again, Diver argued.

"Joan was my favorite person, and she was viciously

killed by a despicable, lying, worthless shell of a person, who should be punished and allowed to grow old and then die in our prisons," Diver told the judge.

"Don't ever forget that Joan was a mother of four children and was their light, and mine," he concluded. "She will never come back to us, and Sanchez should never walk free."

After the families of those he killed spoke, Sanchez stood at the defense table and addressed the court.

"I just wanted to mention that whatever sentence I get today, I deserve," said a barely audible Sanchez, tears running down his face. "I know I'm going to be spending life behind bars, never to see the streets again. But I committed, I did these crimes, and I should pay for these crimes.

"To Mr. Diver and the Yalem family," Sanchez added, "I apologize, but I know I can never bring back your loved ones. But what you said today here in court was true about me. And I will pay for this for the rest of my life. Thank you."

When told of Sanchez's apology, Christine Mazur was not impressed.

"That really was not a very good apology, if you ask me," she said. "Because what he did was sick and horrible. It wasn't like he shot somebody. That's awful too. But what he did was really just sick. He had a family and kids and he still did it. He destroyed so many people."

Frank A. Sedita III, the prosecutor, held up a coil of wire, similar to what, he said, Sanchez used to kill Joan Diver, and told the judge that Sanchez should serve the maximum seventy-five years to life.

"You showed no mercy, and you deserve none," Burns said as he gave him the maximum sentence.

"It is this court's intention," the judge said, "that you shall never see freedom again."

Sanchez's lawyer, LoTempio, said he could offer no explanation for why Sanchez could live so normally and then go out and rape and murder women.

"This is someone who is missing a switch in his head," LoTempio said. "This is not some deep-seated, well-thought-out crime. I really believe there is a part of him that really hated the other part of him."

Frank Clark, the district attorney, said Sanchez's apology did nothing for him either.

"This guy is a cold, hard, vicious killer," Clark said. "Remorseful? Repentant? He feels nothing. I don't think he has an ounce of remorse in his body. I think he feels the same way he did the day he killed Joan Diver."

Steven Nigrelli, one of the task force's co-commanders who had since been promoted to captain in the state police, said Sanchez would never pay for all the rapes he had committed because of the statute of limitations.

"The conviction of Altemio Sanchez for the deaths of these three women stand for all of his victims," Nigrelli said. "Let the healing begin for them, knowing he's not going to ruin the lives of any more families for the rest of his life."

59

Sanchez Speaks

Al Sanchez got a call before breakfast on November 8, 2007, at the Clinton Correctional Facility, a state prison so far north in New York that it's closer to Montreal than Albany, the state capital. The prison guards said they were taking him to the hospital for tests.

Sanchez, because of his sex crimes and his notoriety, was considered high-risk by the State Department of Corrections and was locked up for the rest of his life in the prison's section for high-profile prisoners—the Assessment and Program Preparation Unit (APPU).

It's the same place where prison officials put Tupac Shakur, when the late rap artist served a term in 1995 for sexual abuse. Robert Chambers, "the Preppie Killer" who murdered Jennifer Levin in Central Park, was previously locked up in Sanchez's unit. And Ralph "Bucky" Phillips, who killed a state trooper and shot two others after his escape from the Erie County Correctional Facility, is currently housed there.

The corrections officers (COs) told Sanchez he was going to the hospital for some tests on his high blood pressure, which was discovered after his arrest.

Instead, they drove him to the state police barracks in Plattsburgh. Waiting there for him were investigators from the Bike Path Task Force, who had locked him up, and two profilers from the FBI's behavioral analysis section in Quantico, Virginia.

Agents Bob Morton and Kirk Mellecker had also played a role in Sanchez's capture after thirty years, giving the task force tips that helped lead to his arrest. The profilers make a point of talking to serial killers to better understand what they do.

Sanchez had already admitted his crimes, pleading guilty to the murders of Linda Yalem, Majane Mazur, and Joan Diver. He also admitted committing between ten and fourteen rapes over a thirty-year span.

The task force thought he could have done as many as twenty-two rapes, maybe more. They had DNA evidence on fourteen of them, and Sanchez had admitted the rape of Suzi Coggins.

But he never said why he carried on this terrorism against women since 1977. He never said—except in an interview with a probation department investigator, and later the prosecutor Frank A. Sedita III—what had led him to commit his first rape, and then murder.

His toll was a gruesome one. Besides taking the lives of three women and destroying their families, he raped young girls—two who were fourteen, another who was fifteen, a fourth, who was sixteen—single women, married women, and in the last murder, took the life of Joan Diver, who had four children and was planning to go back to work as a critical-care nurse, helping others.

He not only raped women, he tortured them with his rope garrotes, leaving several women unconscious, not knowing whether he had killed them or not. He made even those he didn't attack look over their shoulders for years as they went for a walk or a run on the bike paths that ring the Buffalo area.

Sanchez looked surprised as he sat at a plain wooden table, handcuffed to a chain around his waist, as Josh Keats, the state police homicide investigator, came in the room and sat across from him.

Keats and Lissa Redmond, the sex crimes investigator from Buffalo, were the last two task force members who were part of the team that interrogated him for nine hours on the day he was arrested, January 15, 2007, the Martin Luther King Jr. holiday.

Even though he admitted nothing in that interview, Sanchez seemed to have developed a rapport with Keats and Redmond, and he greeted Keats warmly as he sat down.

"Why didn't Lissa come?" Sanchez asked Keats.

She's not feeling well, Keats told him.

"She's not on the other side of that glass, is she?" Sanchez said of the two-way mirror. Keats said no; Redmond really did not make the trip.

Later in the interview, Sanchez told Agent Morton that after he had been questioned by Keats and Redmond following his arrest, he went to his cell in the Erie County Holding Center.

"I was sitting there in jail," Sanchez said. "I talked to the sergeant. 'Can I talk to Josh and Lissa again?' I was going to tell them the truth."

But it was too late. Sanchez's attorney, Andrew C. LoTempio, had already called off the questioning. It would be another five months before Sanchez would plead guilty.

Keats explained that he had some questions for him, things that would help him as an investigator. Sanchez told him to ask him anything he wanted. The interview was filmed.

Keats began asking about his background, and Sanchez described how his family had left his native Puerto Rico when he was two, his mother packing up four kids under the age of five and moving to Miami after catching his father in bed with a prostitute.

Sanchez began weeping as he talked about his mother's boyfriend.

"He used her as a punching bag," he said. "Why she ever loved the guy, I'll never know why."

The boyfriend, Sanchez said, also sexually abused him.

"He used to take my pants down. He used to have me hold it," he said. "Two to three times a week. My mother finds out one day. She never did anything, because she was so afraid of him. We were all afraid of him."

Sanchez, his mother, two sisters, and a brother lived with this man, he said, in a van in New York City.

"The whole family got arrested for stealing food," he said. "We lived in a van. The only way we could survive was to go into a store and steal food."

He said the boyfriend's sexual abuse of him and physical abuse of his mother continued until they moved to North Collins, south of Buffalo, where they picked strawberries and other produce with migrant workers.

One day, he said, his mother packed the family's bags, moved to Buffalo, and the boyfriend was never seen again.

Sanchez told Keats that his real father had never been part of his life and that he went to see him in New Jersey one summer when Al was in high school.

"He was a drinker," Sanchez said. "He loved his beer. He was a diabetic. Still, to this day, I don't have respect for my dad."

Sanchez said the sexual abuse continued to bother him, even as he went to high school in Buffalo. He also said his mother told him he was a mistake, and that she had tried to abort him during her pregnancy.

"I had trouble in school concentrating," he told Keats. "I started having blackouts, it started happening in high school. I had all the anger inside, I couldn't control it. After my senior year, I started my rapes."

Sanchez had told Sedita, the deputy district attorney who interviewed him after he pleaded guilty, that he had committed between ten and fourteen rapes.

He had two new attempted rapes to tell Keats about.

He was still a senior in high school, still living with his mother on Plymouth Avenue, in 1977. He attacked the girl on Bidwell Parkway, near Delaware Park.

"I approached the girl," Sanchez said. "I was on a bike. I hit her in the head. I raped her, I pulled her pants down. I know I did not insert my penis in. I laid on top of her, had my sexual fantasy, and that was it."

He attacked the second girl near the Scajaquada Expressway, near Elmwood Avenue and Grant Street, he said. He could hear the cars speeding by.

"I grabbed her by the hair, and told her not to say anything," he said. Again, he did not insert his penis, but he said he had his sexual fantasy by lying on top of her.

Keats is a homicide investigator. When he questions a suspect, he's trying for a confession. Sanchez already confessed, was serving seventy-five years to life. Keats let Sanchez roam from subject to subject.

Sanchez spoke without emotion. As he did in the interview when he was arrested, he went for more than eight hours without a bathroom break. Halfway through, the questioning stopped while they had lunch. Sanchez had pizza, chicken wings, and a diet Pepsi, a break from prison food.

He broke into tears talking about the abuse from his mother's former boyfriend, and when he talked of his wife, Kathleen, or his two sons, Michael and Christopher.

"I wrote a letter to my wife, explaining what happened to me as a child," Sanchez said. "She told me, why didn't I tell her? I tried to tell her so she could explain it to the kids. I didn't get into any of the details of the rapes. It was more about my childhood, what happened to me and my mother. My wife couldn't believe it was really me who did this. She filed for divorce. She never knew anything about it. It was more like a dark secret."

When his sons were young, he said, he worked the night shift at the brass plant so he could watch the boys during the day. He helped coach their youth baseball team; he coached the basketball team at his church. He and his wife paid for private school tuition for the two boys at St. Joseph's Collegiate Institute in Kenmore, just across the city line from Buffalo. His sons had been on the St. Joe's bowling team, he said, both of them carrying 200 averages. Son Michael was manager of a supermarket in Buffalo; Christopher worked for a medical supply company in San Diego.

That part of your life wasn't a lie, Keats suggested.

"No, I was always there for them," Sanchez replied.

You said you wrote a letter to your wife? Keats prodded.

"I wrote a letter to her, explaining what happened to me as a child. She still has trouble understanding. She wants to know the truth. I was very, very shy. I never had a girlfriend, even in high school. To be honest with you, my first girlfriend was my wife. I never had too many friends. I would go to school, come home, do my homework, and then go to the Boys Club."

When FBI agent Morton entered the room, the questions became more specific.

Sanchez, what triggered the attacks? Morton asked.

"I don't know what makes me become one person and another, what makes me commit these crimes," Sanchez said. "Being raped by Mom's boyfriend, watching the abuse he gave my mom."

The agent asked him if there was anger.

"The anger is going out and doing harm to someone," Sanchez said. "Fantasy and anger. I think my fantasy has to do with what my stepfather did to me. My anger had to do with my mom not knowing."

When you are going out, Morton asked, and for lack of a better word, you are hunting somebody, what are you thinking about?

"To let out my sexual feelings, to harm her," Sanchez answered. "It's like I wanted control, control makes me excited. It makes me want to be on the top, being the man. It was more exciting for me in the beginning. But once I committed my first murder, it became worse. Once I knew I could commit murder, I could do another."

Morton asked him about the fourteen-year-old girl he raped in Willow Ridge in 1989 and left unconscious. Had he been trying to kill her?

"No, killing her never crossed my mind," Sanchez said. "I'm going to leave her unconscious so I could get away."

Morton brought up the next victim after her that Sanchez choked out on the Ellicott Creek bike path.

"I had her pants off, I got real scared. I took off," Sanchez said.

Had he wanted to kill her?

"No, I didn't have any thought of killing her," Sanchez said.

Why, then, did he kill Linda Yalem, the first murder?

"I never wanted to kill Linda at all," Sanchez said. "She put up a fight. I lost control. She never gave me control. I took it. I put a rope around her neck and I killed her."

Why kill Majane Mazur, the prostitute he picked up in downtown Buffalo and strangled on Exchange Street?

"We had sex in the backseat, doggie-style," Sanchez said. "She didn't know I had the rope in my pocket. I took the rope out of my pocket and strangled her. What made me take the rope out and kill her, I don't know."

Morton told him that he was a complex person. He was able to compartmentalize. He was the good husband, the good father, the good provider. Then he had the other side. How was he able to do this?

"I don't know," Sanchez said. "It's hard for me, even myself, to know I have these separate lives. I'm good to my wife, and my neighbors, and then I have to have sex with somebody. I've got to play rough with her. It's got to be up here," he said, pointing to his head. "When the urge comes, I gotta do what I gotta do. To me, it wasn't rough sex. It was more fantasy."

Why had he stopped his attacks from 1994 until 2006, when he killed Joan Diver?

"After I did the two murders, I was getting scared," Sanchez said. "I had a talk with myself. 'You've got to stop.' I stopped for twelve years.

"I was still seeing prostitutes. When I was seeing prostitutes, my sexual drive was getting worse and worse. My philosophy was 'I have got to rape somebody and take control.' I didn't have that kind of control with the prostitutes.

"I was seeing prostitutes, two to three times a week. At twenty dollars a pop, I was spending between one hundred and one-twenty a week. I always had protection. I would go to Tops (supermarket) on Amherst and get my box of condoms."

Sanchez used condoms with prostitutes, but never once used one during his rapes. He had a vasectomy before his last rape in 1994.

Why did he start again after twelve years, Keats asked, by killing Joan Diver on September 29, 2006?

"I don't know," Sanchez replied. "That day, September twenty-ninth, it never hit me that it had been the same day as Linda Yalem. It never crossed my mind. I never thought about it until I read it in the paper. Linda Yalem was just another victim that was there at the wrong time, in the wrong place. I never said to myself, 'Well, this is the same day as the Linda Yalem murder.'"

Morton later asked him the same question: why start again?

"I was on the [Clarence] bike path for more than a month," Sanchez said, adding that he went there two to three times a week to ride his bike and scout out locations for an attack.

"I wanted to control somebody," Sanchez said. "I don't think I had any intention of hurting Diver. She put up a fight. She was taking my control away. I just wanted her to stop what she was doing, don't fight. 'Just let me do what I'm doing and I'll go home.'"

Morton asked if Diver had hurt him in the struggle.

"She scratched my face. I had a little black-and-blue mark near my eye. I didn't have any sex with her. After I strangled her, she stopped breathing."

That night, after Sanchez killed Diver and her body had not been discovered, he and his wife went to her former company's reunion. Sanchez had no marks on his face in a picture of the smiling couple, drinks in hand.

Morton asked, how long did Diver's death take?

"A long time," Sanchez answered.

What did he see when he looked at her? Morton wanted to know.

"It's kind of hard to say," Sanchez said. "Why am I doing this? Why am I killing this woman? Her eyes were closed. I kept the rope tight until her breath was getting shorter and shorter. She passed out. I could hear her breathing a little bit. I wasn't waiting for her to take her last breath. I pulled her pants off, pulled her shirt off, and threw her jacket over her. I got my bike that was hidden in the bushes, and had her keys in my hand."

What had he felt like after? the agent asked him. Did he feel relieved?

"I felt . . . I was scared," Sanchez replied.

Of getting caught?

"Oh yeah."

Had it satisfied him? Did he get his rage out?

"I don't know if I felt satisfied," he said. "I didn't rape her, so my satisfaction wasn't there. My anger was there. I took my anger out on her. I did what I did, and I felt better."

Why had he covered her up?

"I felt bad for her," Sanchez said. "Once I committed these crimes, I felt relieved and I could go back to my normal life."

Did he have time to think about all these girls he had raped and the three that he had murdered? the agent asked him.

"Yes, it crosses my mind," Sanchez said.

Morton asked if he ever thought about telling his wife.

"I think if I told my wife about it, and she rejected me, it would have gotten worse. Even though I was married to my wife twenty-seven years, if I didn't have her, it would have been worse. Those crimes I committed, it was more of somebody I didn't know."

Keats asked Sanchez about the time he was questioned by the Amherst police, after coworker Bob Bandish had reported to the police that he had seen Sanchez on Route 990 the day a fourteen-year-old girl was raped in Willow Ridge, and had seen him on the Ellicott Creek bike path the day before Linda Yalem was killed. And Bandish told police the composite sketch looked like Sanchez.

"I was scared," Sanchez replied about his questioning by Amherst detectives. "My heart was beating fast. My body was shaking. They said, 'Are you okay? Why are you shaking?' I just said it was my nerves. They had a tape recorder there. They took my fingerprints. They asked me if I had anything to do with what happened on the bike path that day. I told them no."

He just lied?

"Yeah, I told [them] that I was never on the bike path, even though I was."

Had that given him confidence? Keats asked.

"No, it made me scared. They could arrest me for the crimes that were going on. They had me, they called me in."

How long had it taken?

"I'd say about an hour," Sanchez replied.

Were there any other times the police questioned him?

"That was it. Besides being arrested for picking up a prostitute," Sanchez replied.

Thirty years, and that was the only time he had been called in?

"Yeah, I had a feeling they were going to catch me this time, but I never got a call after that."

Morton later asked Sanchez about the Amherst police questioning. What was he thinking about while he was there?

"This is it," Sanchez replied. "I'm going to get caught. They asked me all kinds of questions. I was scared."

All he had to say was he had done it. Could they have talked to him in a different way so that he would have admitted what he had done?

"I never thought of going in there and telling them what I did," Sanchez said.

The agent replied that was a given. But how should they have talked to him?

"I don't know the answer to that," Sanchez said. "I just went in there with the thinking 'I'm going to walk out of here.'"

Keats asked why he had started murdering his victims instead of just raping them.

"It's so hard to explain why I changed from being a rapist and started being a murderer," Sanchez replied. "I don't know how to explain it to you. When a person gave a description of me in the newspaper, I just got so mad when I read an article in the paper about it."

Keats asked Sanchez to tell him about it.

"I read the next day that they had been raped, there was an article in the paper about it. That's when I said, 'These people have seen my face, they gave a description of me.' And I got madder and madder, and that's when I started murdering victims. They didn't do anything to me. I don't know what made me do this, but I did. What made me start again? What made me go after Joan Diver? I don't know what made me start again. What made me go to the bike path, pick a spot, wait for somebody to come by. That person was Joan Diver."

What did he do to try to stop? Keats asked.

"I tried to tell myself, 'You've got to stop what you're doing or you're going to get caught.'"

"I went to that bike path for a month, three to four times a week," he said "I did it because I knew I was going to [do] what I was going to do."

Keats asked him about the garrote he used.

"It was nylon rope," Sanchez replied. "You get it at Home Depot, they always give you rope when you get lumber to tie on your car. That's the rope I used."

Did he ever use cable? Keats asked. A clerk at a Hector's Hardware store told Detective Alan Rozansky that she had sold a length of cable to Sanchez, and at his sentencing, Deputy District Attorney Frank A. Sedita III held up the cable as the murder weapon. Besides the DNA found on the steering wheel of Diver's Ford Explorer, it was the only piece of evidence tying Sanchez to Diver.

"No, never," Sanchez said. "I told the DA, it's always nylon rope. I cut a broom handle a certain length, take the rope and tie it, then wrapped black tape all around it. I cut it to palm width. Then I put a groove into the middle of the handle. The rope was long enough so I could go around twice. I never ever used a cable. I never bought anything from the place Rozansky said. I've never been to Hector's Hardware. I don't even know where it is in Clarence. Rope is much easier to carry around. Cable never crossed my mind. I always used rope."

Morton asked about the rape in April 1981, when his victim saw him a few days later at the Boulevard Mall and gave police his license plate number.

"I was at the mall with my wife," Sanchez said. "I had my son in my arms. We were looking at clothes. I looked at her and I recognized her. She recognized me too. That was one of the victims I raped in Delaware Park, with a knife. I had covered up her eyes. I got scared, very scared. I told my wife, 'Let's go, we're leaving.' That's when I had my uncle's car. I think about it now, it would have been better for me to have been arrested back then."

Keats asked about his uncle Wilfredo Caraballo, or Uncle Freddy to Sanchez, who lent his car to Sanchez to go to the mall that day, but lied to police about it.

"They asked him some questions," Sanchez replied. "That's when he called me and asked me if I had anything to do with any rapes. I said, 'What do you mean rapes? No, I didn't have anything to do with any rapes.'

"He knew," Sanchez said of his uncle. "He didn't have anything to do with this. He kept this secret for a long time. He knew. Me and Freddy were very close. We played a lot of basketball together. When I started committing these crimes, it seemed he started slipping away, our friendship.

"I can't speak for him," he said. "It's hard to say if he did know what I was doing. I don't know how many times the police went to him. Every time there was a rape in the paper? I don't know if they went to him ten times or twenty. He just kept it to himself. Freddy did lend me the car and he kept it to himself."

Keats asked if he knew that Anthony Capozzi spent

twenty-one years in prison for rapes that Sanchez had committed.

"I never knew that somebody got arrested for the crimes I committed," Sanchez said. "I heard a couple years afterward, he got arrested. I know when I got arrested, I heard that a guy spent twenty years for a crime he never committed.

"This guy spent twenty years in prison for a crime he never committed. Why wasn't his DNA taken? From people I heard that every time he went up before the parole board, he said these are crimes I never committed."

In the 1980s, DNA wasn't like it was now, Keats pointed out.

"Why did it take so long?" Sanchez persisted, getting more and more upset. "Why didn't they take his DNA and see if there was a match? Why did they wait until I was arrested?"

As Sanchez ate his lunch, he talked about the weight he lost when he was awaiting trial in the Erie County Holding Center. Always about 150 to 160 pounds, his weight ballooned after he had surgery on a torn rotator cuff in his shoulder in 2006.

"When I was in the Erie County Holding Center, I lost forty pounds," Sanchez said. "I went from two hundred to one-sixty. Now I'm up to one seventy-two."

After lunch, the questioning resumed. Sergeant Gregory Savage, a task force member from the Erie County Sheriff's Office, asked some questions about Joan Diver's murder.

Savage asked how a bruise on her head had occurred.

"I didn't punch her or anything," Sanchez replied. "I never punched her. My intent was to rape her. She fought, it made me angry, pissed off. She was screaming. Face-to-face. She started scratching me. I pushed her to the ground, and pulled up," he said, showing how he had pulled on the garrote.

The autopsy had shown a blunt-force injury. How had that happened? Savage asked.

"She bounced her head a couple of times," Sanchez said, adding that it was on the ground, not the paved bike path.

Why had he run in the 1996 Linda Yalem Run, a race dedicated to honor the woman he killed?

"Five or six guys had a running team at American Brass," he said. "One time they wanted me to run the Linda Yalem race. It crossed my mind what I did. I don't know what made me do it, but I ran the race."

Brian Moline, a detective from the Town of Tonawanda, came into the room and started asking Sanchez about the killing of Kathy Herold, a fourteen-year-old girl who was found on the railroad tracks in 1985, strangled with a garrote, by the American Brass plant, where Sanchez worked.

How did he choose his victims? Was there a type of woman who interested him more? There were no blacks or Asians among his victims.

"No, I didn't care for blacks," Sanchez said. "I don't know why. There were no age differences. If you were there when I was there, you were going to be one of my victims."

How did he use the garrote, Moline asked.

"I always looped it twice," he replied. "If I had it wrapped once, I wouldn't be able to control her. All my victims I had with a rope, I always had success. Once I used a rope, I never used anything else. Once I wrapped it around the victims, I knew I had control."

How did he come up with that?

"I think it was something I watched on TV," Sanchez replied.

Did he kill Kathy Herold?

"I told my lawyer, I didn't have anything to do with it," Sanchez said.

Sanchez repeated the same thing he had said to Keats

about rapes that he had asked him about in the towns of Evans and Angola.

"I'm behind bars for the rest of my life," Sanchez said. "I have nothing to hide. I'll take a lie detector test, if you want me to."

Epilogue

The Bike Path Killer was behind bars for the rest of his life, but his long reign of terror had put fear into women, who felt they had as much a right to enjoy the peace and solitude of bike paths as men.

It was true that Altemio Sanchez would never again rape or kill, but he had changed the behavior of women in Western New York, perhaps forever.

A few days after Linda Yalem's murder, as the university tried to reassure worried students and parents, and as Western New York realized there was a serial rapist and murderer on the loose, Lois Baker, a freelance writer who worked in the university's news bureau, wrote an opinion piece in the *Buffalo News* on the dilemma facing women.

Last Friday was a thrillingly beautiful fall day, Baker wrote, *so instead of doing my daily run around Delaware Park, as is my custom, I decided instead to put in a few miles on the Amherst Bicycle Path. The wild flowers, I knew, would be lovely, and the change of scene would put a little extra spring in my step.*

I ran alone, as also is my custom, she wrote. *Running is an individual sport. That is one of its special attractions. You don't have to make dates or match schedules.*

And the run turned out to be everything she thought it would be.

Mother Nature had arranged stunning bouquets of wild asters in deep purple and light lavender with goldenrod and tiny white daisies along the path. Little grasshoppers popped up from the grasses around me and I sidestepped mahogany-furred caterpillars sunning themselves on the asphalt.

She said she planned to run there again, on Saturday, September 29, 1990, but the weather wasn't quite so nice, so she ran instead in Delaware Park.

Sunday evening, I heard a young woman had been raped and murdered on the bicycle path Saturday during her daily run.

I went to bed that night, stunned, shaken, angry. Linda Yalem died in broad daylight on a public recreational trail, while minding her own business, for only one reason. She was a woman.

Baker might have added, but did not, she could have just as easily been the rapist's victim.

Baker, who is married to Michael Beebe, one of this book's authors, saw a man during her run who looked out of place. He was not dressed in running clothes, but was jogging slowly on the path anyway. He did not look like a runner.

As Baker approached him, something alerted her, a sense that something about him wasn't quite right. As she passed the man, she turned around and saw that he had turned too, and was staring at her.

Once she had gone as far as she had planned, she turned around on the bike path. And soon enough, here was the same man, short, swarthy-looking, she recalled, with the most prominent heavy, dark eyebrows.

This time, Baker ran a bit off the path to keep her distance. As she ran past him, she once again turned and saw him staring at her again.

She didn't think anything more of the encounter until Monday morning, when a story in the *Buffalo News* on Yalem's murder carried a composite sketch of a man who had earlier raped a fourteen-year-old girl in Willow Ridge, and was suspected of raping a businesswoman earlier that year on the Amherst bike path.

"That's the man I saw on the bike path," Baker told her husband about her Friday run. "That's him. I'd recognize those eyebrows anywhere."

She called the Amherst police, and talked to a detective, but decided, when writing her October 4 piece in the *News,* not to mention it.

Instead, she expressed the frustrations that women everywhere have in deciding where to run.

Instead of protecting women, our governmental leaders tell women to protect themselves. In the process, women are forced to restrict their lives yet one more notch. Be more careful, we are advised. Take more precautions. Always look over your shoulder. And especially, don't go there any more. It's too dangerous.

Women live their days looking over their shoulders. They are hostages in their own society.

So, maybe like Linda Yalem, we peer down a lovely running path and decide we don't want to be scared anymore. As her attacker stalked her from behind, maybe Linda too was telling herself she was tired looking over her shoulder.

During the interview in prison, Sanchez admitted to investigators that he was indeed on the bike path the same day Baker said she saw him.

And six years later, on September 29, 1996, the first

time the Linda Yalem Memorial Run was held on the same day that Yalem died, Baker ran in the race.

After Sanchez was arrested, Baker's husband, a former running columnist for the *Buffalo News,* checked the race results to see if the Bike Path Killer had run the race. Three places behind Baker, the results showed, was Altemio Sanchez.